Substance and Structure
of Language

Published under the auspices of
The Center for Research in Languages and Linguistics
University of California, Los Angeles

Substance and Structure of Language

Lectures delivered before
the Linguistic Institute of
the Linguistic Society of America,
University of California, Los Angeles,
June 17 - August 12, 1966

Edited by
Jaan Puhvel

University of California Press
Berkeley and Los Angeles
1969

University of California Press
Berkeley and Los Angeles, California

University of California Press, Ltd.
London, England

In Memoriam
URIEL WEINREICH
1926-1967

Preface

Three series of Forum Lectures were delivered during the 1966 Linguistic Institute at UCLA: the General Series (fifteen lectures), the Indo-European Series (seven lectures), and the Mathematical-Computational Series (eleven lectures). While the latter two were intended to be transitory in character, the bulk of the General Series was projected for subsequent publication. The purpose of such publication in this volume is, in a narrow sense, to codify and perpetuate some of the substance of an intellectually stimulating summer for the hundreds who heard and absorbed each lecture. More generally, we hope to disseminate even more widely a cross section of current concerns to linguists of various leanings, as seen by a sequence of outstanding scholars.

Each printed contribution from the General Series is a revised, and sometimes adapted, version of what was delivered and discussed. Bar-Hillel's work is based on two lectures delivered on June 22 and 29. Weinreich's study of idioms résumés the spoken efforts of three evenings, July 13, 18, and 20. Lambert's psycholinguistic investigations were presented on June 27 and 29. Morag's lecture on oral tradition was given on August 8. Greenberg discussed "dynamic comparison" on July 11 and 13. To these contributions we have postfixed, unaltered, the traditional Collitz Lecture by the Institute's incumbent Collitz Professor of Comparative Indo-European Grammar, Werner Winter, delivered on July 29.

The two lectures by Roman Jakobson, "Lexical and Grammatical Meaning" and "Meaning and Reference," delivered on July 6, were also to have been included. It must be a source of regret to all who heard those stimulating presentations that Professor Jakobson was unable to furnish written versions of those lectures until the ineluctable editorial processes could be delayed no longer.

The three lectures delivered by Eric H. Lenneberg on July 20, 25, and 27, on the human brain and neurological aspects of language, were intended for publication in his book *Biological Foundations of Language* (New York: Wiley, 1967).

The Chancellor of the University of California, Los Angeles, has favored the issuance of this volume with a substantial publication subsidy. Thanks are due the authors, the many discussants whose comments, sometimes acknowledged in the body of the volume, helped shape these end products, and all who contributed to the considerable success of the 1966 Linguistic Institute.

These lectures are inscribed to the memory of one who nobly added to their substance and to the worth and dignity of the linguist's profession. He himself had dedicated his lectures to Roman Jakobson on the occasion of the latter's seventieth birthday in 1966. He completed the final written version in the last weeks of his life, and his colleagues at Columbia University have contributed their counsel in its *post fata* publication.

Jaan Puhvel

Contents

Contents

Universal Semantics and Philosophy of Language: Quandaries and Prospects

Yehoshua Bar-Hillel
The Hebrew University
Jerusalem

I. Universal Semantics and Logic: A Critique of Some Recent Theories of Semantics

The two Linguistic Institute Forum Lectures I presented in 1965 at the University of Michigan began with a historical sketch of the mutual relationship between logic and linguistics, starting with Aristotle. Since these lectures have not been published, and since the overlap between audiences is negligible, it might help to repeat briefly some of the points I made there before proceeding to my present topics.

At Ann Arbor I tried to stress the fact that, owing to certain extremely interesting but also highly unfortunate historical developments, argumentation in natural languages became a no-man's-land between logic and linguistics. Most logicians and linguists were equally eager to put the responsibility for the treatment of this important field — as a matter of fact, I can envisage few fields that are more important — squarely on the shoulders of their colleagues in the other discipline, with disastrous results. Occasional attempts by philosophers to invade this no-man's-land and to claim it for philosophical (or universal) grammar failed miserably because of utterly inadequate preparations, and served only to create distrust bordering on hatred among linguists, for many of whom "logic" and its cognates in time became almost dirty words.

The resulting splendid mutual isolation was perhaps not too bad for the field of logic. Unhampered by any need to care in particular for natural languages, logic, in the form of mathematical logic, reached incredible heights; recently, and rather unexpectedly, it even achieved a certain amount of applicability, if not in the critical evaluation of natural language arguments, at least in

1

sometimes extremely sophisticated investigations into programming languages. On the other hand, while in the early nineteenth century this isolation put new life and ambition into autonomous, comparative, historical, and descriptive linguistics, in the end it succeeded in choking off linguistics almost completely, leaving its central part, semantics, in an atheoretical, sometimes even antitheoretical, bloodless, and anemic state, with anecdotes the only means of presenting a lifelike front.

Even the recent attempts by Katz, Fodor, Weinreich, Lamb, Hockett, and others[1] — and I shall refer here only to work done by American linguists, not out of parochialism, but because I do not think that linguists elsewhere (with the exception of Lyons[2]) have been able to do noticeably better, although they have certainly performed invaluably in creating new interest in semantics among linguists — were at best only a first step toward the theorization of the field; at worst they were so crudely executed as to harm rather than further the cause. What they all missed (with the partial exception of Weinreich[3]) was that meaning relations between linguistic entities are essentially deducibility relations and, therefore, logical relations. They missed this fact partly because a large number of the rules stating meaning relations can indeed be easily and practically formulated in the form of entries in traditional monolingual dictionaries (or lexica). Each such entry, so at least is the received view, tells that certain linguistic entities, usually words or short phrases, have the same meaning (perhaps only in certain contexts), are synonymous with each other (perhaps only partly so). Many linguists are aware of the innumerable problems that arise in this connection, but few are aware of the strong relationship that holds between synonymy and (mutual) deducibility, which is the basis of the successful performance of lexica. Unfor-

---

[1] I do not aim for bibliographical exhaustiveness. The contributions I have in mind are J. A. Fodor and J. J. Katz., eds., *The Structure of Language: Readings in the Philosophy of Language* (Englewood Cliffs, N.J., 1964); J. J. Katz and P. Postal, *An Integrated Theory of Linguistic Descriptions* (Cambridge, Mass., 1964); J. J. Katz, *The Philosophy of Language* (New York and London, 1966); U. Weinreich, "Explorations in Semantic Theory," in T. A. Sebeok, ed., *Current Trends in Linguistics*, Vol. III, *Theoretical Foundations* (The Hague, 1966), pp. 395-477; S. M. Lamb, "The Sememic Approach to Structural Semantics," *American Anthropologist*, 66, no. 3 (June 1964), pt. 2, pp. 57-78; and C. F. Hockett, "Language, Mathematics and Linguistics: Explorations in Semantic Theory," *ibid.*, pp. 155-304.

[2] J. Lyons, *Structural Semantics: An Analysis of Part of the Vocabulary of Plato* (Oxford, 1963).

[3] *Op. cit.*

tunately, the obvious efficiency of lexica has blinded almost all the linguists who gave any thought to that issue into believing that all of semantics is exhausted by lexicology, though a number of them paid some attention to the fact that other rules were needed at least for the purpose of determining how the meaning of longer linguistic entities is to be composed out of the meanings of their component smaller entities supposedly taken care of by the lexicon; but that the semantics of, say, English can be exhaustively presented in the form of a lexicon plus some meaning composition rules (called by Katz and Fodor, though not very helpfully, "projection rules"[4]), has seldom been doubted, though there has been a lot of discussion about the most appropriate form the lexicon should take, as well as a good deal of criticism of extant dictionaries.[5]

I shall presently repeat and further develop my arguments for the utter inadequacy of this conception. For the moment, let me only recall that in Ann Arbor I went on to say that linguists would greatly profit from the insights of such philosophers and logicians as Reichenbach,[6] Carnap,[7] Quine,[8] Curry,[9] and Putnam[10] (to mention again only Americans), who have lately paid much attention to logical semantics, although a crude application of these insights to linguistic semantics would again mean courting disaster. I voiced my apprehension that the long overdue *rapprochement* between logic and linguistics is in danger of being delayed and even stifled at the outset by overstatements and exaggerated and unsubstantiated claims. If we can beware of these lurking dangers, one may hope that linguists can be persuaded to accept that logic is linguistics' best friend, and that by judicious collaboration with enlightened logicians and judicious applications of their insights, linguistics will be able to reach an adequate degree of theorization. I did not propose a merger of logic and linguistics. There is nothing wrong

[4]See, e.g., Katz, *op. cit.*, p. 153.

[5]See, e.g., Weinreich, *op. cit.*

[6]H. Reichenbach, *Elements of Symbolic Logic* (New York, 1952).

[7]In a very large number of contributions; for the latest, see Carnap's "Intellectual Autobiography," in P. A. Schilpp, ed., *The Philosophy of Rudolf Carnap* (LaSalle, Ill., 1964), vol. 11 of *The Library of Living Philosophers*, pp. 53-66; and "Replies and Systematic Expositions," *ibid.*, pp. 809-943.

[8]Again in a large number of contributions; see, in particular, W. V. Quine, *Word and Object* (Cambridge, Mass., 1960).

[9]H. B. Curry, "Some Logical Aspects of Grammatical Structure," in R. Jakobson, ed., *Structure of Language and Its Mathematical Aspects* (1961), *Proceedings of Symposia in Applied Mathematics* 12:56-68 (1961).

[10]H. Putnam, "Some Issues in the Theory of Grammar," *ibid.*, pp. 25-42.

with a division of labor, so long as it does not lead to a division of hearts and mutual distrust.

(When I discuss these problems before an audience of logicians, I try to present the other side of the picture and insist that logic can be brought back to its original task only by constant contact with linguistics: that logic, as it stands today, is quite inadequate to deal satisfactorily with that task, and that its development and expansion in the proper direction depends upon its receiving clues from linguistic needs.)

With this recapitulation behind us — and I hope that my original talks contained more substance, fewer generalities, and less propaganda for a better world where logicians and linguists might live happily together ever after than this summary may have indicated — let us now turn to our first task, namely a critique of what has come to be known as the Katz-Fodor (KF) theory of semantics. I claim that this theory, even in its improved presentation in Katz's recent book,[11] is utterly inadequate as a whole, in spite of a large number of valid insights.

The major shortcoming of the KF theory has already been mentioned and briefly discussed: the identification of semantics with lexicology (supplemented by "projection rules"). True enough, Katz and Fodor were fully aware of the shortcomings of traditional dictionaries, but they definitely gave the impression that the dictionaries, with their format revamped, could still be made to carry the full burden of semantics — an idea that is disastrously misguided. Let me illustrate in some detail.

On page 152 of his recent book, Katz states: "The hypothesis on which we will base our model of the semantic component is that the process by which a speaker interprets each of the infinitely many sentences is a compositional process in which the meaning of any syntactically compound constituent of a sentence is obtained as a function of the meanings of the parts of the constituent." From this hypothesis he deduces (p. 153) "that the semantic component will have two subcomponents: *a dictionary* that provides a representation of the meaning of each of the words in the language, and a system of *projection rules* that provide the combinatorial machinery for projecting the semantic representation for all supraword constituents in a sentence from the representations that are given in the dictionary for the meanings of the words in the sentence." The

[11] *Op. cit.*

hypothesis sounds extremely attractive, almost tautological (and the reader is invited to test this feeling of mine on himself and see off-hand whether he can find a flaw in it); but it is, in its generality, just plain false. Since it is the basic hypothesis of Katz's theory of semantics, the theory itself simply collapses.

Katz's hypothesis (which has, of course, been formulated many times before) is far too atomistic even to stand a chance of being true. Each dictionary entry, in his view, "pairs a word with a representation of its meaning in some normal form" (p. 154), and "the information in dictionary entries must be full analyses of word meanings." The semantic part of the normal form consists of a set of "semantic markers" (and a "selection restriction"). The "semantic markers represent the conceptual elements into which a reading decomposes a sense" (p. 155). Simply that! The reader will in vain look for any discussion of these "conceptual elements" or their "interrelations." I do not think I remember any recent treatise on philosophy of language in which the most basic notions are treated in such a cavalier and unsophisticated, not to say irresponsible, fashion. And what are these conceptual elements? Here the reader will be in for the surprise of his life! Not only are "physical object", "living", "human", and "male" conceptual elements, which would be reasonable enough for a philosophy of language of antiquity or the Middle Ages, but so are "serving under the standard of another," "without a mate at breeding time," and "having the academic degree for the completion of the first four years of college" (with Katz being parochial enough not even to mention that this holds only for the United States and perhaps a few other countries, but not, for example, for Israel, where we do not have colleges and where the bachelor's degree is awarded upon completion of three years of study at a university, with certain exceptions, nor for many other countries which have no bachelor's degree at all).

But this is not all. Has Katz really never heard of theoretical terms whose meaning is theory-dependent and, even within the framework of a whole theory, only partly and incompletely determined? He uses the term "theoretical construct" (p. 155), but without showing any awareness of the implication of this usage. Though he discusses at length Carnap's contributions to the philosophy of language prior to 1950 — not without a large number of distortions — he quotes, of the 1963 volume *The Philosophy of*

Rudolf Carnap[12] (which, true enough, actually appeared early in 1964), only from Carnap's "Intellectual Autobiography," taking nothing from his "Replies and Systematic Expositions," which contain highly relevant and important views on semantics and the philosophy of language, views that make many of Katz's contributions look rather childish by comparison.

Nowhere does Katz show any awareness of the importance of semantic fields, a conception that makes it abundantly clear that, for innumerable terms, no individual, but only a collective, meaning specification is possible. His neglect is the more amazing since Chomsky has shown full awareness of this importance, though he apparently has had no time to discuss the topic at greater length. In *Aspects*[13] (which Katz mentions in his bibliography), Chomsky says (p. 164): "We have just seen that this account [similar to that of Katz but without the ridiculous commitment to such conceptual elements as "without a mate at breeding time"] is over-simplified in the case of semantic features, further structure being necessary in the lexicon to account for field properties," though even he never mentions the special problems posed by theoretical terms.

When Katz comes to the dictionary entry for *Neg* (the negation symbol), he conveniently forgets all about "normal forms" and presents it (on p. 201) without a word of excuse or explanation, as a sequence of three rules in eighteen lines — and I shall not here go into the adequacy of these rules or into the question of whether, even if adequate, they needed to be presented with such extraordinary complexity. Incidentally, the sense in which these three rules are "entries" for *Neg* is hyper-Pickwickian, as the reader is invited to check for himself.

After these few illustrations of the way Katz handles his tasks, let me come back to my major criticism. I claim that nobody has fully mastered the semantics of English who does not know that from *John is older than Paul* and *Paul is older than Dick* (with the occurrences of *Paul* referring to the same person) one can deduce *John is older than Dick*. A complete semantics of English must contain a rule to this effect, either as a primitive, explicit one, or at least as a derivative, implicit one. Such a rule might, for example, have the form: From X *is older than* Y and Y *is older than* Z, deduce X *is older than* Z. We also need rules to the effect: From X *is older than*

[12]See n. 7, above.
[13]N. Chomsky, *Aspects of the Theory of Syntax* (Cambridge, Mass., 1965).

Y, deduce *Y is not older than X* and *X is not as old as Y* and *Y is younger than X*, and so on. None of these meaning rules can be derived from traditional dictionaries. Any stretching of the notion of dictionary (or lexicon, for that matter) in order to incorporate them would be at best merely pointless and, at worst, a misleading adherence to outmoded terminology, even more than in the mentioned *Neg* example.

Notice that logicians have a way of compressing this multiplicity of rules into very compact formulations. One such formulation would be: *Is older than* denotes an irreflexive, asymmetrical, and transitive relation. A more compact formulation is: *Is older than* denotes a strict partial order. Still more compact and comprehensive is: *Is older than* and *is as old as* together form a quasi-order. (From this formulation it follows, among other things, that these two phrases fulfill the law of strong trichotomy: For any X and any Y, either X is as old as Y, or X is older than Y, or Y is older than X.)

Notice also that these meaning rules can be separated into two parts: one that is specific for a given language such as English, and one that is universal, holding for all languages, or rather is language-independent. That *is as old as* and *is older than* form a quasi-order is, of course, peculiar to the English language, is a rule of specific English semantics; but the fact that, if they do, then *is as old as* is symmetrical, *is older than* is transitive, and so on, has no longer anything to do with English specifically. This implication belongs with "universal semantics" or "logic," depending upon the department you belong to. The first rule would best be published in a volume called *The Semantics of English*, the others, in a volume entitled *Semantica Universalis sive Logica*. That *ist so alt wie* and *ist älter als* form a quasi-order in German belongs with German semantics, but the properties of this quasi-order are, of course, the same as those of any other quasi-order and are discussed only once, in the very same book, *Semantica Universalis sive Logica*.

Lest I be misunderstood, let me stress immediately that I do not believe that there exists a rigid borderline between special and universal semantics. The general tendency would be, for reasons of simplicity, elegance, economy, and "explanatory adequacy," to draw the line so as to include in universal semantics as much as possible. Following this maxim, one might, for instance, ask oneself whether one could not slice off from the mentioned rule of English semantics ("*is as old as* and *is older than* form a quasi-order") another universal ingredient. Let us first assume that not only does *is older than* denote a strict partial ordering, but that every English comparative does likewise. (This assumption is neither trivially true nor obviously false; but a more detailed discussion would require too much space.) Similarly, let us assume that every English *as Adj as* phrase denotes an equivalence (with a similar proviso). Then it should be clear how the semantics of English could be given a simpler form. But if the above assumption is correct (and I think that it could be enforced and therefore perhaps should be), then it is not unlikely that a similar situation should be made to prevail in all languages. (I would tend to believe that, but don't really know whether all languages have constructions that deserve to be called comparatives, or adequative constructions corresponding to *as Adj as;* but what still could be enforced is that no construction in any language should be called a comparative unless it denotes a strict partial order, or an adequative unless it denotes an equivalence.) Such universal similarity would allow the transfer to universal semantics of another part of the semantics of each specific language. We would then have as a rule of universal semantics (in a self-explanatory *ad hoc* symbolism): Compar (Adj) and Adeq (Adj) form a quasi-order. The phonological rules of English would state: Compar (Adj) is realized, depending upon some appropriate subclassification of adjectives, as *more Adj than,* or *Adj-er than,* or in both forms. Similar rules would indicate *Adj-er als* for German, *plus Adj que* for French, and so on.

English semantics must tell us that from *X is a parent of Y* one can deduce *Y is a child of X,* but for this purpose it would be sufficient to have a rule to the effect that *is a child of* denotes the relation converse to the relation denoted by *is a parent of,* with universal semantics (= logic) taking care of the rest. After being told that *is a pupil of* is the converse of *is a teacher of,* I would not only be able to deduce from *John is a teacher of Susan* that *Susan is a pupil of John* with the help of universal semantics, but would also be able to deduce from *Mary is a parent of a teacher of Susan* the statement *Susan is a pupil of a child of Mary,* with the help of my friendly logician who will call my attention to the rule (of universal semantics)

$$\breve{R/S} = \breve{S}/\breve{R},$$

after my equally friendly English linguist will have pointed out that, in accordance with a rule of English special semantics, *is an X of a Y of* denotes (perhaps with some qualification as to the membership of the categories X and Y) the relative product of the relations denoted by *is an X of* and *is a Y of*, respectively.

Let me point out that one must be careful not to push too many linguistic relationships into universal semantics. Husserl,[14] who was greatly impressed by the philosophical grammars of the seventeenth and eighteenth centuries, and was one of the last philosophers to take this conception seriously, regarded "How is the passive expressed in . . . ?" as a good question to ask for any given language. I doubt that many modern linguists will be ready to accept this notion. They would rather regard Husserl's view as one more attempt by a philosopher to impose his a priori schemes on linguistics, and resent his doing so just as much as their forefathers resented earlier such attempts. Indeed I see little justification for wanting to enforce the universal existence of passive constructions; but I think that what Husserl should have insisted upon was that the question "How does one express in . . . the converse relation of a given relation?" is a good one to ask. With this I would fully agree and am sure that attempts to answer this question will lead to progress. For some languages the answer will indeed somehow use the term "passive," but even for languages containing a passive this will by no means be the only way of expressing converse relations.

At this point it might be useful to propose not to treat the terms "general semantics" and "universal semantics" as synonyms, but rather to make use of the opportunity and, by fiat, give those terms, qua technical terms, different meanings. Whereas, I propose, *general* should be used to denote "accidental allness," *universal* should be reserved for "necessary allness." Whereas generality should therefore allow of degrees and enable us to say that certain linguistic phenomena are more or less general, or that such and such a feature occurs generally in all the Indo-European languages (but perhaps not in Semitic languages), universality would be absolute. A given linguistic feature would be termed universal, rather than just general, not simply because the state of affairs was such and not otherwise, but rather because we would not want to call something a language unless it contained that feature, in other words, if the occurrence of that feature was necessitated by the very meaning of the term "language." I realize that if my proposal is adopted,

[14]E. Husserl, *Logische Untersuchungen*, Vol. II (Halle, 1900). Cf. my paper, "Husserl's Conception of a Purely Logical Grammar," *Philosophy and Phenomenological Research* 17:362-363 (1957).

most of the "linguistic universals," including most of the "semantic universals," will have to be termed otherwise, though there are some obvious problems with "linguistic generals."

The semantics of a given language would be presented ideally not in one volume but in a number of them. One volume would contain universal semantics, another the special (idiosyncratic) semantics of the given language, while an indeterminate number of other volumes would contain the (more or less) general semantics of various classes of languages of which the given language is a member, with the optimum organization to be determined by a variety of pragmatic factors which I shall not go into here. The first volume, incidentally, would be written, according to the accepted division of labor, by logicians and, at least in principle, once and for all. Its contents, I submit, would not be subject to linguistic change.

With Katz's outline of a theory of semantics being such a complete failure, where do we stand? Are we back to chaos? Can anything sensible be said at the moment about restrictions on the forms that meaning rules should take? I am afraid that I, for one, have very little positive to say at present that might be of help in this situation. Though we can and should, in general, take many clues from Carnap (as well as, of course, from Reichenbach, Quine, Curry, Putnam, and others), he has very little specific to say about the form of what he calls "meaning postulates." This lack of specifics is not surprising in view of his avowed personal disinterest in the semantics of natural languages, though he fully realizes the importance of this field and merely takes, in the required division of labor, the other side.[15]

We need, then, a fresh start. As a first step, let us forget as quickly as possible Katz's theory; second, let us take it easy with semantic universals; third, let us realize that so far the only sound ingredient in universal semantics is logic, and, in consequence, let us press hard upon the logicians to spend some of their time (and even, for some of them, all of their time) in developing logic so that it will be able to answer the needs of linguists and of everybody else for a theory of deducibility in natural languages that should be as complete as possible and would then turn out to be a full theory of valid argumentation in natural languages. After that, we might perhaps be in a position to attack with better prospects of success the problem of the possibility of putting meaning rules into some normal form.

[15]*The Philosophy of Rudolf Carnap*, p. 94.

II. The Future of Philosophy of Language

Though I shall indeed discuss the future of philosophy of language, I shall not try to forecast this future but rather expand upon what I think should be its development. Though I do belong to a nation of prophets, we also have an old proverb to the effect that, since the destruction of the Second Temple (A.D. 70), the gift of prophecy has been restricted to infants and fools. I, however, plan to do slightly more than pronounce my predilections: I intend to do my share to make them come true.

Let me start with a terminological remark. In addition to the terms "philosophy of language" and "linguistic philosophy," recently also the term "philosophy of linguistics" has been propagated by the ubiquitous Katz-Fodor team (though with an interesting change of mind between 1962 and 1966 on the part of at least one member of the team[16]). I guess that one reason for this innovation was the existence of the triplet "philosophy of nature"–"philosophy of science"–"scientific philosophy"; but I have some doubts whether this particular triple distinction is worth imitating. "Philosophy of nature" is no longer an endeavor that is taken seriously, if I am not mistaken, as a result of the excesses of German *Naturphilosophie* in the early nineteenth century, and survives only in the periphery of philosophical thinking. It would be a pity if the nice term "philosophy of language" would be reserved for wild speculations about the "nature" of language, its "origin," and so on. This seemed indeed to be the destination of the term during the 1930's and 1940's when it was scarcely used in English-speaking academic circles and was replaced by "logic of language" and the like. But now that this danger seems to be over, I at least would propose not to let the term "philosophy of language" go out of use but to apply it in approximately the same responsible way as the term "philosophy of science" is employed nowadays (perhaps adding to it the term "philosophy of communication," if this has not yet been done). On the other hand, for methodological investigations in linguistics and communication theory, the terms "methodology of linguistics" and "methodology of communication theory" (or "of communication science") seem to me apposite, so that I would propose discarding the term "philosophy of linguistics" (just as I am not in favor of such terms as "philosophy of physics," "philosophy of psychology," and the like). Not that the borderlines between these three disciplines, philo-

[16]Katz, *op. cit.*, p. 4 n. 2.

sophy of language, methodology of linguistics, and linguistic philosophy are, or should be, rigidly determined: their interrelation
is so strong that an extensive overlap is to be expected and encour-
aged, rather than frowned upon. It is, after all, one of the main con-
tentions of KF that recent linguistic philosophy (as I propose to use
the term), whether in the form of "(linguistic) constructionism" (as
I shall hereafter call it, following P. F. Strawson and Carnap,[17] re-
placing KF's very unfortunate "positivism"), practiced, say, by
Carnap, or in the form of "(linguistic) naturalism" ("ordinary language philosophy"), practiced by the late L. Wittgenstein, by the
late J. L. Austin, and, at present, by G. Ryle, Strawson, J. O. Urmson,
and a host of other Oxonians, suffers from neglect of the advent of
theoretical linguistics and of its methodology, so that the philosophy
of language on which they base their linguistic philosophy is too
narrow, one-sided, and dated to serve its purpose well. Whether or
not Katz and Fodor like my paraphrase of one of their main tenets,
I like it and am ready to subscribe to it fully.

But exactly because I so heartily welcome this thesis and regard
its acceptance as a necessary condition for a healthy development
of philosophy of language, I am appalled by the extremely poor exe-
cution of this program in the recent book by Katz. I fear there is a
good chance that, because of the prestige acquired by its gifted and
forceful author, both on his own and as the philosophical spokes-
man of the "MIT-niks" as a group, this book will be regarded by
many readers as an authoritative exposition of "the new philosophy of language." They will turn away disenchanted, not from
the book alone, but from the discipline as such, thereby possibly
setting the clock back many years. Let me, therefore, make it perfectly clear that in my view all the many faults and shortcomings
are the author's alone and carry no reflection on the discipline or
even on his main thesis.

I shall first deal with an almost random selection of these shortcomings, and then turn to a list of problems which have been either
entirely disregarded by Katz, or treated in an unsatisfactory manner,
but which seem to me to deserve the closest study by future philosophers of language. No claim is made for the exhaustiveness of
this list. After all, mine is a single lecture and not a book. As one
more preliminary, let me mention that some of the points treated

---

[17]Carnap, "Replies and Systematic Expositions," in *The Philosophy of Rudolf
Carnap*, p. 933; P. F. Strawson's essay, *ibid.*, pp. 503-518.

briefly in this presentation are discussed at greater length in my review of *The Structure of Language*.[18]

My first comment will be rather dogmatic, since I am addressing myself to linguists rather than philosophers, so that I cannot assume any particular familiarity with, for instance, the writings of Carnap. Let me then say that Katz's description of Carnap's views is anything but authoritative. The unquestioned adoption of Quine's well-known (to philosophers) criticism of Carnap's (older) treatment of analyticity (one of the two dogmas Quine so forcefully exposed and attacked in perhaps his most famous article, "Two Dogmas of Empiricism"[19]) is the author's privilege; but I must point out that, since the appearance of this article, many refutations of Quine's argument have appeared, not to mention Carnap's own reply—which for me was wholly convincing—in his "Replies and Systematic Expositions."[20] I already mentioned that Katz, perhaps for such respectable reasons as deadlines and other niceties that bedevil authors, gives no account of the highly significant articles dealing with philosophy of language in the Carnap volume, nor of the equally, if not more, significant "Replies" by Carnap himself. In particular, I can highly recommend a careful reading of Carnap's reply to Strawson (from which I took the terms "constructionist" and "naturalist").

I already commented on the strange and extremely old-fashioned atomistic conception of Katz of the role of elementary concepts in semantics. Since he does not make the slightest allusion to the vast philosophical literature on this topic, the linguist reader will probably end up with the impression that this conception is hallowed by philosophical consensus, while the philosopher reader might think that the existence of such concepts has been demonstrated by linguistic research. In fact, of course, this whole conception is utterly wanton and indefensible, as I showed in my first lecture.

Bordering on the ludicrous are some of the things that, according to Katz, can be done "simply." How, for instance, does one "obtain the *semantic categories of language*, i.e., the semantic categories for all natural languages ... " (p. 234)? Nothing could

---

[18]Review of Fodor and Katz, *op. cit.*, in *Language* 43:526-550 (1967).

[19]W. V. Quine, "Two Dogmas of Empiricism," *Philosophical Review*, vol. 60; reprinted as chapter ii in *From a Logical Point of View* (Cambridge, Mass., 1953); see also Quine's article, "Carnap and Logical Truth," in *The Philosophy of Rudolf Carnap*, pp. 385-406.

[20]Pp. 917-919.

be simpler. It is done in two easy stages. First, "to find the semantic categories of a particular natural language, we *simply* [my italics] check over the list of redundancy rules [i.e., rules stating that a semantic marker subsumes another semantic marker] in the linguistic description of *L* and pick out each semantic marker for which there is a rule saying that that marker subsumes other markers under it but for which none of the rules say that the marker is subsumed under other semantic markers" (p. 234). In the second stage, "the semantic categories of language are those concepts represented by the semantic markers belonging to the intersection of the sets of semantic categories for particular languages [Katz must surely mean "for *all* particular languages"], as obtained in the manner just described" (p. 235).

Should someone be worried by the fact that the semantic markers and the redundancy rules of a particular language have been defined only with regard to a given grammar, with no indication of how to get rid of this relativization (not to mention the fact that the whole idea that the semantics of any given natural language can be presented exclusively in terms of semantic markers, redundancy rules, and projection rules is ludicrous, as I tried to show at some length in the first lecture), Katz has a quick remedy: "Such justification for putative semantic categories is *simply* [my italics] a matter of empirically establishing that no simpler statement of the lexical readings for the dictionary of the language is provided by redundancy rules other than those which, by the given definition of semantic categories of *L,* yield the semantic categories in question" (p. 234).

Should now someone be uneducated or timorous enough to wonder whether it is so simple after all to establish that a certain set of rules is the simplest of *all* possible such sets, perhaps because this set seems to be so undetermined and is presumably infinite, which might create some obvious problems, his confidence is quickly restored by the remark that, after all: "This, it is to be noticed, is the same sort of empirical justification used in other branches of science when it is claimed that some theoretical account is best because it is based on the simplest set of laws describing the phenomena." Let me first state that this account of general scientific procedure is, to put it mildly, vastly oversimplified — I personally

---

[21]See, e.g., my paper, "On Alleged Rules of Detachment in Inductive Logic," in I. Lakatos, ed., *Problems of Inductive Logic* (Amsterdam, 1968), pp. 120-128; see also the discussion on pp. 129-165.

regard it as just plain false.[21] I do not deny that some scientists do on occasion use such formulations, but I do deny that there is any good reason to take such formulations seriously. Let me add, as an *argumentum ad authoritatem,* for whatever it is worth, that Chomsky has recently made it clear repeatedly that his appeal to simplicity as a criterion for evaluating competing grammars has nothing to do with the general notion of simplicity in the general methodology of science.[22] But I am already spending altogether too much time on this combination of browbeating and empty circular reasoning.

I shall pass over in silence Katz's treatment of analyticity (pp. 188-224), which he seems to regard as a kind of showcase for the superiority of his approach. If someone wants to see how this topic can be treated responsibly, let him read, for example, pages 963-966 of Carnap's "Replies" (though in order to understand these passages fully, he will have to read some preceding material) or Hintikka's recent series of four masterful articles,[23] one of which, incidentally, is called "Kant vindicated"; a comparison of this serious vindication of Kant's conception with Katz's attempts is a none too pleasant experience.

I come now to a brief list of real and underdiscussed problems that the future philosopher of language should investigate in depth.

A. UTTERANCE–SENTENCE–STATEMENT

I have many times[24] called attention to the necessity of carefully drawing certain distinctions that are often slurred over even in places where they are required. I shall give it another try, since I would like to solicit help in this endeavor. I am quite sure that neither I nor anyone else has yet said the last word on this issue. None of these distinctions has been invented by me. On the contrary, each single one of them has been drawn on may occasions, and many authors are aware of them in some detached way; but when the chips are down, I have found time and time again that arguments suffer badly and sometimes decisively because of confusions between concepts whose distinctness is, in principle, well known.

---

[22]See, e.g., *Op. cit.,* §7.

[23]J. Hintikka, "An Analysis of Analyticity," "Are Logical Truths Tautologies?" "Kant Vindicated," "Kant and the Tradition of Analysis," in P. Weingartner, ed., *Deskription, Analyzität und Existenz* (Salzburg and München, 1966), pp. 193-272.

[24]My latest attempt is "Do Natural Languages Contain Paradoxes?" *Studium Generale* 19:391-397 (1966).

Who does not know the distinction between an act—in particular, for our purposes, a linguistic act—and its product? Who does not know that the English word "utterance" (and innumerable other words, in English and, I am told, in very many other, and perhaps all, languages) denotes both a certain speech act and the (perhaps only a) product of the act? I believe that this distinction is part and parcel of high school textbooks. A statement can be quick, and it can be carefully formulated; but it is, of course, the statement-act, the particular act of stating, that is quick, and it is the statement-product that is carefully formulated, and any confusion (of categories) can be disastrous, and has been so on untold occasions.

Who does not know that one has to distinguish between a sentence, qua abstract linguistic entity, and the utterance of it, qua concrete physical product of some linguistic act, or even between a sentence and the set of all its actual and possible utterances? (One does not have to make this distinction by using these terms, of course; anything will do, so long as it is realized that one has to deal here with two entities that are different under any name.) But are you really sure that you know how to avoid the trap of regarding (as has been done quite often in the past) this distinction as being of the well-known type-token kind, or of the class-member kind? And are you really sure that you will know how to make this distinction when making it is crucial? I could give you hundreds of quotations, including recent ones from leading linguists, where it is obvious that the distinction was not made in places where it mattered.

Most, though not all, of the people I know understand rather quickly the existence of a difference between a declarative sentence, an abstract linguistic entity, and the statement, if any, that is made by an utterance of this sentence on some occasion. Statements are abstract, nonlinguistic entities that can be made by uttering declarative sentences but also in many other ways. The same statement can be made by uttering different tokens of the same sentence(-type), and also by uttering tokens of different sentences, in one language or in more, even by nodding one's head, and so on. It is statements that are the prime carriers of truth-values (i.e., that are true or false); and in natural languages, truth and falsity should be assigned to sentences or utterances only derivatively and with a number of precautions and provisos. I know quite well that this particular issue is still in flux and that what I said just now will not be generally accepted by all my philosophical colleagues, but it is precisely for this reason that I regard this topic as one of the major items that the future philosophy of language will have to discuss. Of course, many more refinements will need to be introduced and investigated. One will have to distinguish among, for example, the statement intended, the statement understood by some listener to have been made, the statement that is usually made by uttering a certain sentence under standard conditions (and, sometimes, these three statements may turn out to be different and thereby perhaps to be a major source of misunderstandings), and so on. More generally, for a given utterance, the questions of how one determines which sentence was intended to be uttered, which was understood to have been uttered, what kind of linguistic act was performed on that occasion (whether asserting, requesting, demanding, declaring, promising, swearing, or whatever), what was the product of this particular act, how was it intended, how was it understood, and so on, have only begun to be systematically investigated. It is amazing to see absolutely no awareness of this wealth of important issues in Katz's recent book; but I am afraid that even in Chomsky's *Aspects,* for instance, there are a number of points that rest upon nondistinction of distinguishables, and I return to one such point later.

B. THE TRANSPOSED MODE OF SPEECH

Even though linguists are aware of the problematics subsumed under such catch words as grammatical subject (logical subject) and psychological subject (but I agree with Chomsky that extant analyses of this issue are not particularly satisfactory and could not really have been so before some such distinction as that between surface and deep structure, under this or any other name, was made and clearly understood), they have unfortunately paid little if any attention to a phenomenon to which Carnap has, alas too briefly, drawn our attention under the somewhat forbidding name "transposed mode of speech."[25] Briefly and roughly, an utterance is in the transposed mode of speech if it seems to be about *A* but is really about some *B* different from *A*. Of course, certain subspecies of this mode of speech are well known and have been widely discussed by lin-

---

[25]R. Carnap, *The Logical Syntax of Language* (London, 1937), p. 308; cf. my "Carnap's Logical Syntax of Language," in *The Philosophy of Rudolf Carnap,* pp. 519-543.

guists, literary critics, and recently even by some philosophers of science under such headings as "metaphors" and the like. Yet what Carnap had in mind was something much more general than that, which, however, still has enough interesting properties to deserve close study in all its generality.

To present just one, perhaps not too convincing, illustration, which has certainly nothing to do with metaphorical speech: One might want to say that, by uttering *LBJ is famous*, one is not really saying anything about LBJ at all, but rather something about people and their acts, in particular, perhaps, about their speech acts. Such a view may be defended by pointing out that a person may cease to be famous (or, for that matter, may become famous) without any change having occurred in him but rather, and exclusively, through some changes in his environment. All this raises innumerable problems, of course, some of which are well known to philosophers under such designations as "the problem of aboutness" or "the problem of external and internal relations." I would insist, though, that these problems are not really philosophical ones, and certainly not exclusively so, but should be the linguists' direct concern, and that no good understanding of language and speech is possible without an adequate understanding of their nature.

Let me also mention, in an aside, that some subspecies of the transposed mode of speech gained great fame among philosophers in the 1930's and 1940's and were discussed by them with great fervor and, in my opinion, deserve to be discussed some more. In particular, it was the material mode of speech which became, in the hands of Carnap and his followers, an extremely powerful technique for the dissolution of classical philosophical problems. To illustrate: *A rose is a thing* seems to say something about roses, namely, that they are things, but Carnap insists that what is really achieved by uttering (a token of) this sentence (in particular, when a philosopher is the utterer) is to claim of the word rose that it is a noun (a thing-word, *Dingwort* in German). And, believe it or not, this reinterpretation does make a decisive difference in matters philosophical, in particular in so-called ontology. Of course, there is nothing about all this in Katz's book.

C. INDEXICAL EXPRESSIONS

The problems created by the "indexicality" (or "context [-of-utterance] dependency") of most of our utterances — an indexical sentence is one that contains such words as *I, you, here, there, now, then, this,* and the like, or one that contains tensed verbs, but it is not limited in meaning to these two criteria—are numerous, all-pervading, and partly well known and understood. Indexical expressions are both ubiquitous means for effective communications (it is a nice philosophical standby to discuss whether communication is at all possible without them) and the source of many misunderstandings (i.e., of failures of communication). It is my personal view—which I shall, of course, not try to defend here—that this phenomenon is also a major cause of many philosophical pseudo-problems and pseudo-theses; and, in the confusion it creates when not fully understood, is partly responsible for the otherwise almost incomprehensible veneration in which the Cartesian *Cogito* is held.

Needless to say, nothing is said about indexical expressions in Katz's book. Standard dictionary entries for these expressions are altogether inadequate, and a KF-type lexicon is utterly unable to cope with them. To my knowledge, their treatment within such a framework has not even been seriously attempted, and all KF illustrations try to keep away from them, even though the reasons for this asceticism are never discussed. Semantic markers are clearly completely out of place in the characterization of their function, which is an almost exclusively pragmatic one. The occasionally quite confused, but sometimes also rather insightful, discussion by philosophers such as Peirce, Husserl, Russell, Reichenbach, Goodman, and many others is disregarded no less and no more than the treatment by such linguists as Stöhr and Karl Bühler—and I am just mentioning names at random, without any attempt to be even remotely exhaustive.[26] The terms used by linguists for this phenomenon are something like "deictic," but the phenomenon is simply underdiscussed under any name.

D. DEGREES OF GRAMMATICALITY

The jungle of phenomena around degrees of grammaticality, semigrammaticality, semantic anomaly, oddness, bizarreness, category mistakes, type violations, and a host of other related concepts is now in a state of almost utter confusion, after a decade of intense and well-meant discussion which has exhibited linguists, logicians, and philosophers at their dogmatic and insensitive worst. Without

[26]More is said in my paper, "Indexical Expressions," *Mind* 63:359-379 (1954); see also my "Can Indexical Sentences Stand in Logical Relations?" *Philosophical Studies* 14:87-90 (1963).

the many distinctions I indicated above (under A) and a large number of additional ones, it is, in my opinion, almost hopeless to make inroads into that jungle. Because whatever positive statements I have to make on this topic have already been made on another occasion,[27] let me turn to my fifth and last point.

E. INCOMPLETELY DETERMINED MEANINGS

Carnap and other recent philosophers of science have brilliantly called our attention to the fact that scientists are constantly working, and successfully, with expressions whose meaning has only been incompletely determined.[28] (The twin phenomenon of indirect meaning determination, decisive though it is for theoretical terms and the understanding of their methodological status, is so complex that it shall only be mentioned here.) This fact came as a surprise to many people whose conception of science included the notion that science abhors meaning indeterminacies, that in scientific writings each term, at least in principle, has a completely determined meaning. Wittgenstein, Waismann, and other philosophers of the British brand of analytic philosophy had said much about that many years before Carnap, with respect to expressions in ordinary, everyday speech, with Waismann coining the term "open texture" for this phenomenon. (Here, as often before, any identifications of intentions should be taken with a large grain of salt. Nobody will have any difficulties in finding any number of differences, even important differences, between Carnap's conception of partly interpreted theoretical terms and Waismann's conception of ordinary terms with open texture. I would still insist that, on a certain relevant level, they were discussing phenomena belonging to the same class.)

Unfortunately, the phenomenon of partial meaning is not reducible to full meaning in certain contexts and lack of meaning in all remaining contexts. It is only a whole theory that gets a kind of wholesale interpretation, usually through an enormously complex and, in practice, a never explicitly presented network of rules of interpretation whose exact functioning has never been satisfactorily analyzed and understood. In general, there exists no retail basis for this global meaningfulness, so that the partial meaning of the particular theoretical terms cannot be characterized in terms of obser-

[27]In my review of Fodor and Katz, *op. cit.*, in *Language* 43:526-550 (1967).

vational expressions in any more specific form. For lucid and rea-
sonably nontechnical presentation of the issue, let me refer to
Carnap's recent, eminently readable volume, *Philosophical Foundations of Physics*.[28]

POSTSCRIPT
October 1967

Since my two lectures are being published two years after
their delivery in June 1966, a certain amount of updating is man-
datory. During the last sixteen months, a number of publications
have appeared which change somewhat the picture described in
the text. In particular, the new journal *Foundations of Language*
contains a considerable number of highly relevant contributions.
The most important of these is J. J. Katz's "Recent Issues in Semantic Theory" (3:124-194 [1967]) which is considerably more sophisticated than his previous contributions. It is Katz's reply to Weinreich's critique mentioned in note 1 to my lectures. (Cf. also
Weinreich's short rebuttal in the August 1967 issue of that journal.)
I still think my critique remains valid in essence, even with regard
to Katz's more recent, improved formulations, but the sharp words
I used in the text no longer apply to them. There has been considerable and welcome improvement, and it may be hoped that, by
taking into account the achievements of the logical semanticists,
this sophistication will soon be adequate to support a more serious
scholarly undertaking.

---

[28]R. Carnap, *Philosophical Foundations of Physics* (New York, 1966).

Problems in the Analysis of Idioms

Uriel Weinreich
Columbia University

I. Introduction

There is a view, widespread not just among laymen but also among sophisticated practitioners of the verbal arts, that in the idioms of a language lie its most interesting specificities. To urge this view on an audience of linguists today would surely smack of the most outlandish romanticism. If I have, nevertheless, decided to take up so unfashionable a topic,[1] it is not because I think of idioms as a true revelation of the folk soul, but because, as a student of the organization of language, I find them intriguing, as well as sadly underexplored. Idiomaticity is important for this reason, if for no other, that there is so much of it in every language; for a phraseological dictionary in preparation for standard Russian, no less than 25,000 entries have recently been anticipated (Babkin, 1964, p. 29). Idiomaticity is interesting, too, because it appears in many structural varieties and yields certain distinct subpatterns — some perhaps universal, others specific to each language. Finally, to a linguistics that is preoccupied with productivity in the strongest, Chomskyan sense, idiomaticity represents a basic theoretical stumbling block; for under the rubric of idiomaticity we are concerned with complex structures that can be recognized and analyzed but not naturally generated by any explicit machinery so far proposed. Like many facts of word-formation (cf. Zimmer, 1964), idiomaticity serves to remind us how heavily language is laden with

[1] The research on which this paper is based, carried out while I was a fellow at the Center for Advanced Study in the Behavioral Sciences, was supported in part by a Public Health Service research grant (MH 95743) from the National Institute of Mental Health.

semiproductive patterns. Although linguistics was too long and too exclusively obsessed with semiproductivity, these patterns cannot be swept under the rug just because the *main* focus of our attention has been turned to fully productive devices.

Even if the theoretical implications of idiom study seem particularly intriguing against a generative background, the subject *can* be approached from other points of view as well, so that it is rather puzzling that it should have been so long and so thoroughly ignored. The general abeyance in which semantics was held is not the sole explanation, because even works explicitly devoted to semantics have skipped over the topic of idioms almost entirely.[2]

One small phase of the idiom problem was discussed from a machine-translation point of view by Bar-Hillel in 1955. A year later Hockett proposed a rather novel conception of idioms which has failed to gain wide acceptance.[3] Householder (1959), writing about linguistic primes, put forward the notion of an idiom grammar as part of a complete generative system. Whatever the merits of his proposals at the time, they were made with an eye to linguistic descriptions devoid of semantic components, and hence Householder's approach just cannot serve our needs any more. Among students of kinship and folk-scientific terminology, the matter of idioms has also been grazed in a paragraph here and a section there, only to be set aside for a confrontation with componential analysis, to them a more fundamental problem.[4] Finally, a modest stab was made at idioms from a generative-syntactic point of view in a brief paper by Katz and Postal (1963); I have found their contribution an incomplete but useful base to build on, and have suggested some further questions in my "Explorations in Semantic Theory" (Weinreich, 1966b, pp. 450 ff.). All this American work of the past decade has a distinct hit-and-run quality. The only two investigations that are not disappointingly desultory and that actually grapple with a body of diversified material are Malkiel's study of irreversible binomials (1959) and a recent, still unpublished Yale dissertation by Makkai (1965).

In West European linguistics, as far as I am aware, there is little to brighten the picture, except for the chapters on phraseology

---

[2]Ullmann's books of 1957 and 1962, though they reflect a rich literature on various semantic subjects, do not deal with idioms. The topic is also missing from other recent books on semantics, e.g., Ziff (1960), Lyons (1963), and Greimas (1966).

[3]Hockett (1956). This conception, despite its highly experimental status, was incorporated in the author's elementary textbook of linguistics (Hockett, 1958). For a criticism of the approach, see Weinreich (1960), pp. 337-339.

[4]Cf., for example, Lounsbury (1956), pp. 192 f., and Conklin (1962), p. 122.

and idioms in Casares' manual of dictionary making (Casares, 1950). A rather different situation, on the other hand, prevails in the Soviet Union. There, a field called "lexicology" has been developing as a legitimate domain of linguistics (Weinreich, 1963); not surprisingly, a Russion translation of Casares' handbook has been available since 1958. Within lexicology, the study of what are broadly called "phraseological units" or "stable collocations" has enjoyed a particularly boisterous growth in the past few years. That this is a field not merely staked out, but diligently tilled, is evident from a bibliography of Soviet works on phraseology from 1918 to 1961, which contains over 900 items (Babkin, 1964). Of these, incidentally, over a hundred items deal with English alone. In the past few years, book-length studies of Russian and English phraseology by Šanskij (1963), Amosova (1963), and Arxangel'skij (1964) have appeared.[5]

You can't tell a book by its cover, nor a theory by its terminology. The sheer quantity of work carried out by our Soviet colleagues does not guarantee the solidity of its theoretical underpinnings, or the cumulativeness of its results. The samples I have seen suffer, I feel, from syntactic inadequacies of various kinds, and too little of this work has been guided by an attempt to formalize its findings.[6] But the purpose of this presentation is analytical and exploratory: a critique of previous works must be left for another occasion.

II. Idioms and Phraseological Units

The first problem before us is to identify idiomaticity in language structure, to see what idioms are and how they differ from nonidiomatic expressions; the second is to see whether idioms can be "dissolved," by appropriate analytic devices, into nonidiomatic constituents, and what obstacles stand in the way of such dissolution.

To simplify the exposition, I shall begin with examples of the utmost syntactic simplicity. Transformational complications will

[5]Note also the published abstracts and proceedings of recent conferences on the study of phraseology, listed in the bibliography to this paper under *Problemy frazeologii* . . . (1965), and Ustinov (1966).

[6]Most Soviet work follows the classifications and theoretical guidelines first laid down by Vinogradov (1946, 1947). The clearest and most attractive example of this approach seems to me to be Šanskij (1963); however, I find Amosova's critique (1963, pp. 31 ff.) of the approach completely convincing. She has shown Vinogradov's classificational criteria to be too vague and interdependent to yield reliable results.

be encountered soon enough. I should make it clear, too, that I shall not be able, in this paper, to touch on, much less to exhaust, all questions relevant to the subject. I think we have seen eloquent evidence in the past few years of how much more instructive it can be to study small problems under powerful magnification than to try to take in great heaps of phenomena in sweeping surveys.

Let us then begin by trying to represent with some degree of formality the common understanding of an idiom as a complex expression whose meaning cannot be derived from the meanings of its elements. Let us posit for the present that the minimal meaningful units of a language are *morphemes*, and let us symbolize a morpheme as a capital letter (representing some sequence of phonemes) paired with a lowercase letter (representing its sense). Formula 1a then symbolizes a nonidiomatic, or literal, construction, whereas formula 1b symbolizes an idiomatic construction.

$$\frac{A}{a} + \frac{B}{b} = \frac{A+B}{a+b} \tag{1a}$$

$$\frac{C}{c} + \frac{D}{d} = \frac{C+D}{x} \neq \frac{C+D}{c+d} \tag{1b}$$

In formula 1a, the construction of A/a with B/b yields a phonemic sequence $A + B$ and a sense that is in some way a function of the ingredient senses, a and b. In 1b, the obtained sense x is not the expected function of the senses c and d.

It is the job of a semantic theory to account for the derivation of the expressions on the right sides of the equal-signs from those on the left sides. While this theoretical job may seem trivial with regard to formula 1a, it is quite serious with regard to 1b, for it raises the question of how to represent in a dictionary, in which C/c and D/d are entries, the information that if they are constructed with each other they will not yield the predictable result. But even so ridiculously simple a formula as 1a offers a theoretical problem if we endow the plus sign with any intuitively recognizable content. The phonemic forms of the two morphemes A and B may quite typically appear one after the other; if so, the + above the horizontal bar may be a symbol of sequence.[7] If it is, however, we hardly want the same plus sign to connect the senses, as represented by

---

[7]To be sure, there is a great deal of fusion in the phonic representation of signs in most languages, but for purposes of this discussion we may stipulate that deviations from an ideal agglutinative structure are irrelevant.

the lowercase letters under the bar. For the senses of a string of morphemes to form a mere sequence of "meaning pulses" is quite atypical; on the contrary, some nonsequential fusion of the senses is more typical. The cumulative sense is some kind of function of the component senses, but hardly a sequence. One way to symbolize cumulative sense is shown in formula 2, where 2a represents a literal construction and 2b represents an idiom.

$$\frac{A}{a} + \frac{B}{b} = \frac{A + B}{f(a, b)} \tag{2a}$$

$$\frac{C}{c} + \frac{D}{d} = \frac{C + D}{x} \neq \frac{C + D}{f(c, d)} \tag{2b}$$

It is becoming fairly widely recognized that there is in any language more than one combinatorial semantic function f and that a particular f_i is associated with each nonterminal node of the syntax which is capable of dominating a binary branching in the deep structure.[8] For the sake of argument, let us assume that a language has two semantic functions, f_1 and f_2, and that among its nonterminal nodes are M and N, which are associated each with one of the functions, as symbolized by the notation M_1 and N_2. To show semantic combination in at least a minimal syntactic context, we may resort to diagrams such as 3, in which the arrow may be taken to symbolize the passage of the fragmentary phrase marker through the semantic calculator (in the sense of Weinreich, 1966b, pp. 455 ff.).

$$
\begin{array}{ccccccc}
& M_1 & & & & N_2 & \\
\frac{A}{a} & & \frac{B}{b} \to \frac{A+B}{f_1(a,b)} & & \frac{Q}{q} & & \frac{R}{r} \to \frac{Q+R}{f_2(q,r)}
\end{array}
\tag{3}
$$

So far we have looked at the senses a, b, q, and r as wholes; however, there is good reason to analyze many senses further into components. Think of semantic paradigms such as *chair — sit, bed — lie*, or *have — give, see — show*. Such paradigms yield fairly reliable

[8]Katz (1966, p. 165), going a step beyond the vague formulations in Katz and Fodor (1963, pp. 193-205), now asserts that "there is a distinct projection rule for each distinct grammatical relation." In my opinion, this view is incorrect; I have suggested that there are only four semantic functions (= projection rules; cf. Weinreich, 1966a, pp. 164 f., developed in Weinreich, 1966b, pp. 420-428). As was pointed out to me by Jonathan D. Kaye, we may set ourselves a goal of reformulating the phrase-structure component of a syntax in such a way as to contain the same number of nonterminal nodes as there are (independently arrived) semantic functions. Whether such a syntax could indeed be designed is highly problematical.

components of meaning.[9] Traditionally a sense was treated as the logical product of its components, so that the semantic components of a sense formed an unordered set. In recent years it has become increasingly clear that the relation between sense components is not, in general, symmetrical.[10] If we reckon with more than one combinatory semantic function — say, the two functions f_1 and f_2 — then the component of a sense can be related by either of these functions.

We may further assume that there is at least one semantic function that is asymmetrical. This property would be shown formally as in formula 4. (In principle, nothing precludes the existence of more than one asymmetrical function, but we do not pursue this point further here.)

$$f_2 \left(\alpha_1, \alpha_2 \right) \neq f_2 \left(\alpha_2, \alpha_1 \right) \tag{4}$$

Suppose there are two senses, a and b, such that a contains the components α_1 and α_2 related by function f_1, while b contains components β_1 and β_2 related by function f_2. Suppose now that, as represented in 5, morphemes A and B form a grammatical construction dominated by node M_1 (i.e., a node that itself has the semantic effect f_1). The semantic result of the construction, represented in terms of the sense components, is shown on the right of the arrow in 5b.

[9]That the senses of many morphemes (or lexemes) of a language are indeed analyzable into components can, I think, be supported by such evidence as anthropologists have been developing in their studies of special vocabularies and which linguists have been unearthing in certain areas of "general" vocabulary (cf. *Mašinnyj perevod i prikladnaja lingvistika*, 1964; Bendix, 1966). Nevertheless it is sobering to realize that in every language many morphemes or lexemes yield no clear-cut componential analysis, and for many others such analysis is hard to conceive of altogether (Weinreich, 1966*b*, p. 473). On how to deal with the combinatorial effects of such unanalyzable or unparaphrasable sense gestalts, I have at present no suggestions to make. All I have to say in these pages applies only to senses that have been, or possibly can be, componentially analyzed, or at least reliably paraphrased.

[10]In the analysis of kinship terminologies, the need for "relative products" as an alternative to "logical products" has been apparent for some time. (Cf. Burling, 1965, for a comparative utilization of these frameworks.) The rules discovered by Lounsbury (1965) have forced an even more dramatic broadening of our conception of the way in which sense components are related to each other. Katz (1964, 1966) has introduced complex, internally structured semantic markers for the *ad hoc* solution of certain semantic problems; in my own recent paper (Weinreich, 1966*b*), I have gone even further, arguing that any semantic relation that holds between the constituents of a construction may also occur among the "simultaneous" components of a single sense. These semantic relations among components, I have suggested, are exhibited in the snytax of paraphrases and of definitions, so that there is in fact a continuity between the "ordinary" sentences of a language and the definitional sentences.

Given $a = f_1 (\alpha_1, \alpha_2)$

$\qquad b = f_2 (\beta_1, \beta_2)$ $\hfill$ (5a)

then

$$\underset{f_1 (\alpha_1, \alpha_2)}{A} \overset{\displaystyle M_1}{\diagdown} \underset{f_2 (\beta_1, \beta_2)}{B} \rightarrow \underset{f_1 [f_1 (a_1, a_2), f_2 (\beta_1, \beta_2)]}{A + B} \qquad (5b)$$

If it is granted that languages have one semantic function ("predication," or "linking") in which the constituents appear in a symmetrical relation, and if we let f_1 in the present example stand for this function, then further operations (Weinreich, 1966a, p. 199; 1966b, p. 419 and *passim*) permit us to derive 5c from 5b:

$$\frac{A + B}{f_2 [f_1 (\alpha_1, \alpha_2, \beta_1), \beta_2]} \qquad (5c)$$

In a semantic theory I have recently been developing (Weinreich, 1966b), I envisaged the possibility that a nonterminal node might itself contribute some sense or sense component (e.g., "time," "direction," etc.) to the constituents it dominates. To coordinate this view with the present discussion, let me therefore also consider the possibility, symbolized in 6, in which M_2/m is a nonterminal symbol in a grammar which produces the semantic effect f_2 on the constituents it dominates and itself has the categorial sense m. The total semantic result would be as shown on the right of the arrow.

$$\underset{a}{A} \diagup \overset{\displaystyle M_2}{\underset{\displaystyle m}{}} \diagdown \underset{b}{B} \rightarrow \underset{f_2 (m, a, b)}{A + B} \qquad (6)$$

This particular instance, however, is a somewhat tangential matter, and we can safely ignore this possibility in the balance of the present discussion.

And now to return to idioms. In 2b we tried to represent an idiomatic construction; but we did not specify its syntactic form, nor did we indicate in what particular way the sense x may differ from some expected function of the senses c and d. We can now replace 2b by formula 7, a more fully analyzed representation.

$$\overset{\displaystyle M_1}{\underset{\displaystyle \frac{A}{a} \qquad\qquad \frac{B}{b}}{\diagup \qquad\qquad \diagdown}} \to \frac{A+B}{x} \neq \frac{A+B}{f_i\,(a,\,b)} \qquad\qquad (7)$$

This formula shows that in the construction $A + B$, the resulting sense is not the expected semantic function f_i of the component senses a and b. That is what x is *not*, and that inequality is what defines the "phraseological phenomenon" in the most general terms. But what *is* this new semantic object, sense x? Let us look over several possibilities.

The first possibility, symbolized in formula 8a, shows that one of the components in the obtained sense y is distinct from the expected component a.

$$\frac{A+B}{x} = \frac{A+B}{f_i\,(y,\,b)} \qquad (y \neq a) \qquad\qquad (8a)$$

$$\frac{A+B}{x} = \frac{A+B}{f_i\,(y,\,z)} \qquad (y \neq a; \quad z \neq b) \qquad\qquad (8b)$$

This type is extremely familiar and much studied. Thus, *red* in the construction *red hair* does not render the "absolute" sense of *red*— its "abridged dictionary" sense, so to speak—but some variant of it. (A color swatch matching red hair, if abstracted from the hair context, would hardly be called "red.") We can further complicate the example, as in 8b, to show that while two senses related by the function f_i are distinguishable in the construction, *neither one* is the "expected" contribution of the components A and B. Suppose that we take one of the meanings of *red herring* to be "phony issue," with the component senses "phony" and "issue" in a modifier-head relation, as are the literal "red" and "herring." Yet unless we envisage a dictionary in which "phony" is listed as one of the senses of *red* and "issue" as one of the senses of *herring*, there will be a discrepancy between the ingredients and the product, as symbolized in 8b.

For the sake of completeness, we should perhaps also mention the possibility symbolized in formula 8c, in which the component senses are retained intact in the construction, but are related by a

$$\frac{A+B}{x} = \frac{A+B}{f_j\,(a,\,b)} \qquad (i \neq j) \qquad\qquad (8c)$$

semantic function different from the one specified for constructions dominated by the given node (e.g., M_i), as might occur, for example, if a particular verb phrase, which in its literal sense functions as a verb with a direct object, turns up in idiomatic usage as a copula with a predicate noun (contrast *make cookies with flour* and *make friends with a foreigner*). Ordinarily, a deep-structure phrase marker would differentiate sufficiently between the structures involved in such a way that the difference of semantic effect would be redundant with respect to a difference of dominating nodes. We will, however, return to a possible examplification of this form of idiomaticity in Section IV.

The notation used in 8*a* and 8*b* implies that the difference between the expected sense, say *a*, and the obtained sense *y* is an all-or-none difference; however, if we now introduce the devices of componential analysis discussed a little earlier (recall the examples of 5), we can represent the net differences between the expected *a* and the obtained *y* in factorial terms. Suppose that, as in 9, *a* consists of components α_1, α_2, and α_3 related by semantic function f_1.

$$a = f_1 (\alpha_1, \alpha_2, \alpha_3) \tag{9}$$

$$y = f_1 (\alpha_1, \alpha_2)$$

$$y' = f_1 (\alpha_1, \alpha_2, \alpha_3, \alpha_4)$$

$$y'' = f_1 (\alpha_1, \alpha_5, \alpha_6)$$

Sense *y* may differ from sense *a* by just lacking a component, or by having an additional component, or by differing by one or more components. (We could formulate these possibilities even more generally than is done in 9 by using algebraic subscripts rather than integers, but I would guess that in this highly preliminary discussion, such technicalities can be dispensed with.)

The formulas under 9 are again meant to represent phenomena that are all quite familiar. When we compare the "absolute" sense of *coat*, "a covering of some kind," with its sense in the expression *coat of paint*, we may say that in the latter some specifying component is lacking and only those components that render the general meaning of "covering" are present. In comparing *news* in general with *news* in *newsboy*, we might say that a more specific sense of *news* appears. In comparing *red* in general (or in such contexts as *red paper*) with *red* in *red hair*, we may say that a partly different set of components is realized. Since the color of red hair, manifested in anything other than hair, would hardly be called *red*, some of the components of the senses must be different. On the other hand, some are shared: the two senses of *red* are still color names.

To sum up: An idiomatic sense of a complex expression may differ from its literal sense either in virtue of the semantic function (as in 8c), or of the semantic constituents. The difference between expected and obtained constituents may amount to a suppression of some component of meaning, or the addition of some component, or a replacement of components.

We have been at pains to characterize the difference between members of homonymous pairs, one of which is a literal expression, while the other is affected by idiomaticity. We have been stating these differences for pairs of expressions in isolation, but nothing has been said yet about introducing an idiom into a text. This process depends on the status of the idiom in the dictionary. As Bar-Hillel (1955, p. 186) justly observed, an expression is idiomatic not absolutely, but relative to a particular dictionary. For example, if our dictionary contained all three items listed under 10 as entries,

$$\frac{A}{a}, \ \frac{B}{b}, \ \frac{A+B}{f_j\,(y,\,z)} \tag{10}$$

the expression that appeared on the right of the arrow in 7 could be taken intact from the dictionary, so that it would not be an idiom in terms of synchronic process at all. But even if such entries were allowed in the dictionary, we would still have to consider the manner in which they could be "taken" from the dictionary and "put into" a text. For that, an expression would have to be available to a highly explicit syntax, conceived as an abstract automaton. It must have the right handles, as it were, to be grasped by the syntax. One convenient way of describing these handles, explored by Chomsky, is in terms of syntactic features.

To see what we are up against, we must increase the realism of our schematic syntax by showing the node M to dominate appropriate unary nodes, for example, F and G. Let us, for the time being, reckon with a "lexical rule" that substitutes morphemes for dummy symbols. We can now represent three ways in which an idiomatic expression $A + B$ can be related to its literal counterpart. The first way, illustrated in 11, shows M to be an endocentric construction in which F is optional and G is obligatory; the idiom $A + B$ has the syntactic features of the head, G.

$M_i \rightarrow (F) + G$ *Dictionary*: $\qquad\qquad\qquad\qquad\qquad$ (11a)

$F \rightarrow \Delta \qquad\qquad \dfrac{A}{a}\,[+F]\,;\dfrac{B}{b}\,[+G]\,; \qquad \dfrac{A+B}{f_j\,(y,\,z)}\,[+G]$

$G \rightarrow \Delta$

$$
\begin{array}{ccc}
 & M_i & \\
F & & G \\
| & & | \\
\Delta & & \Delta \\
| & & | \\
\dfrac{A}{a} & & \dfrac{B}{b} \rightarrow \dfrac{A+B}{f_i\,(a,\,b)}
\end{array}
$$
(11b)

$$
\begin{array}{c}
M_i \\
| \\
G \\
| \\
\Delta \\
| \\
\dfrac{A+B}{f_j\,(y,\,z)}
\end{array}
$$
(11c)

This formulation might represent fixed adjective-plus-noun phrases, for example, *hot potato*, meaning "highly embarrassing issue." A second way in which an idiomatic expression can be related to its counterpart is shown in 12.

$M_i \rightarrow \left\{ \begin{matrix} F+G \\ \Delta \end{matrix} \right\}$ *Dictionary*; $\qquad\qquad\qquad$ (12a)

$F \rightarrow \Delta \qquad\qquad \dfrac{A}{a}\,[+F]\,;\dfrac{B}{b}\,[+G]\,; \qquad \dfrac{A+B}{f_j\,(y,\,z)}\,[+M]$

$G \rightarrow \Delta$

$\qquad\qquad\qquad$ Same as 11b $\qquad\qquad\qquad\qquad$ (12b)

$$
\begin{array}{c}
M_i \\
| \\
\Delta \\
| \\
\dfrac{A+B}{f_j\,(y,\,z)}
\end{array}
$$
(12c)

This second way requires a more unconventional grammar in which particular nodes, such as M, may function either terminally or non-terminally. Such descriptions as 11 and 12 would generate both the literal and the idiomatic expressions; however, they would not exhibit the fact, characteristic of most idioms, that $i = j$, that is, that the semantic function over the constituent senses of the idiom does in fact agree with the one associated with the dominant node. (The counterexample above, *make friends*, is rather atypical.) Still another possibility is represented under 13.

$$M \rightarrow F + G \qquad Dictionary; \tag{13}$$

$$\ldots \rightarrow \ldots Q \ldots \qquad \frac{A}{a}\,[+F]\,; \frac{B}{b}\,[+G]\,; \frac{A+B}{f_j\,(y,\,z)}\,[+Q]$$

Here the idiom has syntactic features unrelated systematically to those of the literal counterpart. We find this where a combination of noun and noun functions as a manner adverb: *(fight) tooth and nail, (go at him) hammer and tongs*. It is an interesting empirical finding that such syntactic deformities are altogether rare among idioms and are confined to a very few types, whereas the theoretical possibilities of unconstrained deformation are very great.

And so, we have seen that we can, as Bar-Hillel (1955) noted, eliminate idioms simply by listing them in the dictionary. For rare instances such as 13, this solution seems nearly inevitable. For frequent cases, as exemplified under 12, however, the listing of idioms, as such, in the dictionary entails grammars of unusual design — in addition to other "costs" of which we have yet to speak. Moreover, in the instances outlined in 11 and 12, semantic infornation must be redundantly given as the f_j is specified in each. We therefore want to see whether we cannot get rid of idioms by some less costly alternatives. The obvious machinery to try is, of course, *polysemy*, or disjunction of senses in dictionary characterizations of the morphemes.

Let formula 14 include a morpheme A that is marked as ambiguous in the dictionary: it has senses a or y. In an M-construction

$$\tag{14}$$

$$
\begin{array}{ccc}
 & M_i & \\
F & & G \\
| & & | \\
\Delta & & \Delta \\
| & & | \\
A & & B \\
\overline{a \vee y} & & \overline{b} \rightarrow \dfrac{A+B}{f_i\,(a,\,b) \vee f_i\,(y,\,b)}
\end{array}
$$

such as $A + B$, we expect to find the corresponding ambiguity, as shown in the formula, to the right of the arrow. We may now impose still more structure by allowing our notation to show that two possible senses of morpheme A, namely a and y, have specialized environments such that sense y is realized in constructions with B, while sense a is realized elsewhere. The contextual specialization of senses is shown by means of a notation familiar from phonology. We now have the results shown in formula 15.

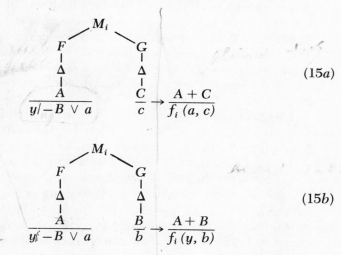

$$(15a)$$

$$(15b)$$

The selection of the special sense y in the context $-B$ may be optional or obligatory. We have here treated it as obligatory, so that the resulting reading in 15b is free of ambiguities. If we marked the selection as optional by means of a dotted diagonal, for example, as in formula 16,

$$(16)$$

we would obtain an ambiguous reading. For example, suppose that *blind* in construction with *date* has the sense "not previously introduced." The selection of this sense is optional. Hence *I had a blind date* means either "a companion I had not previously seen" or "a sightless companion." (I am thinking of the personal sense of *date*, as in *I kissed my date good-night.*)

The solution in terms of polysemy is free of the major disadvantages of listing whole idioms in the dictionary. It specifies the appropriate structure for the phonological component to operate on and accounts for the agreement between the subscript i of M_i and the semantic function f in the vast majority of idioms in which there is, in fact, such agreement.[11]

Shall we then go ahead and dissolve all idioms, as *can* be done? Such a procedure hardly can be adopted across the board. Some "dissolutions" of idioms seem to be too counterintuitive to offset the lexicographic economies achieved. We, therefore, must look at some instances where the dissolution makes us uneasy and see what formal features they contain that might be at the roots of our intuitive objections.

Let us take the English phrase *by heart*, which functions as a manner adverbial with a highly restricted set of verbs, and has the meaning "from memory." In order to make it insertible in a sentence, *by* would have to be marked as a preposition and *heart*, as a noun. Since our dictionary already has a preposition *by* and a noun *heart*, we want to consider analyzing the expression into the *by* and the *heart* already noticed. (For the sake of simplicity, let us ignore the fact that the other *heart* is a count noun, whereas this one, judging from the lack of an article, is a mass noun.) Now, the preposition *by* has several disjunct senses, but *he said it by heart* does not seem to exhibit either the sense of *he said it by the window* (location) or that of *he said it by today* (deadline), or *he said it by phone* (vehicle), or *by whispering it* (manner). Let us assume that the sense of *by* in *by heart*, paraphrasable perhaps as "from," is unique, and is determined by the contextually following word *heart*. Now, the sense of *heart* as "memory" is also unique here. We cannot say *his heart failed him* and mean "his memory conked out," nor do we say *he has an excellent heart* of someone who can sing all four stanzas of "The Star-Spangled Banner." It seems then

[11]Katz and Postal (1963, p. 275) see the "essential feature of an idiom" in the fact that "its full meaning . . . is not a compositional function of the idiom's elementary grammatical parts." But this takes the set of idioms of a language as given; it offers no criteria for deciding between idiom treatment and the polysemous resolution of an expression. It is safe, I think, in the present context to avoid a discussion of alternative forms of the lexical rule for inserting morphemes into preterminal strings. For my countersuggestions to the proposals made by Chomsky, Katz, and Postal, see Weinreich (1966*b*), p. 434.

that the special sense of *heart,* namely "memory," is here determined by the contextually preceding *by.*

Schematically this mutual selection would be shown in the dictionary as in formula 17.

$$Dictionary: \frac{A}{y/-B \lor a} \, [+F] \, ; \, \frac{B}{z/A-\lor b} \, [+G] \tag{17a}$$

$$
\begin{array}{c}
\overset{\displaystyle M_2}{\diagup \qquad \diagdown} \\[2pt]
\begin{array}{cc}
F & G \\
| & | \\
\Delta & \Delta \\
| & | \\
A & B \\
\hline
y/-B \lor a \quad & z/A- \lor b
\end{array}
\; \rightarrow \; \dfrac{A+B}{f_2\,(y,\,z)}
\end{array}
\tag{17b}
$$

(I have marked the selection as obligatory, although such marking may be an artifact of our disregard of the *ad hoc* "massness" of *heart;* if the idiom were *by the heart,* there would be ambiguities showing that the selection is optional).

Be that as it may, let us scrutinize the analysis to see what aspect of it may be held accountable for its absurdity. Actually there are several possiblities. The first possibility is that the selection of special senses here goes both ways: morpheme *A* selects a subsense of *B* and morpheme *B* selects a subsense of *A.* In other domains of description, two-directional selections (properly ordered) seem to be inevitable. Consider the morphophonemics of *broken:* the stem determines the allomorph of the suffix (*-en,* rather than *-ed),* while the suffix determines the allomorph of the stem (*broke,* rather than *break).* In the semantic component, on the other hand, we may want to prohibit two-directional selective restrictions. If I propose this constraint with some hesitation, it is because I have noticed that its violation is, in practice, almost invariably connected with the violation of other, equally reasonable constraints.

A second feature in our example to which we may attribute the awkwardness of its dissolution is the fact that the contextually specialized subsense *z* of *heart* (i.e., "memory") has no semantic components in common with the "otherwise" subsense, *a* (i.e., "blood pumping organ"). We might rephrase this statement by saying that there is here homonymy, not polysemy. Now, the distinction between homonymy and polysemy is notoriously elusive. There are pairs of like-sounding morphemes in a language, such as the English verbs *pour* and *pore,* which do share some very abstract semantic feature, such as "activity," but no others, and yet might most conveniently be classed as homonyms. It is still possible that as polysemy shades into homonymy, some clear break should be postulated at which the relative preponderance of shared features over separate features drops markedly. At the moment we have no criteria for distinguishing homonymy from polysemy, but the suppletiveness of the subsenses seems to be involved in the absurdity of our analysis.

A third possible source of the absurdity is that the context of the special senses of *heart* and of *by* has been stated in terms of particular morphemes, symbolized in the formula by the capitals *A* and *B* under the diagonals, and could not be restated in terms of semantic components. What I mean is that if the subsense of *by* which is here evoked is "from," then *heart* should function similarly with synonyms of *by*, for example, the word *from* itself; but it does not. We cannot sing "The Star-Spangled Banner" *from heart*. The example is rather delicate, but in the syntactically more complex material to be dealt with below, we have completely unmistakable evidence. If, for example, the special sense of *cats and dogs* were dependent, not on the morpheme *rain*, but on its sense, we would not expect the raised eyebrows we get at *pour cats and dogs*, nor the howl of protest at **snow cats and dogs*. Again I mention this factor as a *possible* source of absurdity of the analysis, although I am not sure how decisive it is, because some idioms do come in quasi-synonymous pairs of sets. We return to this also below.

We have been discussing three properties of the situation under 17: the two-directionality of subsense selections, the suppletive relation among subsenses, and the impossibility of identifying the significant semantic components of the selector. Let us note that these three properties conspire to destroy any natural isomorphism between the syntactic organization of the idiomatic expression and its semantic analysis, its paraphrase. This conspiracy to destruction may not be so obvious in our extremely simple example, *by heart*, for all its weirdness, where we might settle for the analysis that *by* in the expression corresponds to "from" in the paraphrase, and *heart* in the expression corresponds to "memory" in the paraphrase. In more complex examples, the arbitrariness of such pairings would be more evident. Who would presume to correlate the constituents of the expression *cats and dogs* with the constituents of a paraphrase such as "in an intense manner"? Is *cats* "intense" and *dogs* "manner"?

In getting ready to conclude this section, let me raise one further point about selecting contexts. We have considered the possibilities that the determinant of a subsense of an ambiguous morpheme A may be either another morpheme, or a sense (or subsense) of another morpheme with which A is constructed; but it is common for a morpheme to have two or more senses and two or more syntactic characterizations. Suppose, as in formula 18,

$$\frac{A}{y[+F] \vee a[-F]} \tag{18}$$

a morpheme A has two sets of syntactic features, schematically symbolized as $[+F]$ and $[-F]$, and two senses, such that sense y is paired with the syntactic feature $[+F]$, and sense a is paired with the syntactic feature $[-F]$. The example is purposely schematic and the further analysis of F is irrelevant, regardless of how many selectional or strict subcategorization features F stands for. Obviously our dictionary will contain many such pairs of associated syntactic and semantic disjunctions (e.g., to represent the partial semantic differences between the noun *mother* and the verb *mother*, the noun *father* and the verb *father*, etc.).

This mechanism would help us "dissolve" in a natural way some idioms that are ill-formed with respect to syntactic subcategorization. In fact, we can apply it to our example straight away, as in 19, and obtain a solution by associating the special sense of *heart* with its syntactic feature $[-\text{count}]$.

$$\tag{19}$$

$$\frac{\text{HEART}}{\text{``memory'' } [-\text{count}] \vee \text{``blood pumping organ'' } [+\text{count}]} \, [+\text{noun}]$$

But this is really no solution, because *heart* cannot be used as a mass noun freely to mean "memory"; so we have not eliminated the dependence of sense selection on a particular contextual morpheme, namely the preposition *by*. Moreover, although the syntactic feature does give us a peg on which to hang our semantic distinctions, the associations are completely arbitrary. In this instance, the relation between "memory" and "blood pump" is nothing like the full semantic-syntactic correlation we find among other English nouns straddling the +count/−count categories.

In any event, as one looks through collections of idioms, ill-formedness with respect to strict subcategorization turns out to play a very minor role; the major, pervasive type of ill-formedness among idioms consists rather of some transformational defect. Some of these defects are examined in the next section.

To summarize and restate the preceding analysis, we have tried to contrast the semantic structure of an idiom with that of a nonidiomatic expression. Idiomaticity turned out to be an extreme example of contextual semantic specialization, defined by a cluster of characteristics that also occur separately.

We have proceeded on the assumption that, for our purposes, the ultimate constituents of constructions are *morphemes*. Many morphemes appear in a dictionary with more than one sense each: we call them *polysemous* dictionary entries. The subsenses of a *polysemous morpheme* can be compared with each other to see whether they share semantic components. If they do not, or at least if they fail to do so to any significant degree, we refer to the subsenses as *homonymous*. The amount of overlap between subsenses (the ratio of shared to unshared components) is one of the variables with which we are concerned.

Now, it often happens that when a polysemous morpheme appears in a construction, the construction is not correspondingly polysemous; that is to say, only one of the subsenses of the polysemous morpheme is realized, depending on the context. We can study the nature of the contextual specialization of subsenses. One possibility we may find is that each subsense of a morpheme is associated with a different set of inherent syntactic features of the morpheme; for example, the English word *row* has the subsense "series, linear arrangement" associated with the inherent feature "noun", and the subsense "move oars, paddle" associated with the feature "verb." Here the nominal and verbal subsenses are mutually suppletive — they share no semantic components — but this condition does not necessarily exist in all instances; the subsense of *father* as a noun does share components with the subsense of *father* as a verb. Alternatively, the syntactic features with which a subsense is paired may not be inherent in the given morpheme, but contextual. The contextual features may, in turn, be of several kinds. They may be syntactic: for example, a verb with the contextual feature corresponding to transitivity may have one subsense, and another subsense in its intransitive function. (Cf. the subsenses of intransitive *walk* and transitive *walk*: *walk a dog*, etc.) Or else the contextual features may be semantic. For example, the adjective *blind* has at least these two subsenses: "unseeing" and "without exit at opposite end." The selection of the second subsense is associated with a contextual semantic feature: it depends on the adjective *blind* being constructed with a noun signifying some passageway. The dictionary illustrates it by such phrases as *blind alley, blind tube, blind valley, blind shaft* (in mining), *blind door* (one that does not lead anywhere), and so on. What is important here is that if the subsense really depends on a contextual semantic feature, its selection is accomplished by any member of a synonymous set. Thus, if the selection of the subsense of *blind* depends on the presence of a semantic component "passage" in *blind tube,* other nouns synonymous with *tube* (i.e., sharing this component) should accomplish the same selection; and I believe they do: *blind pipe* would work just as well as *blind tube.* But sometimes the selection of a subsense depends not on any semantic fact in the context, but on an individual morpheme being present; then synonyms do not all have the same effect. Let us exemplify this instance by still a third sense of *blind,* which we find in *blind date* and which may be paraphrased "with a stranger." The selection of this subsense depends on the contextual presence of the morpheme *date,* and not on some component of the meaning of *date* as seen from the fact that synonyms cannot be substituted: *blind appointment,* *blind rendezvous* do not work, except as playful allusions to the original phrase. The contextual features of a subsense may thus vary in nature and in narrowness, and then they are another variable in this area. The context, as we have seen, may be syntactic, semantic, or morphemic, that is, the limiting case in which an individual morpheme functions as the selecting feature.

A third variable, in principle independent of the others, is whether the contextual specialization of subsenses works both ways when a polysemous morpheme is constructed with another polysemous one. For example, in *blind date* the selection is definitely two-directional; *date* itself also has at least two senses (e.g., *What's today's date?),* but only one of them is selected in construction with *blind.*

There appears to be general agreement among various scholars, working without awareness of each other, that the highest degree of idiomaticity is registered when all three variables have their limiting values, that is to say, when the subsenses of a morpheme are suppletive, when the selection is determined by a unique contextual morpheme, and when the contextual selection works both ways. When all these criteria are satisfied, there results an expression such that there are no limits to the difference between its semantic structure and the semantic structure of its paraphrase.

The phrase *red herring* has been cited as an example of a minimal triplet (Amosova, 1963). On one possible reading, no selection of specialized subsenses takes place; a *red herring* is a fish of a certain kind, colored the color of blood. On another reading, a special subsense of *red* is selected; the word then means "smoked and cured with saltpeter" and contrasts with *white (herring),* which designates a fresh, uncured herring. Notice that the selection is here determined by a unique contextual morpheme; other kinds of fish or meat can also be cured with saltpeter and smoked, but none of their names seems to select this subsense of *red.* Lastly, we have the sense of *red herring* that can be paraphrased as "phony issue." If, for the sake of argument, we ascribe a subsense "phony" to the adjective *red* and a subsense "issue" to the noun *herring,* the selection is two-directional; the relation between the subsenses, suppletive; and the selecting feature, again morphemic.

At this point, let us stabilize our terminology, calling any expression in which at least one constituent is polysemous, and in which a selection of a subsense is determined by the verbal context, a *phraseological unit.* A phraseological unit that involves at least two polysemous constituents, and in which there is a reciprocal contextual selection of subsenses, will be called an *idiom.* Thus, some phraseological units are idioms; others are not. Expressions that are not phraseological units we will call *free constructions.* In the triplet of readings of *red herring* mentioned above, one was a free construction, the other two, phraseological units. Of the latter, one was idiomatic ("phony issue"), the other was not.[12]

We noted before that the difference in sense between idioms and their nonidiomatic counterparts — whether or not they are phraseological units — can be remote. So it is with the present example, where the semantic connection between the idiomatic *red herring* ("phony issue") and the other two homophonous phrases has no synchronic value for most speakers. Few people know that smelly red herrings were dragged by hunters across trails to put animals off the real scent. But at the same time let us note that an

[12]The terminology I am proposing is a combination of various usages. In my classification of phenomena I have been most deeply influenced by Amosova (1963). I employ "phraseological unit" as it is used by Arxangel'skij (1964) and "idiom" as it is used by Amosova. For Arxangel'skij himself, idioms are a subclass of phraseological units not important enough to be assigned a distinctive name. I feel this attitude of his is unwise.

idiom (i.e., a phraseological unit with two-way subsense selection) does not *necessarily* have a meaning that is suppletive in relation to the literal meaning. A fine gradation of specialized senses can be found among the coordinate binomials studied by Malkiel. As he justly notes (1959, p. 138), there stretches "between the two extremes of literalness and symbolism . . . a continuum of finely graded possibilities." I suppose that the binomial *Latin and Greek*, if it really has this favored formulaic order, is nevertheless semantically literal. In *milk and honey*, on the other hand, there is nothing literal whatever. A country may have plenty of cows and bees, but nowadays if it does not have oil or iron deposits, it will hardly be flowing with milk and honey in the idiomatic sense. Between these extremes lies the great majority of binomials, whose semantic peculiarity seems to be just a slight modification of the sense of each constituent—or, perhaps, a specially enhanced meaning of the conjunction. In *bacon and eggs*, I suppose that the eggs must be fried or scrambled, and the bacon, cooked. We would be somewhat startled if *bacon and eggs* were applied to a closed package of bacon and a carton of raw eggs, although it is precisely the legitimacy of this possibility that brings out the ambiguity of the binomial and confirms the fact that it does have a phraseologically bound sense in addition to its literal one.

Is every phraseological unit *necessarily* ambiguous, that is, has every nonliteral expression a homophonous literal counterpart? Let us pause briefly at this question, which has two aspects. The first is whether "odd" or "deviant" meanings should be taken into account in counting ambiguities. For example, if we wanted to ask how many meanings the phrase *blind alley* has, should we say one, or should we reckon with the meaning "an alley that cannot see" as well? On this matter, opinions diverge. Katz (1966), at first with Fodor (1963), and Chomsky (1965) have been constructing a theory to deal only with well-formed sentences. Consequently, they let contextual features play a completely passive role, and wherever obligatory contextual features are satisfied, unambiguous constructions result. Since the subsense "unseeing" of *blind* would presumably be marked with the contextual feature "animate," the theory would predict that the phrase *blind alley* is unambiguous, because *alley* is inanimate and cannot select the other subsense. In my own approach (Weinreich, 1966*b*), more ambitious and more risky, a semantic theory must be powerful enough to account as well for many types of expressions which are understandable in spite of their deviance. This task is accomplished by interpreting the same features not as passive and contextual, but as transfer features. *Blind alley* would, by my reckoning, come out as ambiguous; in one of its senses, the transfer feature "animate" would be imposed from *blind* onto *alley*. Since I reject the Katz-Chomsky thesis that anomalous expressions have null readings,[13] I consider *blind alley* to be ambiguous, one of the "readings" being phraseologically specialized; in the Katz-Chomsky approach, on the other hand, *blind alley* would not be ambiguous, but neither would it be a phraseological unit. Thus the principle that all phraseological units are ambiguous can be upheld; the difference is only as to whether a given item should be classified as phraseological.

The question of ambiguity has yet another aspect on which a consensus seems to be emerging, the matter of expressions with unique constituents. I have in mind such phrases as *luke warm, runcible spoon, spic and span, kith and kin, hem and haw, cockles of the heart,* and so on. These are hardly ambiguous, since the unique occurrence of, say, *luke* with *warm* guarantees that *luke* has only one subsense—whatever that may be; similarly for *kith, cockles,* and so on. I find that the most careful students of the problem, Amosova (1963) and Makkai (1965), both agree that expressions with unique constituents should not be called idiomatic. Makkai has dubbed them "pseudo-idioms." From this point of view, ambiguity is an essential characteristic of true idioms.

The difference between the two kinds of phenomena is, I think, fairly clear. One much-discussed attempt to pin it down was made by Mel'čuk (1960), who proposes to distinguish idiomaticity from stability of collocation. The stability of a collocation with respect to a particular constituent is measured by the probability with which the given constituent predicts the appearance of the other constituents. In the examples I have mentioned, this probability is a certainty: *runcible* must be followed by *spoon; cockles* must (in ordinary English) be followed by *of the heart*. Idiomaticity, on the other hand, is defined as uniqueness of subsense. What Mel'čuk calls "stability of collocation" is thus a high degree of contextual restriction on the selection of a monosemous dictionary entry; what he calls "idiomaticity" is a strong restriction on the selection of a

[13]The two approaches have been contrasted informally as follows: Chomsky and Katz match a square peg against a round hole and state that it does not fit. My theory presses the peg into the hole to see whether the peg is thereby tapered, or the hole stretched.

subsense of a polysemous dictionary entry. Let us note in passing that both types of restriction—on entries and on subsenses—may be one- or two-directional. We made this observation in distinguishing idioms, with their two-way restrictions (e.g., *red herring*, "phony issue"), from other phraseological units, with their one-way restrictions (e.g., *blind alley*). Among Makkai's "pseudo-idioms" and Mel'čuk's completely stable collocations, we also find one-way restrictions (as in *kith and kin*, where *kin* is free) and two-way restrictions, as in *spic and span* (where neither constituent is free.) This theoretical point, with Russian examples, was first made, I think, by Arxangel'skij (1964).

Before resuming the discussion of the grammatical properties of phraseological units (including idioms), it may be relevant to note that while the semantic difference between idioms and their literal counterparts is, by definition, *arbitrary in principle*, languages show a tendency to develop certain families of expressions in which the difference is reutilized, so that the semantic uniqueness of an idiom is put into question. One class of expressions which has been recognized is exemplified by such pairs as *bury the hatchet* and *bury the tomahawk*, both glossed as "make peace, abandon a quarrel." On the one hand, *hatchet* and *tomahawk* obviously share the bulk of their semantic components; the special sense of the construction would therefore seem to be attributable to the components of the object nouns. Yet other synonyms cannot be substituted: **bury the axe* does not work in the same way, so that the determination of the special meaning would seem to be due to specific lexemes after all. Such pairs of expressions have been called "idiom variants" (Amosova, 1963, pp. 97 ff.). We may take it that the existence of idiom variants does not affect the integrity of the idiom concept any more than the existence of morpheme variants (e.g., /ekanámiks/-/íkanámiks/) affects the integrity of the morpheme or the phoneme. An even more curious apparent exception to the arbitrariness of idiomatic senses may be observed in connection with antonymous pairs, such as *bury the hatchet* versus *dig up the hatchet* ("resume a quarrel"), also noted in the variant *take up the hatchet*. The two idioms are antonymous, as are their literal constituents *bury* and *dig up*, yet the relation of each literal constituent to the idiom is still arbitrary. This phenomenon is perhaps characteristic of a class of expressions that literally describe symbolic behavior in some nonlinguistic (e.g., gestural) semiotic system (e.g., *take off one's hat to, shake hands on, lift one's glass to;*

cf. *raise our heads* ["act proudly"] vs. *lower our heads* ["express shame"]).[14]

At this point we resume the question of the grammatical properties of phraseological units (including idioms).

III. Idioms in a Generative Framework

As a general principle, one may say that the well-formedness of expressions is relative to the crudeness or delicacy of the syntax. When, in Section II, we considered phraseological units from a very simple grammatical point of view, viz. in terms of strict subcategorization alone, we found very few that were not well formed. There are some isolated oddities in any language, such as the English *by and large*, or *to blow somebody to kingdom come;* there are also recurring patterns of oddity, such as adverbials consisting of coordinated noun phrases: *to fight tooth and nail, to run neck and neck, to go at something hammer and tongs.*[15] But every investigation I have seen confirms the fact that such categorial anomalies account for only a small fraction of the phraseological resources of a language. On the contrary, if we increase the delicacy of the syntactic analysis, if we require that each phraseological unit not only be provided with a phrase marker, but also pass some transformational tests, we can probe its grammatical structure more deeply. We then do not accept *blind date* as a well-formed adjective-plus-noun phrase if we cannot have an insertion (e.g., *blind boring date);* nor can *eat crow* pass muster as a well-formed expression if we cannot passivize it to **crow was eaten* without destroying its phra-

---

[14]Still another type of idiom family has been noticed by S. Robert Greenberg. In criticism of my claim that the difference between *hit the sack* (literally, "collide with the cloth container") and *hit the sack* (idiomatically, "go to sleep") is arbitrary, Greenberg (1966) points out the existence of the series *hit the road* ("get going"), *hit the bottle* ("take to drink"), *hit the silk* (of parachutists, "jump out of the plane"), and the like. That *hit* here recurs in some constant, specialized meaning is not difficult to grant; but whether the pattern is indeed productive, or even whether the difference between the literal and contextually specialized meanings of the nouns can be conceived of as a constant ratio, can be determined only after much careful analysis of validated paraphrases of the expressions.

[15]In the lecture on which this paper is based, I used *to rain cats and dogs* as a paradigm example of categorial ill-formedness of an idiom, a coordinate noun phrase functioning as a manner adverbial; however, Paul S. Cohen has subsequently pointed out that the existence of such expressions as *it rained arrows and rocks, it rained torrents,* etc., establishes a grammatical framework for noun phrases functioning after *rain.*

seological properties. Superficially well formed, these expressions turn out to be transformationally defective.

It would be extremely gratifying if transformational defectiveness were a reliable syntactic correlate of phraseological units, semantically defined. Indeed, among the hundreds of idioms and other phraseological units I have looked at in four or five languages, I have not found a single one that did not have some transformational defect. But it also turns out that transformational defectiveness is not restricted to phraseological units. It is often a feature even of single words.[16] It seems to me, therefore, that phraseological units are at best a subclass of transformationally deficient structures.

In looking at examples, it will be convenient to begin with adjective-noun phrases. Many phraseological units with such structure have this nonsuperficial grammatical defect, that there are no underlying source sentences in which the same adjective occurs with the same sense as a predicate. We do not have *the lie is white, *the alley is blind, *the date is blind, *the potato is hot, at least not in the special senses we are concerned with. From this fact, several possible conclusions may be drawn. One is that generative grammar does not work. For example, Winter (1965) found a glaring error in Chomsky's Syntactic Structures (1957), namely the claim that all attributive adjectives in English are derivable from predicate adjectives. Winter concludes (p. 488) that "multiple solutions, not necessarily clearly set off against each other, must be admitted." I do not agree with the inference, though in general, when one thinks of the pompousness with which some workers in generative grammar proclaim their preliminary findings, one can appreciate the Schadenfreude of a critic: after all, the temptation to puncture is directly proportional to the inflation of the balloon. Still the discovery of analytic puzzles does not seem to me an argument against generative grammar if we take it, not as a fixed doctrine, but as a way of asking precise questions about certain aspects of language. Generative grammar is a challenge to say all we know about the grammatical behavior of forms, and to say it in a strictly controlled, condensed language. It is far too soon to conclude that the challenge cannot be met. The existence of "transforms without kernels" (Winter's title) can be described by well-tested analytic devices. Thus transformationally deficient adjectives could be generated (i.e., accommodated in the description) by being viewed as predi-

[16]See Lakoff (1965).

cates that are subject to a set of obligatory transformations. But the adjectives we have been considering not only fail to occur as predicates; they also do not yield nominalizations such as *the whiteness of the lie, *the blindness of the alley, *the hotness (or heat?) of the potato. They would, therefore, have to be marked not only as requiring the transformations that would reduce them to attributes, but also as prohibiting the transformation that would make them into nouns. It might, therefore, be more economical all around to introduce these adjectives directly in attribute position. As a matter of fact, English and other languages contain strictly attributive adjectives that are not involved in phraseological specialization at all. Well-known examples are *elder (sister), right (hand), (the) late (Churchill), (the) third (door)*, and so on. For these examples, too, we have neither predicates (*Churchill is late, *the hand is right, . . .) nor nominalizations (*the lateness of Churchill, *the rightness of the hand, . . .); nor do any of these allow free formation of comparatives or superlatives (*the blindest alley, *a blinder date, *the righter hand).

I am suggesting, then, that adjectives of this type be introduced into preterminal strings as manifestations of an optional constituent, adjective, between the determiner and the noun of a noun phrase. This treatment could be used for all adjectives with the described transformational defect, whether involved in contextual semantic specialization (such as *blind* in *blind date*), or not so involved (as *right* in *right hand*).

Consider a grammar containing rules such as those under 20.

$$
\begin{aligned}
&\text{NP} \rightarrow \text{Det} + (\text{Adj}) + \text{N}\\
&\text{Det} \rightarrow \text{Art} + (\text{S})\\
&\text{VP} \rightarrow \text{copula} + \text{predicate}\\
&\text{Predicate} \rightarrow \text{adjective} + (\text{complement})
\end{aligned}
\tag{20}
$$

dull [+Adj, +copula_____]
right [+Adj, −copula_____]

A strictly attributive adjective like *right* or *left* would be marked as prohibiting a preceding copula; while ordinary adjectives like *dull* or *happy* would be inserted by the lexical rule only if a copula did precede. (I omit the details necessary to show modifying adverbs, such as *very happy*.) These predicate adjectives occurring in embedded sentences would be transformed through relative clauses and postnominal modifiers into prenominal modifiers, in ways that are by now well known, with the copula being deleted in the process.

Adjectives such as *right* and *dull* would be distinguished by the contextual feature [−copula_____] and [+copula_____]. Now, in a polysemous adjective like *blind,* one subsense would be associated with the syntactic feature [+copula_____] (the subsense "unseeing"), while the other subsenses would be associated with the feature [−copula_____]. The diagram in 21 shows how the

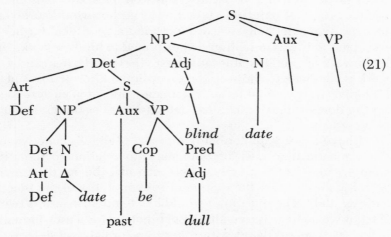

(21)

blind [+Adj, +copula_____], "lacking sight"

blind [+Adj, −copula_____ + __ DATE], "with someone not previously introduced"

blind [+Adj, −copula_____], "lacking exit"

sentence *The dull blind date bored him* might be derived: the adjective *dull* is introduced one way; *blind,* another. On the other hand, in *the blind dog bit him,* the adjective *blind,* with its subsense "unseeing," would be introduced through the predicate of an embedded sentence, *the dog is blind.*

It may be of some interest to report the finding that among polysemous English adjectives, the vast majority are characterized precisely by this phenomenon, that one subsense goes with the contextual feature [+ copula _____] , while another subsense, or a great many others, go with the opposite feature. In fact, this discovery may give us a syntactic correlate, at least for English adjectives, for the semantic contrast between basic and derived meaning.

A good deal could be said at this point about other types of transformationally defective noun modifiers, such as possessives. Again we would find expressions (such as *Parkinson's disease, baker's dozen*) that are involved in contextually specialized sense selections and are syntactically defective. But let me pass on to a rather different class of examples, the ones that Malkiel (1959) has studied under the heading of "irreversible binomials." This study is most suggestive because it includes material from many languages other than English and because the examples are cross-analyzed from a variety of points of view. But its author would surely agree that the syntactic analysis can be carried a good deal further than was done in the examination he performed in his own work, "in the framework of grammar at its austerest" (p. 160). That austere framework is adequate to show up the exceptional illformedness of a few binomials in categorial terms; the framework is too austere to show up the deeper transformational defectiveness of the great majority of binomials.

I have already quoted with approval Malkiel's conclusion that the semantic deformity of binomials (in relation to their literal counterparts) varies greatly. There can also be no disagreement with his finding that the degree of irreversibility of the binomials varies widely. The question I would like to propose now is twofold: First, if we analyze irreversibility of binomials as a transformational defect, is this correlated with other transformational defects? And second, if transformational and semantic oddities are both variable characteristics of binomials, are they correlated?

Let us see, first, what it means to interpret irreversibility as a transformational defect. In general, most expressions linked by co-ordinate conjunctions appear to be derivable from pairs of underlying sentences containing partly identical constituents in the same syntactic relationship. For example, we relate *I bought eggs and milk* to the pair of sentences *I bought eggs and I bought milk*. It has recently been shown by Schane (1966) that the derivation of such conjoined expressions from pairs of sentences is beyond the generative power of a transformational grammar. Instead Schane proposed a schema of nontransformational phrase structure rules which, together with a set of transformational rules of deletion (secondary conjunction rules), would be capable of generating a great many conjoined sentences.

Whatever one's final evaluation of this new schema, it is admitted by Schane himself that some conjoined expressions still remain unaccounted for. The recalcitrant expressions are of various types, and their difficulties cannot all be solved in the same way. What is relevant in the present context is that "binomials" such as (*sit*) *on pins and needles* ("*be highly impatient*") cannot be derived from *sit on pins* and *sit on needles* by means of the proposed schema, despite the superficial wellformedness of *pins and needles*. The deeper defectiveness of the binomial is evident not only from its irreversibility (**on needles and pins* fails to do the expected semantic job), but also from the impossibility of repeating the preposition (**on pins and on needles*; cf the nonidiomatic *on paper and* [*on*] *cardboard*).

According to Malkiel, some binomials are fixed in their order because they describe a cause and effect, or a sequence of events. For example, the normal order is *eat and drink*, not *drink and eat*; but the same is equally true of the underlying sentences. If some ungrammatical person drinks first and eats later, it would be only proper to say that *he drank and ate*. This binomial is a good example of one whose irreversibility is very weak and in which the semantic deformity is barely perceptible. As a matter of fact, if we compare it with *on pins and needles* in the sense of "impatiently," we find that *on pins and needles* is not only more idiomatic and more irreversible than *eat and drink*, but is beset with a whole family of transformational defects of which *eat and drink* is free. Thus, we can vary the conjunction to produce *eat or drink, eat but not drink*, but we cannot, in the idiomatic sense, form *pins or needles, **pins, but not needles*. We can introduce modifiers and quantifiers in the first, as in *eat well and drink a lot*, but not in the second. Thus it appears that transformational deficiencies are correlated with semantic specialization, and that the one deficiency most carefully considered by Malkiel, namely irreversibility, correlates well with other transformational deficiencies.

Comparing now the results of our analysis of two classes of expressions, adjective-plus-noun phrases and coordinate binomials, let me underscore the difference between them: In binomials, the connection between grammatical defect and semantic specialization seems to run both ways; for adjective-plus-noun phrases, semantically specialized expressions form only a subclass of grammatically defective phrases. I am interested in stressing this difference expecially because of my friendly dispute with Roman Jakobson on the congruence of semantic and syntactic categorization (see Weinreich, 1966*b*, p. 469). According to Professor

Jakobson's frequent assertions, the reliance on syntax in semantic study is a survival of distributional, "antisemantic" linguistics. Refracted in the prism of his magnificent poetic imagination, the correlations between syntactic and semantic categories appear perfect—and predictable. I must confess that, to my naked, prosaic eye, these correlations are not all that perfect; and when a good correlation is found, I am still capable of surprise. In the present example, where we consider the relation of transformational defectiveness to contextual specialization of meaning, Professor Jakobson would probably say, "I told you so." At the risk of pedantry, I would answer that he could not have told us so, because what we found were two different things: a two-way correlation in one class of expressions (binomials), and a one-way implication in another class (adjective-noun phrases). I would urge similar pedantic cautions in approaching other problems as well.

Schane (1966), like others before him, pinpointed some of the theoretical difficulties that conjoined sentences put in the way of explicit (generative) syntax; but it is worth pointing out that, for all their syntactic recalcitrance, coordinate constructions make a remarkably powerful heuristic device for the exploration of *semantic* structure. Take coordination by means of *but*. In an expression of the form *A but B*, the element *B* states something that is surprising in light of *A* (see, e.g., Strawson, 1952, p. 48). Therefore, *A-but-B* statements that are semantically odd show that what is represented as surprisingly related is "in reality," so to speak, or "as a rule," either unrelated or not surprising. If *A but B* is paradoxical, we know that *not-B*, rather than *B*, was to be expected from *A*. If *A but B* is tautologous, it means that *B* is entailed by *A* in the first place. Thus *A-but-B* statements that are interpreted as paradoxical or tautologous reveal a good deal about entailment relations between *A* and *B*. Where such entailment is mediated by specialized theories or private knowledge, it is not linguistically relevant; but in many instances such entailment reflects precisely the common-knowledge semantic relations between words, the covert semantic system of the language. *A-but-B* tests are, therefore, enormously helpful in revealing the componential semantic structure of terms. Is giggling a kind of laughing? Is smiling a kind of laughing—in English? You can find out quickly: *She giggled but did not laugh* is paradoxical; *she smiled but did not laugh* is perfectly acceptable. So giggling *is* a way of laughing; smiling is not.

I have sung the praises of *but* on other occasions, and I think that Bendix's recent book (1966, pp. 23 ff.) exemplifies the potential of what I have called "the *but* method" as a semantic research tool. Let me note here that the conjunction *and* is, in its own way, also a powerful analytic device, expecially in instances of polysemy. Is the sense of *eat* the same in *eat soup* and in *eat spaghetti*? The actions referred to are hardly identical, but are we to say that we have here two senses of *eat*? What about *practice* in *he practiced medicine* and *he practiced piano*? I think we can reach a decision after a test by means of *and*: *He ate soup and spaghetti* seems perfectly normal, so the sense of *eat* is the same in both instances. *He practiced medicine and piano* is a joke; apparently *practice* is used in two different senses. The *A-and-B* test strikes me as perhaps a firmer basis than others yet proposed for controlling the degree of delicacy to which subsenses are legitimately to be differentiated in the dictionary. In turn, the deletion rules for coordinated sentences will have to be so formulated that their structural conditions specify not just identity of syntax and identity of constituent morphemes, but also identity of *semantic features* of morphemes. This fact supports the suspicion (Weinreich, 1966*b*, p. 454) that the transformational processing of a terminal string is not indifferent to the semantic features of the lexical material in it. (I do not know whether this matter is controversial or trivial or "sort of interesting.")

In Section II we came to the conclusion that if phraseological units were well formed categorially — and the vast majority are — they could be stored in a dictionary in terms of their constituents, and if provided with the correct syntactic features, they would be available to the lexical rule. We have now seen, further, that phraseological units have transformational defects; but these defects can be marked, I think, along with other syntactic features of the dictionary entries, so that prohibited transformations would be blocked and obligatory ones would be applied. The decision as to whether a phraseological unit should be stored in the dictionary as a whole, or dissolved into its constituents, still rests on a balance of the same factors as those with which we ended up in Section II: the semantic awkwardness of the separate listing on the one hand (especially for parts of idioms), supporting the treatment of the expressions as wholes; and against that, certain "costs" of treating them as wholes of which we were still to speak.

The phraseological phenomena are so diversified that no single example can illustrate all the problems by itself. We must, therefore, guard against generalizing from single examples; but we must begin somewhere. Let me exemplify at least some of the issues by analyzing the idiomatic *shoot the breeze* ("chat idly") as part of the sentence *The boys shot the breeze*. This example will give us a chance to look at yet another syntactic form in which phraseological specialization and idiomaticity are rife in many languages, verb phrases consisting of verbs and noun phrases. Let us see what generative problems arise with each treatment of the idiom, first if it is listed in the dictionary constituent by constituent, and then if it is listed as a unit.[17]

The unit treatment is exemplified below. The diagram in 22*b* represents a dictionary fragment treating *shoot the breeze* as a unit entry.

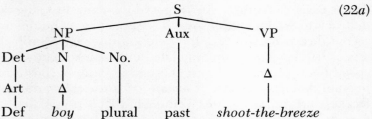

(22*a*)

shoot the breeze /šútɗəbríz/   (22*b*)
[+ V, + animate _____ , + plural _____ , − _____ NP]

    "chat idly"

The first line is a representation of its phonological form. The second line gives its syntactic characterization: the item is a verb requiring an animate plural[18] noun as a subject and prohibiting a following object noun (in other words, it is an intransitive verb). The third line is a paraphrase to suggest its semantic features. The identical paraphrase might, in principle, recur with some one-word synonym, for example, *confabulate*. The advantages of the unit treatment are that it prevents the inadmissible insertion of modifiers adjoined to *breeze* (e.g., **the boys shot the light breeze*), guarantees

---

[17]This discussion in part follows an earlier statement of mine (Weinreich, 1966*b*, pp. 450-454), although the conclusions reached there have here been partly reconsidered. The analysis owes a good deal to Katz and Postal (1963); divergences will be mentioned as they are encountered.

[18]The plurality of the subject represented here is probably not an entirely adequate way of rendering the feeling that it takes more than one person to have a chat. Of course, one person can chat—or shoot the breeze—*with* someone else, and the mention of the interlocutor can, in turn, be suppressed. I trust that in the present schematic context, these incompletely worked out details can be overlooked.

the singular definite of *breeze,* and prevents passivization, since
our expression is treated as a one-piece intransitive verb. (We do
not want to generate **The breeze was shot by the boys.*) The disadvantages of the unitary treatment are much more formidable. In
the phonemic representation, sequences of sounds are introduced
which do not otherwise occur within simplexes (*tð̵*), and which
would force us to give up certain redundancy rules in the phonological component, thus complicating the phonologic representation of the rest of the vocabulary. Moreover, stress information has
to be specified for parts of the entry which would otherwise be
assigned automatically by phonological rules that could act on the
syntactic features of *shoot* and *breeze.* In larger idioms, such as *hit
the nail on the head,* a good deal more stress information would
have to be given in the dictionary. The syntactic disadvantages are
even more serious, for we have not yet made any dictionary entry
to indicate how this alleged verb is inflected for tense. Why is not
a tense marker, *-ed,* added at the end of our putative verb (i.e.,
*shoot the breeze-d)? If nominalized, how would we obtain *shooting the breeze* and not *shoot the breez-ing?* And even if we were
somehow to show that with strange verbs of this type the tense formative is infixed, why is the formative the "replacive" *ū → o* and
not *-d?* Actually, the inflectional irregularities of verbs involved in
idioms are almost always the same as of the homophonous verbs in
literal expressions. If the dictionary is not to be cluttered with repeated specifications of morphophonemic irregularities, it is clearly
disadvantageous to list idioms as unanalyzed units. As one more
point against this treatment, let us recall that in languages with
case systems, the accusative (or other appropriate case) would have
to be assigned to the constituent *breeze,* and the appropriate inflectional forms specified.

   The other procedure that is feasible, as far as I can see, within
existing theory is outlined under 23.

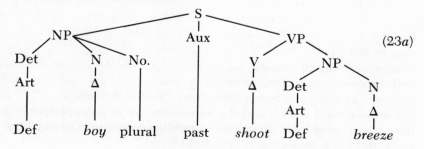

(23a)

shoot   /šū̆t/

$$[+V, +\underline{\quad\quad}NP; \quad IC_8] \qquad\qquad (23b)$$

$$\left\{ \begin{array}{l} \text{``chat''} \quad [-^TNom\text{-}of; \ +\text{animate}\underline{\quad\quad}, \ +\text{plural}\underline{\quad\quad}, \\ \qquad\qquad\quad +\underline{\quad\quad}\text{THE BREEZE}, \ -\underline{\quad\quad}...\text{passive}] \\ \text{``fire a projectile at''} \end{array} \right\}$$

breeze   /brīz/

$$[+N, +\text{count}, -\text{animate}, ...]$$

$$\left\{ \begin{array}{l} \text{``idly''} \quad [\text{SHOOT THE}\underline{\quad\quad} \text{``chat,''} \ -\underline{\quad\quad}\text{plural;} \\ \qquad\qquad -\text{adjective}\underline{\quad\quad}] \\ \text{``light wind''} \end{array} \right\}$$

It compensates for the phonological and grammatical disadvantages of solution 22. With *shoot, the,* and *breeze* identified respectively as verb, article, and noun, the phonological component can automatically assign them their correct stresses. The redundancy rules can take full advantage of the word boundaries after *shoot* and before *breeze*. The inflectional specificities of *shoot* can be shown in a routine way by listing its conjugational class—here arbitrarily labeled IC_8, which is the same as that for *shoot* in any free construction. In a case language, such as Russian, the proper case (i.e., accusative) would be assigned to the noun phrase *the breeze*, and the proper allomorphs of the stem *breeze* and the accusative suffix would be generated in a routine way. The impossibility of the phrase undergoing certain transformations, for example, *the boys' shooting of the breeze took all afternoon*, could be marked as a special syntactic feature associated with one of the subsenses of *shoot*. (Here it is shown in square brackets on the third line of 23*b*.)

But this solution, too, has crass disadvantages, this time on the semantic level. We have encountered them all before. Notice that the segmentation of the paraphrase "chat/idly" is arbitrary in relation to the idiom itself. Why not "chat idly / ϕ"? The expression is idiomatic on all counts: the selection of unique senses of *shoot* and *breeze* is two-directional; it is determined by specific morphemes, as synonym tests prove (thus, *fire at the breeze* or *shoot the wind* do not work); and the subsenses are in a suppletive relation, since "chat idly" shares no semantic components of any interest with "fire a projectile at" or "light wind."

The awkwardness of both solutions, 22 and 23, is what I had hinted at as "the high cost of idiomaticity." Both procedures are beset by intolerable disadvantages. As Katz and Postal (1963) pointed out, a slight modification of linguistic theory is necessary if this type of idiom[19] is to be made accessible to a generative grammar without semantic absurdities.

The syntax as here conceived[20] contains a categorial component that generates preterminal strings (Chomsky, 1965, p. 84). A *preterminal string* is a string of grammatical formatives and "dummy symbols" or "complex symbols" (i.e., slots for the insertion of lexical items from the dictionary [p. 122]).

A *dictionary entry* is a set of phonological, syntactic, and morphophonemic features and a sense description. The linguistic theory contains a "lexical rule," which is a transformation that substitutes dictionary entries for dummy or complex symbols in the preterminal string if certain contextual conditions for each are met. After the lexical rule has operated as many times as there were "slots" in the preterminal string, the result is a terminal string, which enters the transformational-phonological components to be mapped into a surface structure of a sentence (unless blocked by the transformational filter) and enters the semantic process in order to receive a semantic interpretation (or, in Katz-Fodor terminology [1963], a derived reading).

This conception is now modified as follows: The description of the language is to contain, in addition to the dictionary, an *idiom list*[21]. Each entry in the idiom list is a string of morphemes, which may be from two morphemes to a sentence in length, with its associ-

---

[19]Katz and Postal (1963) distinguish "phrase idioms" from "lexical idioms"; the latter are compound or complex words formed by derivational patterns that are not fully productive. Their discussion, like mine, deals mainly with "phrase idioms." But they err, it seems to me, in regarding the class of phrase idioms as homogeneous, and in creating a theory that has been tested against only one example—*kick the bucket*.

[20]Katz and Postal's paper on idioms antedated Chomsky's *Aspects* (1965) by two years. The incompatibilities between their approach of 1963 and the syntactic framework assumed here are not, of course, to be taken as inherent defects of their proposals.

[21]In Katz and Postal's terms (1963, p. 277), the dictionary itself is divided into a lexical item part and a phrase-idiom part. The difference between their scheme and mine is not much more than terminology; however, the introduction of the lexical rule as a component of linguistic theory, a move with which Katz and Postal would, in all likelihood, agree, and the possibility that idiomatic meanings would be assigned after the operation of the lexical rule, provide motivations for a more clearcut separation of nonidiomatic and idiomatic storage devices.

ated phrase marker and a sense description.[22] An example of an entry in the idiom list is given under 24, the idiom *shoot the breeze*. The entry contains, in addition, contextual features and instructions for obligatory or prohibited transformations. In this example, the

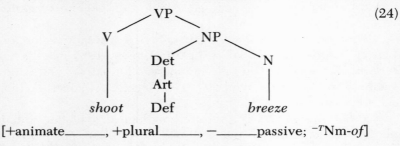

(24)

[+animate_____, +plural_____, −_____passive; $^{-T}$Nm-*of*]

"chat idly"

contextual features specify an animate plural noun for a subject and prohibit the presence of the passive morpheme; the entry is also marked as prohibiting *of*-nominalization, since there is no **the boys' shooting of the breeze* in the idiomatic sense. The idiomatic sense is paraphrased as "chat idly."

The order in which entries are arranged in an idiom list is of minor interest in the present connection. If a physical searching procedure were envisaged, certain ordering conventions could be established, for example, that entries be first identified by the highest dominating node, etc.

We now add to the linguistic theory, diagramed under 25, an "idiom comparison rule," which operates on a terminal string before it has entered the transformational component or the semantic process. The idiom comparison rule[23] matches a terminal string against the idiom list. If it finds an entry in the idiom list which is identical with all or part of the terminal string, the idiom comparison rule deletes the semantic features of the matched fragment of the terminal string and substitutes the semantic features and transformational instructions specified for the matching entry in the

---

[22]Katz and Postal (1963, p. 277) require that an entry in the phrase-idiom part of the dictionary have the constituent specified that "must dominate the idiomatic stretch." Clearly, this requirement is insufficient, since the phonological and transformational rules could not operate correctly unless the nodes lower than the dominant one were also fully enumerated.

[23]Katz and Postal's relatively informal treatment (1963) contains no analog of the idiom comparison rule and thus does not indicate how a sentence containing an idiom might actually be generated.

(25)

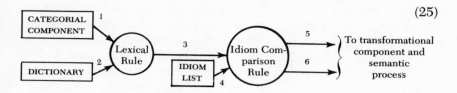

1. Preterminal strings
2. Dictionary entries
3. Terminal strings
4. Idioms
5. Literal terminal strings
6. Idiomatic terminal strings

idiom list. (I said that the matching entry in the idiom list must be identical; actually, we would probably want to define it as non-distinct in a technical sense—but more in Section IV.) What is important to note is that the idiom comparison rule is optional. The optionality of the rule accounts for the fact that each idiomatic expression has a homophonous literal counterpart.

Suppose the base (i.e., the categorial component and the dictionary) has generated at random terminal deep-structure strings for the four sentences under 26. For sentences 26a and 26d, the idiom comparison rule finds no

The *boys shot* the *wind.*   (26a)

The toys *shot* the *breeze.*   (26b)

The *boys shot* the *breeze.*   (26c)

The toy fired a projectile at the light wind.   (26d)

match in the idiom list. For 26b the rule finds a match for the verb phrase portion, *shoot the breeze*; however, the entry in the idiom list specifies an animate subject, a condition that is not satisfied here. For sentence 26c the idiom comparison rule again finds the matching verb phrase in the idiom list; this time the contextual features of the idiom list entry are satisfied. The rule now option-ally replaces the semantic features of the original sentence with those that yield the paraphrase "chat idly." If the optional rule does not operate, the originally generated features remain, eventually yielding a sense paraphrasable as "the boys fired a projectile at the light wind."

The solution outlined here, and schematized under 25, has the advantages of retaining all the phonological, syntactic, and morphophonemic information with which a literal expression is furnished by the grammatical base and the dictionary, so that the automatic conversion of the deep structure into a surface structure can proceed normally. At one stroke it accounts for the ambiguity of literal expressions having idiomatic counterparts, and for their specific idiomatic senses. It further wipes out any expectation of syntactic isomorphism between an idiomatic expression and its paraphrase; the syntax of the sense description of an idiom list entry need not correspond to the formal syntax of the expression itself.

The solution also has at least two disadvantages. One specific disability is that it takes care of the transformational defects of idioms, but not of strictly categorial defects. For example, if a terminal string existed in which *fight the enemy tooth and nail* occurred, the generated sense of "bony appendage on the jaw and pointed metal spike" could be replaced by "vigorously," in the context *fight* (NP) _____, through the operation of the idiom comparison rule; but *tooth and nail* could not be generated after *fight* by the base in the first place, there being no productive rule of the form "adverbial — manner → N-*and*-N." Thus, as we will see in Section IV, additional machinery will be needed for some kinds of idioms.

Another characteristic of the theory diagramed under 27 which will strike many people as unattractive is the prospect of an unordered idiom list and the awkward notion of endless matching operations. To be sure, a certain amount of searching could be obviated by letting the dictionary function as an index to the idiom list. Each dictionary entry that occurs in the idiom list might be tagged in the dictionary and in the terminal string by a symbol that would trigger the idiom comparison rule to search; in the absence of such a symbol, the idiom comparison rule would not be activated. For example, the words underlined in the examples under 26 are all involved in some idioms in English; on the other hand, sentence 26*d* has perhaps no words involved in idioms, so that if it were generated by the base, the idiom comparison rule would not be triggered. But we must admit that the majority of words occurring in a text *can* be involved in idioms, so that the amount of searching which can be obviated by this device may be rather insignificant.

The evaluation of my proposal perhaps hinges on one's commitment to its abstractness. To me personally the prospect of a rule searching through an idiom list is no more dismal than the conception, in Chomsky's *Aspects*, of a base generating strings at random, including an endless number of potential embedded clauses that are not sufficiently well formed to pass the transformational filter. It seems to me that if we are seriously committed to a truly abstract conception of generation, and if we honestly disclaim any relation between the generative account of a sentence structure and a description of how a real sentence is produced or understood, there is no harm in any amount of idling on the part of our abstract automaton. And yet I realize that, in spite of the most vigorous and unambiguous disclaimers, the temptation to give the generative analysis a psychological interpretation is extremely difficult to resist. If one yields to that temptation, blocking grammars and list searchings will be highly unattractive aspects of linguistic theory.

IV. Further Questions of Idiom Analysis

A syntactic component that contains a lexical rule could conceivably be so arranged as to obviate the necessity of an idiom list. The dictionary itself could contain complex entries, such as that exemplified under 27. Note that a V node here dominates a VP node, a relationship that is not generated by the part of the grammar which is under control of the categorial component but can be stored in fixed form for specific lexical entries. Such an entry would be available to the lexical rule for insertion into a phrase marker slot at a node dominated by V, yet it would provide all the additional syntactic structure needed for the phonological component to operate correctly.

The complex dictionary entry 27 may

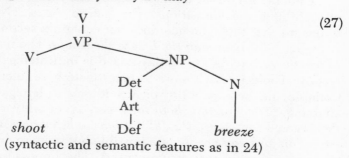

(27)

(syntactic and semantic features as in 24)

be contrasted with 24, which represented an entry in an idiom list : in which VP dominated. The entry exemplified in 24 is well formed, and the problem there is merely to make the idiomatic sense description accessible to some operation that would transfer it to the generated phrase marker. If entries of the unorthodox form of 27 were permitted in principle, we would have to decide, in describing a language, which items would receive this analysis. But in any event, if entries of this form were allowed, we could contrast the derivation of a free construction (28a) and an idiom (28b).

(28a)

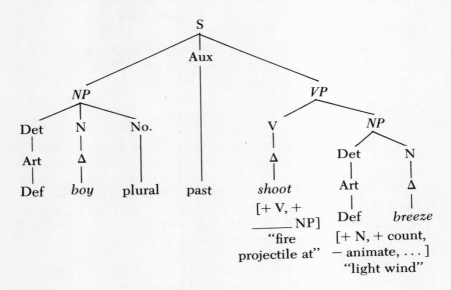

Under (28b) we see a complex entry carrying with it indications of prohibited transformations. The feature — _____ NP is needed to ensure that the sentence does not contain a second object, for example, *The boys shot the breeze the rumor. The inability of the idiomatic verb phrase to be passivized is indicated as a contextual feature. There is much more to investigate here, incidentally; for example, the incompatibility of such idioms with negation is worth studying. *They did not shoot the breeze is certainly most unusual; the negated sentences, He did not have a blind date and He is not sitting on pins and needles are possible but seem to presuppose an unusually specific contrastive context. The impossibility of nominalization by of, that is, The boys' shooting of the breeze, is here also indicated as an inherent morphophonemic feature. It is quite possible that there are some ways to generalize all these restrictions which I have not noticed.

(28b)

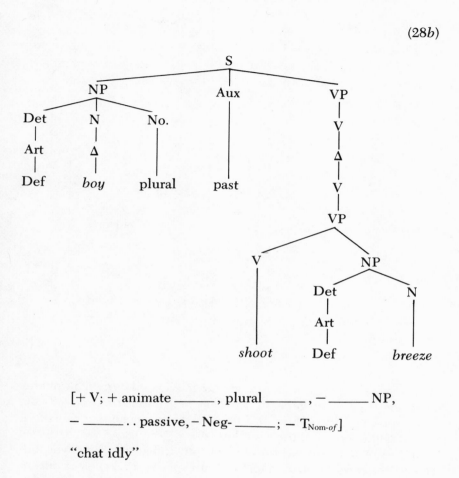

$[+ V; + \text{animate} \underline{\quad\quad}, \text{plural} \underline{\quad\quad}, - \underline{\quad\quad} NP,$

$- \underline{\quad\quad} .. \text{passive}, - \text{Neg-} \underline{\quad\quad}; - T_{\text{Nom-}of}]$

"chat idly"

So far so good. If forms such as 27 and 28b are allowed, the complex entry is still in the running as a possible way of bypassing the need for an idiom list; but let us consider next a slightly more complex form, one that Katz and Postal did not deal with. I am now thinking of idiomatic constructions that dominate nonidiomatic ones, such as *make fun of, pay attention to, take offense at, take charge of,* and the like. If these are complex dictionary entries, they are presumably transitive verbs; but the dictionary entries representing them must be allowed to contain optional dummy symbols, for example, for the insertion of a quantifier (or other prenominal modifier) in *pay little attention to,* illustrated under 29.

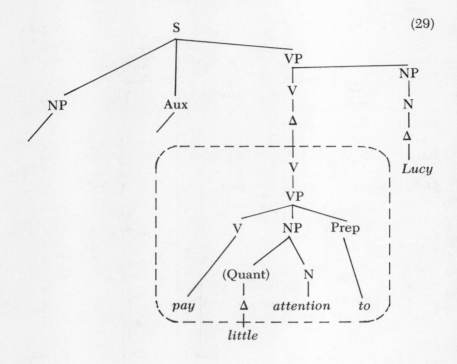

(29)

The lexical rule must then operate recursively on its own output for such sentences to be generated as *They paid little attention to Lucy, They took serious offense at Tom,* and so on, if the mechanism of complex dictionary entries is allowed.

We are not quite at the end of our difficulties, however, because, in terms of semantic form, such expressions as *pay attention to* are atypically simple. Their simplicity lies in the fact that the object of the idiomatic "verb" also functions as a direct object or prepositional object in the paraphrase (cf. *They heard Lucy, They listened to Lucy*). In connection with 8c, I mentioned the possibility that the semantic function within an idiom may or may not correspond to the semantic function associated with the dominant node in the syntax of free construction. Here we have idioms in which this correspondence is upheld, but take something like *to pull _____'s leg* or *get _____'s goat.* Here the correspondence breaks down because what is represented in the expression as the possessor of the direct object is, in any reasonable paraphrase, represented as a direct object. Speaking even more informally, the element *the* *boy* in *They pulled the boy's leg* or *They got the boy's goat* "feels" very much like the direct object of some action done to the boy, not like a reference to the possessor of certain objects or even moods or psychic states. This problem is apparent in such reasonable paraphrases as "They teased the boy" for *They pulled the boy's leg* and "They provoked the boy" for *They got the boy's goat.* Here, then, we have idioms with a semantic peculiarity that was anticipated in Section I, a discrepancy in the semantic functions of the constituents in the free and in the idiomatic constructions. A rather similar problem would arise with idioms that represent as quasipossessors an element that functions in the paraphrase as a reflexive object: *to pull in one's horns* (where *one* = subject), *to burn one's bridges,* and so on.

It is convenient to reconsider here, very briefly, the place of the idiom comparison operation in the generative process. Katz and Postal (1963) thought that the semantic interpretation of a sentence should proceed from the bottom up and that the derived reading reached at a certain node should be discarded for the meaning of the idiom; but this approach fails if the derived reading by that time contains components that should be retained. The Katz-Postal analysis could not, even if elaborated, specify the part of the derived reading which should be retained because it was based on a semantic theory (Katz and Fodor, 1963) which destroys syntactic structures as it amalgamates readings (Weinreich, 1966*b*, p. 410). This failing is corrected, I think, if we provide instead that the idiom list should be consulted before the semantic interpretation begins. In a type of linguistics in which ordering is important, this point does perhaps deserve to be made.

But let us go back to the notion of a complex entry which has become possible as a consequence of the subsequently developed theory of the lexical rule. The *complex entry* contains elements that are subject to morphophonemic alternation, so that morphophonemic features must be specified for them. Consider *shoot the breeze* as a possible complex dictionary entry. The morphophonemic features (i.e., the inflectional class) of *shoot* in this entry are precisely the same as those of the noncomplex verb *shoot.* In fact, if there are in the language two homonymous literal verbs, the verbal constituent of an idiom is identical with a specific one of them. For example, the morphophonemic features of *ring* in *ring the changes* are identical with those of the verb *ring* ("to make the sound of a bell"), and not with those of the other *ring* ("to encircle"): we say *He rang the changes,* not **He ringed the changes.* So, as I indicated on an earlier occasion (Weinreich, 1966*b*, p. 453), we would have to devise a way to represent in the dictionary the fact that *shoot the breeze* is associated with the entry *shoot*, in order to avoid the redundant specification of the conjugational features of *shoot*. I now realize, however, that the difficulty is even greater, for even if we had a dictionary in which *shoot the breeze* were a "branch" of the entry *shoot*, we could not, as far as I can see, show the idiom simultaneously to be a "branch" of another simple entry, *breeze*. Yet this is exactly what would have to be done in the general case, as becomes obvious if we get away from English as a model and think of more highly inflected languages. In Russian, for example, an idiom of the type *shoot the breeze* would involve an object noun in the accusative, and the morphophonemics of the noun would also have to be specified; for if the sentence were negated, the noun would appear in the genitive; if it were passivized (for idiomatic phrases that permit passivization), the noun would be in the nominative. In fact, the noun would participate in a good part of a regular declension, while the verb participated in the conjugation. I do not see how a complex entry could be simultaneously a "branch" of more than one simple entry. The problem is similar with adjective-plus-noun idioms such as *hot potato*. If one were stored in the dictionary of an inflected language as a complex entry with the syntactic feature "noun", the full inflectional morphophonemics of the literal (i.e., the independently entered) adjective would have to be repeated under the complex entry, and likewise under every complex entry of which the adjective was a constituent.

I come now to my last, and strongest, argument against treating idioms as complex entries. If the syntactic structure of complex entries were not governed by the same syntax as free construction, we would expect to find among the complex entries a great many, or at least some, that are "asyntactically" constructed. In other words, if the rules of syntax (i.e., of sentence formation) did not hold for the inert entities stored in the dictionary, we would expect random structures in the dictionary, or at least a good proportion of structures that would be ill formed with respect to the rules that govern the generation of free phrase markers. If the syntactic structure of complex dictionary entries were not bound by the grammatical rules of the language, what would prevent us from having some of them in the form shown under 30? And yet, among hundreds and hundreds of idioms in many languages, we do not find any such monstrosities. (The number of exceptions, as I mentioned before,

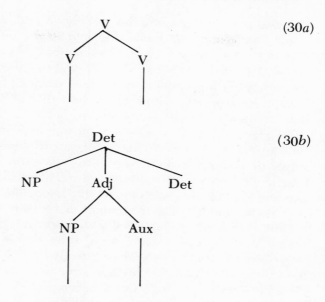

(30a)

(30b)

is infinitesimal.) By postulating complex dictionary entries that are exempt from the rules of grammar, I think we quite needlessly renounce the possibility of accounting for their impressive structural regularity.

Let us pursue this point in just a little more detail. Suppose we formulate a grammar of English so that markers like 31 can be generated; that is, a constituent — let us call it verbal — is written as a

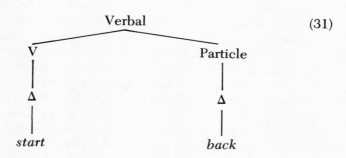

(31)

verb and a particle. Among the particles would be such indicators
as *up, down, in, back, forward, away,* and so on, which could be
selected if the verb were a "verb of motion" (as indicated by appropriate syntactic features). Since *start* qualifies, it could be constructed with any such optional directional particle, for example *back.*
Now there are many idiomatic verbals that utilize the same particles in highly specialized senses. According to Makkai's evidence
(1965), few of them designate motion, but there are some examples,
such as *set out.* (In a theory such as we are discussing, *set out* would
surely be a complex dictionary entry, since semantically it cannot
be resynthesized from the verb *set* modified by *out* in any independently given senses.) Now, by the theory of complex dictionary
entries, it would be sheer accident that a complex entry, such as
set out, could not be combined with productively generated directional particles, such as *in.* To put it another way, it would be a
sheer accident that there were practically no verbs of motion among
the idiomatic verbals that had the structure verb-plus-particle. On
the other hand, if we did away with complex dictionary entries and
accounted for the meanings of such items as *set out* by means of an
idiom list, the reason there are no terminal strings containing a sequence of particles would be perfectly clear: the appropriate rule of
the syntax only permits the generation of, at most, one particle after
each verb.

In an earlier paper (Weinreich, 1966*b*), I used the notion of
complex dictionary entries in the hope that they were the correct
way of harmonizing the Katz-Postal analysis of idioms with the subsequently developed conception of lexical rule. On further reflection, it appears to me that the mechanism of an idiom list, proposed
by Katz and Postal (1963), is indispensable after all—subject, of
course, to at least the modifications proposed in this paper.

There are two classes of phrases for which complex dictionary
entries do seem appropriate. They are an ideal representation, first,
of expressions that are not categorially well formed, for example,
blow (NP) *to kingdom come* or *by and large.* In fact, these could not
be generated in any other way. Since their equivalents in inflectional languages are hardly, I suppose, liable to inflection, the frozen
representation as a complex dictionary entry seems just right. Incidentally, they would not be idioms in our theory because they do
not have any literal counterparts and *cannot* have them in view of
their ill-formedness.

(32a)   (32b)

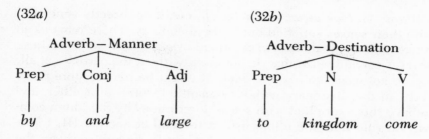

The second class of expressions that should, perhaps, be retained as complex dictionary entries are binomials of which both
constituents are unique, of the type *spic and span, hem and haw,
tit for tat*. These, too, would not be idioms by our definitions, since
their uniqueness excludes the possibility of ambiguity and of literal
counterparts. Note that if inflectional detail had to be specified, as
in English *hem and haw*, or in adjectival binomials corresponding
to *spic and span* in inflectional languages, they could be listed
under the complex entry without redundancy, again because there
is no simple entry elsewhere in the dictionary where the same information is repeated.[24]

And so I am proposing that we have in the description of a language both complex dictionary entries and an idiom list, each for
its appropriate purpose. Let us go back briefly to the verbs with
particles to see how they would be treated. Since they are not
doubly unique binomials or categorially ill formed, they do not, I
say, belong in the dictionary as complex entries. Rather, they should
then be generated as free constructions, and those that require idiomatic meanings will have them superimposed from the idiom list.
You will recall that the idiom list is reserved for constructions of
which two or more constituents are polysemous and where the
selection of subsenses is two-directional. From this it follows that
expressions such as *throw up* ("vomit"), *look out* ("be careful"),
water down ("dilute"), *set off* ("explode"), and *pipe down* ("lower
one's voice") would be idiomatic; each constituent is polysemous,
and the selection of subsenses is two-directional, as demonstrated
by their ambiguity. On the other hand, *stay out* and *keep in*, as well

---

[24]The syntactically most intricate doubly unique binomial that I have so far
come across is the pair of Yiddish impersonal "reflexive" verbs, *kristlen zikh–
yidlen zikh*, which occur exclusively in the proverb *Vi es kristlt zikh, azóy yidlt
zikh*, roughly paraphrasable: "As the Christians fare, so fare the Jews."

as *throw in, look away,* and *send off,* could be directly generated with their senses supplied out of the dictionary. There remains an interesting residual class, exemplified by *eke out* or *cave in.* These phrases contain verbs that do not occur without the particles at all; we do not have **to eke, *to cave.* It might be best to store these verbs in the dictionary without semantic features altogether, and to have them supplied with sense descriptions by the idiom comparison rule from the idiom list. At the end of Section III, I suggested that some dictionary entries might be keyed to trigger the idiom comparison rule for optional operation. If we decide to store such verbs as *eke* and *cave* in the dictionary without semantic features, we might stipulate that segments of terminal strings that have semantic blanks automatically trigger the idiom comparison rule for *obligatory* operation.

I surmise that some readers will feel uncomfortable with my proposals because such diversified treatment for different types of expressions is contemplated; but if the phenomena are heterogeneous, the analysis will also have to be diversified. It happens that just the semantic problem of adverbial particles is common to many Indo-European languages, and has puzzled analysts for over two millennia. The same problem arises in connection with Sanskrit verbal prefixes. In regard to them, the great Patañjali, who taught in the second century B. C., supported the lexicographic dissolution of idioms. Verbal roots, Patañjali argued, are subject to polysemy. To account for a verb like *throw up* in the sense of "vomit," he would, therefore, say that the root *throw* has two meanings: first, "to cast, fling, or hurl"; and second, "to vomit." The particle *up* performs the service function of indicating that in *throw up,* the second subsense is selected. Patañjali's opponents, on the other hand, sought to pin down a more material semantic contribution of the particle. According to Chakravarti's *The Linguistic Speculations of the Hindus,* an intriguing but frustrating book, the controversy continued until Bhartṛhari put a stop to it by showing that some particles *are* "directly expressive of sense," while others are auxiliary and merely "enlarge the denotative power of roots" (Chakravarti, 1933, p. 171). In some instances the sense of the root is assigned to the united form, particle-plus-root. In our terms, this fact would mean that some prefixed verbs were idiomatic, others were not. Bhartṛhari is now known to have taught in the eighth century. If it took the Indians a thousand years to settle the issue, we might allow ourselves a little time to ponder it, too.

V. Some Further Implications

The kind of revised linguistic theory I have been advocating (25) raises a number of broader issues, two groups of which I would like to comment on informally. The first concerns the differential familiarity of generated expressions; the second concerns the semantic relation between literal and idiomatic senses of ambiguous expressions.

Let us consider the matter of differential familiarity first. If we follow Mel'čuk's distinction (1960) between idiomaticity of expressions and stability of collocations, we can agree with those investigators who have taken pains to eliminate from phraseological study expressions that are distinguished by nothing but their familiarity, and have no grammatical defects or semantic properties related to their specialized subsenses. Such binomials as *assets and liabilities* and *Latin and Greek*, and such sentences as *Two wrongs don't make a right* and *Colorless green ideas sleep furiously* fall into this category and have nothing idiomatic, or even phraseological, about them. They are merely stable and familiar. But the fact of their familiarity cannot be presented in the theory as we have sketched it so far.

To represent the fact of familiarity, we would have to enlarge the function of the idiom list, perhaps in the following way. Every entry in the idiom list would be accompanied by a familiarity rating. Let us, for the moment, arbitrarily assume two such ratings, "familiar" and "very familiar." In addition, most entries would contain specifications as to obligatory or prohibited transformations, if we were to reckon with the fact that the familiarity or unfamiliarity of an expression relates to a particular transformational version of it, not to its deep structure. (For example, if our previous example is embedded to yield the sentence *For two wrongs to make a right is rather unusual*, it seems to lose the "familiar" feature that we are trying to represent.) Finally, some but not all entries would contain sense specifications; those that did would be the idioms of the idiom list discussed before.

The idiom comparison rule would be correspondingly modified. Its general function would remain that of matching generated terminal strings against the idiom list. For each fragment of a string for which a match is found in the expanded idiom list, the idiom comparison rule would now

1) attach to the string fragment the familiarity rating specified in the expanded idiom list;

2) attach the specified transformational restrictions;
3) substitute sense specifications for semantic blanks where they occur (recall the type *eke out*);
4) substitute sense specifications for the generated sense specifications already associated with the terminal strings.

Operations 1 through 3 would be obligatory; operation 4 would be optional.

Now, if this kind of mechanism is allowed, a rather intriguing prospect opens up before us for accommodating yet another range of phenomena in an explicit grammar, namely, word derivation. Word derivation, too, like idiomaticity, has constituted a stumbling block for generative linguistics because of its conspicuously restricted productivity. That is to say, for the large majority of compound and derivationally complex words, the speaker of a language recognizes the rulelike manner in which they are made up, but he cannot produce new items without changing the language. For an arbitrary sentence, it is not part of a speaker's competence to know whether he has heard it before; for the typical compound or complex word, on the other hand, being or not being an element of an inventory is as important a characteristic as the phonological, syntactic, or semantic features of the item. This point, missed by Lees (1960) in his pioneering book on English nominalizations, was forcefully made by Karl E. Zimmer in a study of affixal negation in English and other languages (1964).

Suppose we were to build all productive, as well as semiproductive, word-forming processes into the syntax in a uniform way, and we included in our dictionary only the ultimate primes of such a grammar, that is, only single morphemes and complexes of completely unique, ungeneratable structure. Let us call this list the Simplex Dictionary. The Simplex Dictionary would contain such nouns as *brush, cabbage, hair, leaf,* but not *hairbrush* or *cabbage leaf.* Among the transformations of the language would be the one that reduces certain sentences containing pairs of nouns to compounds, for example, *The brush is* Prep *hair* (or the like) to *hairbrush,*[25] *The cabbage has a leaf* to *cabbage leaf,* and so on. The

---

[25]In order to avoid the mistake of attributing excessive structure to a compound such as *hairbrush* (i.e., of determining arbitrarily that it is derived from *The brush is for hair, The brush is (made) of hair,* etc.), we envisage the possibility of deriving the compound from an underlying string that is nonterminal in the sense that the lexical rule has not operated on the node dominated by preposition. Alternatively, one may provide that the specific "relational" content of prepositions in terminal strings becomes neutralized under the compounding transformation, just as tense, mood, and similar details under the auxiliary node become neutralized in some instances of nominalization of verb phrases.

language description would also contain a Complex Dictionary in which would be entered all compounds, complex words, idioms, phrases, and sentences familiar to speakers of the language. A matching rule would operate on each terminal string and on the Complex Dictionary. For idioms and for familiar strings of size greater than words, the operation of the rule would be as described before. But we want to see what it might do with compound and complex *words*.

What we are after is an operation that would pass, let us say, *hairbrush* or *cabbage leaf*, but would frown on some arbitrary output of the compounding transformation, such as *cabbage brush* or *hair leaf*. For compounds, the object to which the matching rule must react is a pair consisting of the terminal string that contains two constituent nouns and the transformation that creates the compound (including the structural description of the input). Assume now that the matching rule, like the idiom comparison rule described before, operates on terminal strings before they have passed through the transformational component of the grammar. Suppose that there occurs, in the range of the rule, a terminal string containing the nouns *brush* and *hair* and a phrase marker satisfying the structural description of the compounding transformation. We would now expect the rule to take from the Complex Dictionary and to attach to the string, a potential familiarity rating that would signify that if the string undergoes the compounding transformation, the result will be marked as "familiar." Since, however, many familiar compounds are also idiomatic, and since the matching rule must substitute idiomatic for generated senses, it would perhaps be simpler to place the entire matching process, the comparison of terminal strings, with the Complex Dictionary, *after* their transformational processing. If the process were so placed, the entries of our Complex Dictionary would consist of truncated underlying, or derived, phrase markers, each terminating in at least two simplexes and any number of blank or dummy nodes. Some of these entries would be words (i.e., compound or complex words), while others would be larger constructions, up to whole sentences. Each entry would be accompanied by a familiarity rating, and some entries—namely idioms, whether a single word in length or longer—would be accompanied, in addition, by sense descriptions. See the diagram under 33.

Thus the categorial component in conjunction with the Simplex Dictionary would generate all possible complex words of the language, as well as all sentences. The Complex Dictionary in conjunction with the matching rule would lead to a marking of those that are not familiar. Such marking, incidentally, would not

(33)

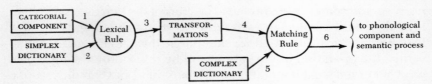

1. Preterminal string
2. Morphemes, unanalyzable
   complexes, ill-formed
   phrases, doubly unique
   binomials
3. Terminal string

4. Derived marker

5. Familiarity ratings
   for analyzable com-
   plex words and clichés;
   idiomatic senses
6. Literal and
   idiomatic
   strings with
   familiarity
   ratings

block the strings from entering the morphophonemic and phono-logical processing. That is to say, the description would also gen-erate phonetic representations of sentences like *Give me the cab-bage brush,* but the compound *cabbage brush* would lack the "familiar" mark that *hairbrush* would have.

Is there anything objectionable in this generated surplus? Nothing that I know of if, again, we are seriously committed to the abstractness of the description. Having a base that generates too much is tantamount to accounting for the structure not only of exist-ing sentences and words, but also of possible sentences and com-plex words (made up of existing simplexes). The role of the filtering device is to differentiate, among possible words, those that are established from those that are not.

I can hardly go into the numerous ramifications and implica-tions of these suggestions here; they could easily form the subject of a separate series of papers. Let me note only three points. First, not every word-forming process is of restricted productivity. The formation of adjectives like *unchangeable* from underlying phrases such as . . . *cannot be changed* is, according to Zimmer's finding (1964), far more productive than the prefixation of *un-* to adjective stems, as in *unobvious.* Consequently we may want to show that some word-forming transformations rely more heavily on the match-ing rule than others; some are more insecure, as it were, and need greater reassurance that their output is familiar (in the technical sense of being entered in the Complex Dictionary).

Second, the Complex Dictionary, as I have depicted it, would mark certain fragments of strings as "familiar" (perhaps "familiar" to a certain degree). Such marking implies a general convention that whatever is not marked as familiar is simply unfamiliar, or equally novel. But if word-formation rules are incorporated into the productive syntax, some of their output would not be simply unfamiliar, but reprehensible. We do not want *cruelness* generated on the pattern of *suppleness*, since *cruelty* is required; we do not want *unhearable*, since *inaudible* is required; we do not want *butcherer*, like *slaughterer*, since *butcher* is already fixed; to take a graphic example, we do not want *collecter* because what is required is *collector*. Thus, if word-formation rules are incorporated in the syntax, the entries in the Simplex Dictionary will have to be supplied with morphophonemic specifications of the correct derivational class; the suppletive stem *-aud-*, for example, will have to be listed under *hear*, so that the transformation that reduces . . . *can be heard* to *audible* operates correctly.

Third, this scheme would have important implications for language learning. The most primitive component of a child's linguistic competence would be represented as a miniature Simplex Dictionary. As his mastery of the language progresses, the categorial component of the child's internalized grammar becomes enriched; consequently certain previously unanalyzed entries in the Simplex Dictionary are assigned internal structure. It is their constituents that become, in turn, entries in the child's Simplex Dictionary, while the complex expression as a whole takes its place in its incipient Complex Dictionary, obtaining the appropriate familiarity rating. As the child learns to perform the matching operation, he increases the calibration of his own norms with those of the speech community as to what is "familiar" and what is not.

And now to the concluding point, the question of similarity between basic and derived senses of polysemous units, and between literal and idiomatic senses of constructions. I have tried to design the theory of idioms in such a way that there could be unlimited distance between literal and idiomatic meanings. In doing so, I realize that I have gone against the spirit of the Saussurean concept of semantic motivation.

Saussurean semantics, as is well known, classifies signs into arbitrary and motivated (cf. Ullmann, 1952, pp. 87-89). Motivated signs display some connection between the sound and the sense. The motivation may be phonological, as in onomatopoetic words; it may be morphological, as when a teacher is called *teach-er* because he is someone who teaches; finally, it may be semantic, as when a saltpeter-cured herring is called *red* because it acquires a red coloring in the process of being smoked.

It seems to me that semantic motivation in Ullmann's sense is something that can only be established a posteriori. Take the example *eat crow*. If we try to visualize the connection between the literal sense ("to consume the flesh of the bird *corvus*") and the idiomatic one, which my dictionary renders as "to accept what one has fought against," each of us is surely imaginative enough to come up with a plausible account: both are rather unpleasant acts. (It is only incidentally relevant that we are dealing with a convergence of two etymologically unrelated *crow's*.) But like the symbolism of dreams or of poetry, the relation is extremely weak. Why should *eat crow* signify the acceptance of what one has fought against, rather than some other nauseating act? Conversely, why should the acceptance of what one has fought against be signified by *eating crow*, and not *eating dog* or *drinking mud* or *smelling rotten eggs*? In short, I feel that the relation between idiomatic and literal meanings is so unsystematic as to deserve no place in the theory.

This phenomenon of superimposed meaning would be awkward and surprising if the doubling up of functions were not so familiar in other fields of human endeavor. I take a hammer and use it as a paperweight; its nail-driving functions are suspended while it functions to hold sheets of paper in a draft. A statue of a goddess holds up the roof of a temple. A horn on a car, as it warns pedestrians, sounds a melodic figure subject to esthetic evaluation.

It seems to me that only in exceptional instances can we conceive of rules governing the relation between basic and superimposed functions. The absence of such a body of rules—a grammar, so to speak, of functional extension—does not mean that in a particular instance the relation cannot be perceived; but this perception is, in each instance, a separate act of historical analysis or of poetic evocation. No general predictions can be made. What is it about the goddess' statue that fits it to hold up the roof? Its sturdiness and height—qualities that, I submit, are unrelated to its basic ritual and esthetic functions. The logic is the same as in the question: Why does *eat crow* signify acceptance of what one has fought against? It is an essentially arbitrary relation, which looks plausible only in retrospect. The purely retrospective plausibility of such connections is easily felt with regard to foreign-language idioms. Yiddish has the verb phrase *makhn zikh harts* (literally, "make heart for one-self") and the impersonal *shlogn* Dative-NP *tsum hartsn* (literally, "beat [somebody] to the heart"). I can conceive of no correct finite analysis of the entry *harts* ("heart") in a Yiddish defining dictionary from which a learner of the language could infer that the first idiom actually means "to give oneself courage," and that the latter means "nauseate, disgust."[26] Semantic rules to connect basic with derived meaning, it seems to me, are chimerical. If formulated they would have no generality whatever; far from resembling phonological rules (such as those that determine the contextual variants of phonemes), they would not even have the limited generality of morphophonemic rules of the type "*break* → *broke*- in the context -*en*." "Rules" of semantic extension would be like "rules" of suppletion, for example, "*go* → *wen*- in the context -*t*."

A number of critics of generative grammar have argued that, in the extension of meanings, in the formation of idioms, in the vagueness of the reference of words, lies the true "creativity" of language, not in the formation of an infinitude of sentences out of a finite stock of primes. We have heard the so-called novelty of the arbitrary sentence ridiculed with eloquence by Roman Jakobson. In this vein, too, Bolinger (1965, p. 567) has recently written, in rebuttal of Katz and Fodor (1963): "A dictionary is a frozen pantomime. . . . A semantic theory must account for the *process* of metaphorical invention—all the more so, a theory that stems from generative grammar with its emphasis on creativity. . . . It is characteristic of natural language that no word is ever limited to its enumerated senses, but carries with it the qualification 'something like.'" I feel that the kind of "theory" that Bolinger has in mind is utopian, for if he is right, if every word carries with it "the qualification 'something like,'" then it follows that there are *no* specifiable constraints *no* serious theory to do the job he calls for. There can be no such theory any more than there could be a grammatical theory if words could be combined at random.

To be sure, creativity comes in different degrees. The Lord's creation of the world is a more spectacular act than the car-

---

[26]No other collocations occur in which *harts* so directly signifies "nausea," although *untern hartsn* ("under the heart") is, of course, the anatomical region where nausea is felt. As for the meaning "courage," we do find (*nit*) *hobn dos harts tsu* ("[not] have the heart [= courage] to")—very much as in English—and *bahártst* ("courageous, valorous"); but no productive use of *harts* in this meaning is permitted.

penter's creation of a table; but let us not forget how much more researchable are the laws of carpentry than the principles of world creation. In disparaging the allegedly minor regularities of language that generative linguistics has set out to study, our poetic critics run the risk of dissipating every advantage of explicitness and rigor that linguistics has gained, at no little effort. As far as I am concerned, there is mystery aplenty in the productive rule systems of language, and beauty enough in their elegant descriptions. We would do well to guard against a loosening of the notions "theory" and "rule," lest linguistics be debased to a pseudoscience comparable to the interpretation of dreams.

Bibliography

Amosova, N. N.
   1963 *Osnovy anglijskoj frazeologii.* Leningrad.
Arxangel'skij, V. L.
   1964 *Ustojčivye frazy v sovremennom russkom jazyke; osnovy teorii ustojčivyx fraz i problemy obščej frazeologii.* Rostov-on-Don.
Babkin, A. M., ed.
   1964 *Problemy frazeologii.* Moscow and Leningrad. Includes the editor's essay "Frazeologija i leksikografija," pp. 7-36.
Bar-Hillel, Y.
   1955 "Idioms." In W. N. Locke and A. D. Booth, eds. *Machine Translation of Languages* (New York and London), pp. 183-193.
Bendix, E. H.
   1966 *Componential Analysis of General Vocabulary: the Semantic Structure of a Set of Verbs in English, Hindi, and Japanese.* Bloomington, Ind., and The Hague. Originally Pt. II of the *International Journal of American Linguistics* 32:2.
Bolinger, D.
   1965 "The Atomization of Meaning," *Language* 41:555-573.

Burling, R.
  1965 "Burmese Kinship Terminology." In E. A. Hammel, ed.,
       Formal Semantic Analysis, pp. 106-117 (=*American
       Anthropologist* 67:5, Pt. II).
Casares, J.
  1950 *Introducción a la lexicofrafía moderna.* Madrid.
Chakravarti, P.
  1933 *The Linguistic Speculations of the Hindus.* Calcutta.
Chomsky N.
  1957 *Syntactic Structures.* The Hague.
  1965 *Aspects of the Theory of Syntax.* Cambridge, Mass.
Conklin, H. C.
  1962 "Lexicographic Treatment of Folk Taxonomies." In F. W.
       Householder and S. Saporta, eds., *Problems of Lexicography*
       (Bloomington, Ind.), pp. 119-141.
Greenberg, S. R.
  1966 "Families of Idioms in American English." Unpublished
       paper presented to the Linguistic Society of America,
       December 29.
Greimas, A. J.
  1966 *Sémantique structurale.* Paris.
Hockett, C. F.
  1956 "Idiom Formation." In *For Roman Jakobson* (The Hague),
       pp. 222-229.
  1958 *A Course in Modern Linguistics.* New York.
Householder, F. W., Jr.
  1959 "On Linguistic Primes," *Word* 15:231-239.
Katz, J. J.
  1964 "Semantic Theory and the Meaning of 'Good,'" *Journal
       of Philosophy* 61:739-765.
  1966 *The Philosophy of Language.* New York and London.
Katz, J. J., and J. A. Fodor
  1963 "The Structure of a Semantic Theory," *Language* 39:170-
       210.
Katz, J. J., and P. M. Postal
  1963 "Semantic Interpretation of Idioms and Sentences Con-
       taining Them," Massachusetts Institute of Technology
       Research Laboratory of Electronics, *Quarterly Progress
       Report* 70:275-282.
Lakoff, G.
  1965 *On the Nature of Syntactic Irregularity.* Harvard Uni-
       versity, Computation Laboratory, *Mathematical Lin-*

guistics and Automatic Translation, Report No. NSF-16
to the National Science Foundation.

Lees, R. B.
1960 *The Grammar of English Nominalizations.* Bloomington,
Ind.

Lounsbury, F. G.
1956 "A Semantic Analysis of Pawnee Kinship Usage," *Language* 32:158-194.
1965 "Another View of the Trobriand Kinship Categories." In
E. A. Hammel, ed., *Formal Semantic Analysis,* pp. 142-185
(= *American Anthropologist* 67:5, Pt. II).

Lyons, J.
1963 *Structural Semantics.* Oxford.

Makkai, A.
1965 "Idiom Structure in English." Unpublished Ph.D. dissertation, Yale University.

Malkiel, Y.
1959 "Studies in Irreversible Binomials," *Lingua* 8:113-160. Reprinted in *Essays on Linguistic Themes* (Berkeley and Los
Angeles, 1968), pp. 311-355.

Mašinnyj perevod i prikladnaja lingvistika
1964 No. 8. Published by Moskovskij Gosudarstvennyj Pedagogičeskij Institut Inostrannyx Jazykov.

Mel'čuk, I. A.
1960 "O terminax 'ustojčivost'' i 'idiomatičnost'," *Voprosy
jazykoznanija,* no. 4, pp. 73-80.

Problemy frazeologii i zadači ee izucenija v vysšej i srednej škole
1965 *Tezisy dokladov mežvuzovskoj konferencii 30.V.-2.VI. 1965.
Čerepovec.*

Šanskij, N. M.
1963 *Frazeologija sovremennogo russkogo jazyka.* Moscow.

Schane, S. A.
1966 *A Schema for Sentence Coordination.* Bedford, Mass.
(= The Mitre Corporation, *Information System Language
Studies* 10).

Strawson, P. F.
1952 *Introduction to Logical Theory.* London and New York.

Ullman, S.
1957 *Principles of Semantics.* 2d ed. Glasgow.
1962 *Semantics.* Oxford.

Ustinov, I. V.
1966 *Voprosy russkoj frazeologii.* Moscow. (= Moskovskij ob-

lastnoj pedagogičeskij Institut im. N. K. Krupskoj, *Učenye zapiski* 160.)

Vinogradov, V. V.

1964 "Osnovnye ponjatija russkoj frazeologii kak lingvističeskoj discipliny." In *Trudy jubilejnoj naučnoj sessii Leningradskogo Gosudarstvennogo Universiteta,* (Leningrad), pp. 45-69.

1947 "Ob osnovnyx tipax frazeologičeskix edinic v russkom jazyke," *Sbornik A. A. Šaxmatov (1964-1920)* (Moscow and Leningrad), pp. 339-364.

Weinreich, U.

1960 Review of Hockett (1958), *Romance Philology* 13:320 – 341.

1963 "[Soviet] Lexicology." In T. A. Sebeok, ed., *Current Trends in Linguistics* (The Hague), I, 60-93.

1966a "On the Semantic Structure of Language." In J. H. Greenberg, ed., *Universals of Language,* 2d ed. (Cambridge, Mass.), pp. 142-216.

1966b "Explorations in Semantic Theory." In T. A. Sebeok, ed., *Current Trends in Linguistics* (The Hague), III, 395-477.

Winter, W.

1965 "Transforms Without Kernels?" *Language* 41:484-489.

Ziff, P.

1960 *Semantic Analysis.* Ithaca, N. Y.

Zimmer, K. E.

1964 *Affixal Negation in English and Other Languages: An Invetigation of Restricted Productivity.* (Supplement to *Word* 20:2).

Some Current Psycholinguistic Research:
The *Tu-Vous* and *Le-La* Studies

Wallace E. Lambert
McGill University

I. Implications of the Pattern of *Tu-Vous* Usage in French Canada

Depending on how we choose to address others, we can very clearly, although subtly, indicate whether we consider them close associates or whether we want to keep them at a certain social distance, either because they are not yet perceived as friends, or because we are never likely to become that intimate with them. Thus in English we may keep a proper social distance by using titles (Mr. or Mrs.) and last names, rather than first names, or we may indicate a status difference by using first names only, with hired help, for example. Other languages, such as French, German, Spanish, and Italian, afford greater precision and flexibility in expressing the desired intimacy of social interaction, because the languages themselves have recognized provisions — namely, the use of *tu* and *vous* or their equivalents — for indicating differences in solidarity and/or social status.[1]

Roger Brown and A. Gilman[2] have recently traced the fascinating story of how the use of *tu* and *vous* (or their equivalents) developed in various countries and how this usage has changed through time. For example, it has only been within the past decade that French army officers have been told to refrain from the practice of using *tu* when addressing their men while expecting them

---

[1]The several investigations reported here were supported by grants from the Canada Council and the Canadian Defense Research Board, grant 9401-10. G. R. Tucker is the coinvestigator for this project.
[2]R. Brown and A. Gilman, "The Pronouns of Power and Solidarity," in T. A. Sebeok, ed., *Style in Language* (Cambridge, Mass., 1960). See also R. Brown, *Social Psychology* (New York, 1965).

to use *vous* in return. Likewise, European residents in French Africa have been advised since 1957 only that it is no longer appropriate (or safe) to use nonreciprocal address forms when conversing with native Africans. During the same time span, it apparently has become socially uncomfortable for a Frenchman patronizing the very best restaurants to use *tu* with his waiter and expect the *vous* form in return.

From a wide array of evidence, including interviews with samples of informants from France, Germany, and Italy, Brown and Gilman have drawn several important conclusions about this trend. They argue that the nonreciprocal use of address forms has given way, through time, to a symmetrical use of the same form by both interlocutors, *tu* being used by both to indicate solidarity and *vous* being used to indicate social distance. This trend suggests that the importance of expressing status differences in this manner has diminished in recent times relative to the importance of expressing degree of solidarity, reflecting, it is presumed, basic changes in value systems. At the same time, Brown and Ford[3] have found that other, more subtle, ways of expressing status differences are still frequently used. For instance, one person may use the first name of another and expect a title plus last name in return, as is evident in such an exchange as: "Is that you, Max?" "Yes, Mr. Adams." However, the central idea of interest here is that nowadays there is very little expression of status differences through the nonreciprocal use of *tu* and *vous* as forms of address.

A question about the generality and universality of these conclusions arises for those who live in French Canada, where it is not uncommon either to encounter directly, or to hear about, parents who use *tu* with their children and receive *vous* in return. We undertook a study to examine, for the first time, how French Canadians use these terms in addressing others. Our informants were 136 French-Canadian boys, sixteen to nineteen years of age, who were attending a *collège* (similar to an American junior college) in Quebec City. They were asked by their teachers to complete a questionnaire concerning both their own use of *tu* and *vous* when speaking with various other people, and the form of address others typically used when speaking with them. First they were asked: "When the following people speak with you, do they use *tu* or *vous*?" Then: "When you speak with each one of the following

[3]R. Brown and M. Ford, "Address in American English," *Journal of Abnormal and Social Psychology* 62:375-385 (1961).

people individually, do you use *tu* or *vous*?" Finally, they were asked to describe their father's occupation in as much detail as possible.

Noteworthy instances of nonsymmetrical usage of address forms were found, two of particular significance. First, most of these boys received the *tu* form from their grandparents but used the *vous* form in addressing them. Second, the vast majority received *tu* from their parents (and from "mother"), while half of them used *vous* in addressing their parents. (Over 97 percent of the boys gave exactly the same responses to "mother" as to "parents.")

What does the first finding suggest about children's relations with grandparents in French Canada? There appears to be a widely accepted standard of nonreciprocal usage here, much more general than that found with parents. On the grandparent's part, it may reflect the accepted standard for expressing respect toward elders, while from the perspective of the boys it may be (or become) an index of social distance from grandparents. The difference between the two older generations may, in turn, be a symptom of a value change that could, in time, dictate a more general use of the address pattern for solidarity. And what might underlie the two different manners of responding to parents, when nearly all are receiving the *tu* form from their parents? We anticipated that social class differences would play an important role, but we saw many forms this relation might take. The middle- and upper-class parents might be more traditional, in this sense, and expect their children to show respect for parents by using the more formal *vous*. On the other hand, it is just as reasonable to argue that the working-class parents might have reason, because of their lower status in society, to expect, or even to demand, that their own children, at least, show them respect by using the *vous* form of address. Of course, the use of *vous* and *tu* may have some other and specific meanings in French Canada. For example, it may not indicate formality or demand for respect as much as social distance or lack of intimacy between children and parents. None of these issues will be settled with a pilot study, but the following analysis is statistically strong enough to indicate that social class differences should be examined more carefully in future studies of this aspect of French-Canadian social interaction.

Using the descriptions each boy gave of his father's occupation, we were able to classify 113 of the 136 boys into one of three socioeconomic categories: *professional*, if the father was, for example, a doctor, lawyer, engineer, dentist, or college professor; *white-collar*, if the father was, for example, a bank manager, a journalist, a salesman, an accountant, a store manager, or a businessman; and *blue-collar*, if the father was, for example, a foreman, a mechanic, a baker, a railroad worker, or a farmer. These categories were so distinct that a panel of French and English Canadians acting as judges encountered very few disagreements in making classifications.

The results of this analysis show a very strong relation between socioeconomic background, as measured here, and the forms of address used; the contingency analysis indicates that it is the higher social class families that encourage the reciprocal use of *tu* between parents and children and the lower class parents (actually, families where the father works mainly with his hands) that encourage the use of the nonreciprocal *vous* form when being addressed by their children. The pattern when "mother" was addressed was nearly the same as that for "parents" and is equally statistically significant.

Further research on this problem was clearly called for. It was necessary to determine how extensive this pattern is in French Canada (i.e., in centers other than Quebec City), at what age it starts, whether it is similar for girls and boys, whether some particular social class characteristics are typically associated with it, whether it was more pronounced with former generations in French Canada, and whether it is likely to hold up with the next generation. For these purposes, a more detailed questionnaire was used and more differentiations in social class background were made. The purpose of the follow-up study, then, was to investigate more extensively second person pronoun usage among French-speaking Canadians.

In this instance, the subjects, or informants, were fifteen hundred male and female French-speaking students enrolled in Catholic public schools in Montreal and in Alma, Quebec, a city in the Lake St. John region several hundred miles north of Montreal. Students were selected from grades 3, 5, 7, 9, and 11 of schools located in all areas of the two cities. The social class representation in each site was approximately proportional to that of the total French-Canadian population (Blishen, 1951[4]).

The informants were asked to complete a detailed question-

[4]B. R. Blishen, F. E. Jones, K. D. Naegele, and J. Porter, eds., *Canadian Society: Sociological Perspectives* (rev. ed; Toronto, 1964).

naire that touched on various aspects of language usage and family relationships. Specifically, we asked for information concerning the pronoun form that the young person typically used to address, individually, other people such as: father, mother, a teacher, a bus driver, among a list of others; and the pronoun form that he, in turn, expected to receive from each of these people. Thirty-four possible social interactions (in the areas of home, school, recreation, church) were studied in this manner. The preliminary results to be reported today concern the interaction between the informant and several members of his family—his father, mother, paternal and maternal grandparents, male and female, first and second cousins, uncle, aunt, godfather, godmother, and brother-in-law. These results provide an interesting picture of linguistic usage with both close and more distant family members. The child also gave a detailed description of the father's occupation, which was used, in part, to determine the social class status of the family.

So that the results could be analyzed, the subjects were divided into groups according to grade, sex, urban versus rural setting, and social class, and the instances of reciprocal and nonreciprocal usage for each of the fifteen interactions described above were tabulated. The chi-square statistic was used to test the relation between linguistic usage and social class, age, sex, or social setting.

Information obtained from large samples of boys and girls at all grade levels, in both public and private schools in Montreal, indicated that the pattern of linguistic usage is significantly affected by social class. The pattern noted in the Quebec City study was found again, that is, French-Canadian youngsters whose parents came from higher social classes tended to use predominantly reciprocal *tu* with both mother and father, while those whose parents were members of the lower social classes tended to establish nonreciprocal relationships.

With regard to age of subjects, there was a stronger relation noted between social class and pronoun usage with elementary school children than with high school children; the chi-square values ranged from 60 to 70 for the younger children and were approximately 14 for the older. All of these, however, are significant well beyond the 0.001 level. In general, about 60 percent of these children had established reciprocal pronoun relations with both parents, while about 40 percent maintained a nonreciprocal relation.

In contrast, more than 90 percent of a smaller sample of European French children attending private schools in Montreal were found to use reciprocal *tu* with both parents; however, a potentially confounding fact in this instance is that these students came from predominantly upper social class families. Thus, it is not clear whether social class or European background determined the pronoun usage for this subsample. Because of this lack of clarity, we have now extended our survey to France where we can more easily examine the European pattern through various social class subgroups.

In regard to urban differences in the French-Canadian pattern; the results obtained in Alma, Quebec, differ from those found in Montreal and in Quebec City. In this rural area, social class background is *not* related to usage. Instead, approximately equal numbers of young people, at all social class levels, use *tu* as use *vous* when addressing their parents. It should be noted that, as with the urban sample, nearly all parents from Alma use *tu* when addressing their children.

Pronounced rural-urban differences are also apparent when other family interactions are examined. In general, the rural youngsters, regardless of the specific people involved in the interaction, established nonreciprocal relations more often than urban youngsters did. This difference was especially marked for rural girls when interacting with their grandparents, aunts, and uncles, and for rural boys when interacting with their aunts and godparents. These same rural students, however, had reciprocal relations with cousins and brothers-in-law more often than did urban students.

Interesting patterns also emerge when social class influences are investigated for the other social relationships, especially when comparisons are made between rural and urban children. First, with regard to parents, we have noted that social class affects the pronoun usage of urban, but not rural, youngsters. On the other hand, where grandparents, uncles, aunts, and godparents (that is, the extended family members) are concerned, social class affects the pronoun usage of rural, but not urban, children. For extended family members, the general pattern for both rural and urban children is to use *vous*. In fact, about 80 percent of the French-Canadian youngsters use *vous* when interacting with grandparents, uncles, aunts, and godparents, while receiving *tu* in return. A different pattern emerges, however, when the social interactions between our informants and their cousins and brothers-in-law are examined. In these interactions, reciprocal *tu* usage tends to predominate for both rural and urban boys and girls, when they are interacting with either male or female first and second cousins, as well as with brothers-in-law. The proportion using the reciprocal *tu* form in these instances is around 75 percent. Thus, within the family there is a point where a shift occurs, from using *vous* with mother, father, uncles, aunts, grandparents, and godparents, to using *tu* with cousins and brothers-in-law. This place along a dimension of social intimacy where *tu* usage commences will be studied more systematically as we complete our analyses of the outside-family interactions.

These results indicate that previous research had not gone far enough in investigating the patterns of pronoun usage to fully justify Brown's conclusion that a "solidarity semantic" has replaced nonreciprocal relations. We do not find on the French-Canadian scene that there is a simple, universal trend toward reciprocal usage. In fact, the study of French-Canadian pronoun usage reveals a rather complex set of results which are of sociopsychological importance. Over 40 percent of the children surveyed established nonreciprocal relations even with their parents, and in many family interactions, nonreciprocal relations were predominate. Furthermore, the role of socioeconomic background is an important one. For urban children, it is clear that those from lower-class families have markedly more nonreciprocal relations within the family than do those from higher-class backgrounds. Thus, in urban centers there may be a gradual movement toward reciprocation with parents when people move up through the social classes, but this trend does not seem to be apparent in rural settings. The effect of social class is complicated in this instance because it influences the manner in which rural children interact linguistically with extended family members, a trend not apparent with urban children. There is also some evidence that the rural social system sets a more normative pattern for pronoun usage, one that is independent of socioeconomic background. The search must, of course, continue in order to determine what it is that accounts for the variations in usage from one family to another.

The premature statement of a universal "solidarity" theme draws attention away from the dynamics of pronoun usage in French Canada. (Our preliminary studies in other cultures, e.g., in Spanish-speaking Bogota, Colombia, in Spain, and in Sweden, indicate that the Canadian findings are not unique.) We have two further types of evidence on this point. First, we measured children's identification with mothers and fathers, using rating scales. Then we studied the relationship of degree of identification and reciprocal and nonreciprocal pronoun usage among parents and children. Preliminary

results indicate that groups maintaining reciprocal and nonreciprocal relations have very similar identification scores, suggesting
that youngsters using *vous* with their parents can establish parental
ties that are as close and strong as those of children using *tu*. Second,
we have examined the differential judgments children make of
families in which either *tu* or *vous* is the typical form of address.[5]
For this purpose, a substudy was conducted in which eleven-year-
old judges listened to professional actors playing the role of mother,
father, and son. Comparable groups of judges heard exactly the
same family discussion differing in only one aspect: in one instance
the son used *tu* with his parents, and in the other, he used *vous*.
The judgments of the children listening to these recordings markedly favored the family in which the boy used *vous* to address his
parents. In fact, the children found "the *vous* family" to be relatively more respectable, to get along together better or have better
family spirit, and to be more progressive or more modern. Furthermore, the son in the family was considered more likely to receive
a bicycle or a dog that he had requested in the taped family discussion. This pilot study is currently being repeated.

In addition to suggesting that significant class differences in
social behavior can be studied through this aspect of speech, these
findings also give us some insight into the linguistic demands made
on children who must learn to switch pronoun and verb forms from
one social setting to another. Children from working-class homes
apparently face a difficult problem, relative to those from families
of higher socioeconomic standing, since they are taught to use
different pronoun and verb forms from those their parents use in
what must appear to them as the same social setting. For example,
it would be difficult for a child to comprehend why, when his mother
asks "Lequel veux-tu, mon garçon?" he should have to shift to
another form to ask her the same question, for example, "Après
vous, maman, lequel voulez-vous?" If started from infancy on, the
task of language acquisition might be all that more exacting, especially for the lower-class children, if these results are representative.

One can also examine the effects of this difference in linguistic
usage on the way the child develops his generalizations about when
to use one form of address or the other. The French-Canadian
youngster, in learning the rules of usage, has a complicated set of
rules to master. He must learn that interaction with certain mem-

[5] We are indebted to Denis Runcie, now at the University of Western Ontario,
for his participation in this phase of the investigation.

bers of one's own family, parents as well as grandparents, calls for nonreciprocal usage. This rule is troublesome because it involves the parents, the very ones who are most instrumental in teaching him the language. The rules are apparently much more complicated for French Canadians than for the European French, who, if Brown's sample is representative, have a much simpler task in balancing their forms of address with established degrees of familiarity. On the other hand, if by chance Brown's samples are not representative, then it is possible that similar demands are made on certain subgroups in the European countries already studied.

II. Does Some Systematic Pattern Underlie Gender Distinctions in French?

There are two major reasons why psychologists might become interested in grammatical gender.[6] First, from a practical point of view, the mastery of gender is perhaps the most difficult and frustrating feature of the study of French as a second language, not only for those whose native language lacks gender distinctions, but also for those who have already mastered some other form of gender classifications; that is, the English speaker studying French must learn not only the French words for things, but also whether the new words are masculine or feminine. Since no rules for distinguishing gender classes are taught him, the whole process seems completely arbitrary. In contrast, the French speaker, even the very young child, seems to have no difficulty with gender. To the non-French speaker, this ability is amazing, and it becomes all the more so when one thinks about the typical explanations offered to account for it: "Through experience one knows it, that's all," or "One just has to learn it, I guess."

This enviable skill which cannot be explained or transmitted can be regarded as a potentially interesting example of rule usage in language, analogous to the rule usage involved in syntax. However, the example of gender may prove to be less mysteriously re-

[6]This research was supported in part by a Canada Council grant to W. E. Lambert, and in part by a Canadian Defense Research Board grant, number D77-9401-10. G. R. Tucker, A. Rigault, and N. Segalowitz collaborated in the study and are co-authors. Mr. Tucker will present a more extensive study of this matter as his doctoral dissertation. We are particularly grateful to Jenny Spire, now at Yale University, for her assistance with the phonetic analyses involved in this investigation.

lated to environmental experiences than syntax is said to be.[7] Thus, the study of gender may be an example of a relatively more tractable form of rule acquisition in language, serving both practical and theoretical ends.

One can regard the insufficient explanations offered by French speakers for their skill with gender assignments as examples of the linguistic myopia most native speakers have for the regularities existing in their own languages. If this step is taken, then a potentially important alternative comes to mind; there may well be some systematic pattern to gender distinctions in French; certain reliable clues may reside in the words themselves that assist native users in making gender assignments; French speakers may at an early age learn to make appropriate differentiations so as to abstract gender-determining regularities in their language.

As a preliminary step to testing this hypothesis, we interviewed experienced French teachers and consulted the most comprehensive French grammars. An interesting hypothesis was advanced by one informant, a specialist in teaching French. According to this person, the native French speaker associates *le* or *la* (or any other gender markers, such as *un*, *une*, *de la* or *du*, all of which apparently function in distinctive coordinate systems) with each noun, as a type of prefix. Thus, he simply learns the word *lamain* (as one word) for *la main* or *lemari* for *le mari.* Even this explanation, however, seems insufficient. Prefixing with *le* or *la* in paired-associates fashion would not very likely be economical or efficient, since there are more than forty thousand nouns in the French language. The explanation also suggests that French speakers would be unable to judge correctly the gender of novel nouns; however, informal tests of French children's skill at "guessing" gender indicate clearly that some method other than paired-associate memorization is available to them for making gender distinctions.

Although most grammars consulted indicate that the *endings* of French nouns may be related in certain fashions to gender distinction, still those grammarians who have systematically examined these relationships (e.g., Byrne and Churchill,[8] Grevisse,[9] and Sonet

---

[7]See e.g., T. Bever, J. A. Fodor, and W. Weksel, "On the Acquisition of Syntax: A Critique of 'Contextual Generalization,'" *Psychological Review* 72:467-482 (1965); D. McNeill, "Developmental Psycholinguistics," in F. Smith and G. A. Miller, eds., *The Genesis of Language* (Cambridge, Mass., 1966).

[8]L. S. R. Byrne and E. L. Churchill, *A Comprehensive French Grammar with Classified Vocabularies* (Oxford, 1950).

[9]M. Grevisse, *Le bon usage* (Paris, 1964).

and Shortliffe[10]) have arrived at the rather discouraging conclusion that noun endings are of limited value and are generally unreliable indicators of gender. With these thoughts in mind, a series of studies was conducted for the purpose of exploring the French speaker's skill with grammatical gender.

Since grammarians had suggested that a noun's ending might actually help to indicate gender to a speaker of French, lists of words with various endings were developed. These lists included both frequently occurring and rarely occurring nouns taken from the *Petit Larousse*[11] and the *Dictionnaire inverse de la langue française* (Juilland[12]). In addition, a large sample of "invented" words was compiled, with attention given to both the endings and the beginnings. These invented words were permissible French phonetic sequences that do not actually occur as words in the language (e.g., *florillon*). The invented words were constructed so that the beginning of the word (e.g., *flor-*) occurred either predominantly in masculine words (as determined from dictionary counts), in feminine words, or equally often in words of either gender. In the final list, words were also chosen so that various endings (e.g., *-aie, -aix*) were represented. Lists with words arranged in random order were presented to the subjects in either an oral or an oral-graphic form. In both instances, the subjects had only to indicate whether they thought each word was masculine or feminine by circling *un* or *une*.

The subjects were eight hundred French-speaking boys and girls from Catholic public schools in Montreal and in Alma, Quebec. Their ages varied so that approximately equal numbers were chosen from grades 2, 3, 4, 5, 6, 7, 8, and 10. They ranged in age from eight to sixteen years.

Since the subjects responded to each item with one of two alternatives (i.e., *un* or *une*), the data were considered to approximate a normal binomial distribution. Using standard statistical procedures (Ferguson[13]), confidence limits were easily defined, indicating whether words, or groups of words, were consistently or reliably chosen as masculine or feminine.

In the initial study 91 grade 2, 3, 4, and 5 students were tested using the oral-graphic method of presentation. They made gender

[10]E. Sonet and G. Shortliffe, *Review of Standard French* (New York, 1954).
[11]*Petit Larousse* (Paris, 1959).
[12]A. Juilland, *Dictionnaire inverse de la langue française* (The Hague, 1965).
[13]G. A. Ferguson, *Statistical Analysis in Psychology and Education* (2d ed., New York, 1966).

assignments for 66 nouns representing a wide variety of endings. Their overall accuracy was quite high — especially since many of the words used were extremely rare. The number of correct gender choices increased from more than 60 percent of the words presented for grade 2 subject to more than 85 percent for those in grade 5. Furthermore, several of the endings were extremely reliable markers of gender, even for the youngest subjects. For example, words ending with the suffix -*illon* were consistently chosen as masculine, while those ending with -*aison* and -*ence* were chosen as feminine.

These results suggested that we should enlarge our sample of word endings and pay attention to both real and invented words, so, in the second study when a group of 145 grade 4 and 8 students was tested, a list of 122 words, including common, rare, and invented words, was developed, using the same criteria as before. The endings were varied along two gross sound dimensions: [5] as in the French word *maison*, and [e] as in *ambiguité* and [ɛ] as in *palais*. Again, results indicated that certain endings (some of which were actual suffixes) reliably distinguish or mark gender, that is -*ais*, -*aix*, -*et*, -*illon*, -*ion*, -*on*, -*çon* were consistently chosen as masculine, while -*aison* was chosen as feminine. The endings -*é* and -*ée*, however, proved to be relatively ambiguous markers.

It is interesting to note that confusion occurred when oral presentation was used with words ending in -*aie* and -*ais*. These endings are, of course, indistinguishable when pronounced, and words marked by both were chosen as masculine. When the words were both heard and seen, however, -*ais* became an even stronger masculine cue, while -*aie* moved from masculine to feminine.

In the third study, 217 grade 10 students were tested with 147 rarely occurring and invented words. Several additional endings were included, and an attempt was also made to examine the effect of varying the beginnings of the invented words. The results were encouraging. For both oral and oral-graphic presentation, the endings -*on*, -*illon*, -*ion*, -*çon*, -*ais*, and -*et* reliably indicated masculine gender in both real and invented words. Similarly, both real and invented words with the endings -*tion*, -*ission*, -*ession*, -*aison* were consistently chosen as feminine. The endings -*stion* and -*xtion* proved to be ambiguous. The importance of oral plus graphic presentation was noted again with the endings -*é* and -*ée*. In no case did oral presentation alone result in example words being chosen as masculine; however, when presented in written form, words ending in -*é* were chosen as masculine except when preceded by *t*, where -*té* was a reliable feminine marker.

With regard to the beginnings or roots of invented words, those that began with *flor* (a root that is essentially feminine, since seven of the ten nouns with *flor* as their stem are feminine according to the *Petit Larousse*), even though paired with typically masculine suffixes, became ambiguous or were chosen as feminine (e.g., *florillon, *floriçon, *floré).

The subjects in the fourth study were 402 grade 4, 5, 6, and 7 students. Stimuli were 84 real and invented words selected with certain considerations in mind. Fourteen endings were studied: -*aie*, -*ais*, -*é*, -*ée* -*eur*, -*eure*, -*illon*, -*oi*, -*oie*, -*oir*, -*oire*, -*ssion*, -*stion*, and -*tion*. These particular endings were chosen because a separate analysis of *all* the nouns listed in the *Petit Larousse* indicated that they were predominantly masculine, feminine, or ambiguous markers for the language as a whole. One purpose, then, was to check on the behavioral implications of these statistical facts about French. Six words were selected as exemplars of each ending according to the following design: one group was made up of frequently occurring words (from *Français fondamental*[14]); two groups were composed entirely of rare words chosen by a French phonetician; one group consisted of invented words that began with the "ambiguous" initial syllable *feuill-* (six entries in the *Petit Larousse* are feminine, and nine are masculine); another group consisted of invented words that began with the "feminine" initial syllable *flor-*; and finally there was a group of words having in common the "masculine" initial *déb-* (sixty-three entries in the *Petit Larousse* are masculine, and seventeen are feminine). Each group of words exemplified each of the fourteen endings (e.g., *floraie, *floralé, *florateur, etc., appeared somewhere in the randomized list).

The results strongly suggest that endings reliably mark gender in particular instances, and that the initial syllables also have an influence on gender, although probably a less powerful one. For all six groups of nouns, the following endings (with the results for all exemplars combined) were statistically reliable ($p < 0.01$) markers of masculinity in both oral and oral-graphic presentations: -*ais*, -*eur*, -*illon*, -*oi*, -*oir*. The following endings were statistically reliable feminine markers: -*ssion*, -*stion*, and -*tion*. The ending -*aie* indicated masculinity when presented orally, but femininity with oral-graphic presentation.

[14]*Français fondamental* (Paris: L'Institut Pédagogique National, 1954).

We can compare these empirical findings with the statistical counts of endings suspected to be related to gender for all nouns listed in the *Petit Larousse*. These counts were undertaken in order to make just such comparisons with a very good approximation to the total corpus of French nouns. In order to facilitate the counting, all nouns listed in the *Petit Larousse* were put on I.B.M. cards with a tag for their gender. These were then compiled as a type of inverse dictionary of nouns, with all nouns ending in a particular syllable congregated in groups. Using this approximation to the total corpus, we find the following number of masculine to feminine exemplars for each of the endings mentioned above: *-illon*, 64 M, 1 F; *-ais*, 70 M, 0 F; *-oir*, 220 M, 0 F; *-eur*, 1490 M, 88 F; *-oi*, 148 M, 10 F. Furthermore, the following number of feminine to masculine exemplars are found in the corpus for the endings our subjects judged to be feminine: *-tion*, 1688 F, 4 M; *-ssion*, 33 F, 0 M, *-aie*, 58 F, 0 M. Note how well these occurrences agree with the behavioral evidence reported when these endings are placed in various novel wordlike constructions. These endings, then, all represent stable, reliable markers of gender.

We noted some degree of confusion and ambiguity with the endings *-é*, *-ée*, *-oire*, *-eure*, and *-oie*, that is, exemplars of these endings are sometimes thought to be masculine and sometimes, feminine. It is of interest that this ambiguity actually exists in the language. From the counts we note the following distribution: *-oire*, 47 F, 52 M; *-eure*, 7 F, 9 M; *-oie*, 5 M, 16 F; and [e] 1398 M, 1393 F. It was noted that *-ée* always reliably indicates femininity with the oral-graphic form of presentation, and we find in the corpus that there are, in fact, 357 F and 30 M nouns ending with *-ée* in the language.

The effect of manipulating the initial syllable is evident in particular instances where the type of beginning strengthens or weakens the effects of a particular ending. The importance of beginnings also appears when one considers the exemplars with the *ambiguous* initial syllable as the base line for responding. If we compare the responses in the ambiguous case with those when masculine and feminine beginnings are used, it is seen that with oral presentation the exemplars with masculine roots become "more" masculine for nine of the fourteen endings, and the exemplars with feminine roots become "more" feminine for nine of the fourteen endings. With *oral-graphic* presentation, ten of the fourteen endings beginning with the masculine root become more masculine and seven of the fourteen beginning with the feminine root become more feminine. Thus, it is clear that the initial syllable of the noun can also have an effect in marking gender, expecially in instances where the ending provides an ambiguous clue.

These preliminary studies have shown that particular endings reliably mark gender in French nouns and that the initial syllables apparently play a supportive role in the same regard. The findings can be of relevance for those concerned with the acquisition of French, either as a first or later language. For first-language learning, it seems apparent that the French child is able to distinguish and utilize, by induction from the recurring regularities in the language, those patterns of cues that mark gender. He appears to be very skilled in generalizing from these patterns to novel occurrences.[15] This line of reasoning is supported by the close correspondence found between the distribution of gender in the total corpus of French nouns and the behavioral evidence that has been reported. If one presents French children with words they have never before encountered, they can consistently determine the appropriate gender form of masculine and feminine exemplars, and they reflect in their reactions the lack of clarity of the ambiguous exemplars. It is obvious, therefore, that the French speaker is sensitive, although apparently at some level far below awareness, to these recurring patterns of regularities in his language. Much more research of a similar nature is needed to describe in detail the basic nature of these patterns, and we have several such studies now underway.

As research progresses, it may turn out that certain important sound continua exist in French that provide higher-order cues to gender. Consider, for example, the results presented above for the ending -on [ɔ̃]. We noted that the endings -illon, -on, and -çon reliably indicate the masculine form, whereas -aison, -ssion, and -tion indicate the feminine form. The ending -xtion was ambiguous. If one considers both the common final sounds and those immediately preceding, one can refer to a phonetic continuum, the extremes of which indicate masculinity and femininity, and whose central area indicates ambiguity or ambivalence. Continua of this sort could be particularly instructive.

With regard to second-language learning, the results suggest that French grammarians have been hasty in their conclusion that

[15] I am assuming that no linguist will want to argue that *this* type of rule usage is *also* under the control of some special "faculty" for French gender or something of that sort!

there are no useful regularities, or only minimal ones, for gender determination. Quite to the contrary, it now seems possible to make the problem of gender acquisition a much easier one simply by "chunking" the vocabulary for presentation. For example, words with distinctive ending and beginning characteristics could be congregated so that the regularities would be highlighted. The language learner could then infer the underlying pattern of regularities for himself in a fashion analogous to that used by the native speaker of the language. Of course, the gender cues could be explained to him and, later, the exceptions brought to his attention. (Although one may be confident that the lists of exceptions can be reduced, we have already noted one of their characteristics: exceptions to the ending and beginning cues are usually frequently occurring monosyllabic nouns in the French language. Thus they could be relatively easily learned as separate items.) Furthermore, vocabulary could be taught with somewhat more leniency; that is, students could be permitted to make "errors" on the far-out exceptions (such as *bastion*,[16] which is actually masculine), so that the basic regularities could be learned and the associated changes in sentences attendant on gender made and used with more confidence.

The training procedures could be adapted, too, for young French speakers, permitting them to master more efficiently the basic rules for gender residing in their own language.

---

[16]The example of *bastion* is of interest. Its pronunciation is not typical of the feminine *-tion* ending, and its historical roots are unique; it is a variant of *bastillon* (A. Dauzat, J. Dubois, and H. Mitterand, *Nouveau dictionnaire étymologique*, Paris, 1964]), and we have found the *-illon* ending to be a reliable cue for masculinity.

Psychological Studies of the Interdependencies of the Bilingual's Two Languages

Wallace E. Lambert
McGill University

For some time now[1] a rotating group of students and I have been interested in the bilingual person's capacity to use one or the other of his two languages efficiently, that is, with surprisingly little interference from the other. When one thinks for a moment about the psychology and neuophysiology of this capacity, its complexity and its intrigue become clear. How is it that the bilingual is able to "gate out" or, in some fashion, set aside a whole integrated linguistic system while functioning with a second one, and a moment later, if the situation calls for it, switch the process, activating the previously inactive system and setting aside the previously active one? Both linguists and psychologists have been attracted to this phenomenon because an understanding of it would likely shed light on various aspects of bilingual behavior, linguistic, psychological, and neurological. In fact, Uriel Weinreich[2] suggests that any comprehensive or useful theory of bilingualism must account for this "effectively separated use of the two languages," as well as for the interferences that take place between the two languages. We have attempted to contribute to the psychology of such a theory by analyzing different features of the bilingual person's skills. My plan for this paper is to review and discuss these research efforts, giving more attention to ongoing studies than to earlier ones, and yet making it evident that the earlier ones gave us the experience needed to make what we feel is some progress in this field.

[1]The research reported herein has been supported by research grants from the Canadian Defense Research Board and from the Canada Council.
[2]U. Weinreich, *Languages in Contact* (New York, 1953).

In 1954, Susan Ervin and Charles Osgood[3] developed several notions about bilingualism which suggested to us that language-acquisition contexts may contribute importantly to the interdependencies of the bilingual's two languages. Ervin and Osgood believed that a bilingual could develop either a "compound" or a "coordinate" relation between his two languages, depending on how he acquired the two. The compound relation would apparently be engendered through experiences in mixed acquisition contexts, for instance in settings where the same interlocutors used two languages interchangeably to refer to the same environmental events. A coordinate relation would be developed through experience in two distinctive linguistic settings where interlocutors rarely switched languages. They suggested that translation equivalents would have a more similar meaning and would likely have a more common neurological representation for compound bilinguals than they would for coordinate bilinguals who, presumably because of the distinctiveness of their language-acquisition contexts, would be more likely to develop two functionally separated systems of meanings, one attached to each of their languages.

We have considered the differences between compound and coordinate bilingualism more as an interesting contrast than as a rigid typology. Certainly a typical sample of the bilinguals we have worked with would distribute themselves along a continuum of compoundness-coordinateness, and one should only expect to find differences of a comparative sort in the behavior of selected groups of compound and coordinate bilinguals. It is also probable that any particular bilingual will develop a compound relation between his languages for certain of his experiences and a coordinate relation for other experiences. Nevertheless, if the underlying theory is correct, there are many interesting comparisons that should emerge when groups selected to represent the extremes of the continuum are contrasted. Furthermore, those comparisons should satisfy the psychologist's interest in learning as well as his curiosity about the neurophysiology of mediating processes.

[3]S. M. Ervin and C. E. Osgood, "Second Language Learning and Bilingualism," *Journal of Abnormal and Social Psychology* 49:139-146 (1954).

The Earlier Studies

In our first studies[4] we argued that if there was anything to these notions about compound and coordinate bilinguals, then extended experience in separated language-acquisition contexts should enhance the functional separation of the bilingual's two languages, while experience in mixed contexts should reduce the functional separation of the two language systems. More specifically, we sought out groups of bilinguals with different acquisition histories and tested them, anticipating that those with experience in separated contexts would give evidence of (1) comparatively greater semantic distinctiveness between a word in one language and its translation equivalent in the other, (2) more associative independence of translation equivalents in their two languages, and (3) relatively less facility in translating.

In general the results confirmed the first two predictions. It was found that semantic differences of translation equivalents, measured with semantic rating scales, were greater for coordinate than for compound bilinguals. Then, in recalling a list of words, compound bilinguals profited more from rehearsing in advance with the translation equivalents of these words, indicating dependencies across languages which did not appear with coordinate bilinguals. In the third instance, there was no difference between the groups in speed of translation. The pattern of results suggested that both groups could move from one language to the other equally well when directed to, but that compound bilinguals had a stronger proclivity to do so in situations where it was not required, possibly because, for them, there was greater semantic similarity for words in the two languages.

These findings prompted a further question. We had been reading about aphasia among bilinguals, some of whom would apparently lose the functioning of only one of their languages following a cerebral "insult" or accident of one sort or another, while others would lose complete or partial facility with both languages. Since coordinate bilinguals were presumed to have more functionally separated neural structures underlying their two languages than compound bilinguals do, we should expect that brain damage leading to aphasia would be more likely to affect both languages of the

[4]W. E. Lambert, J. Havelka, and Cynthia Crosby, "The Influence of Language-Acquisition Contexts on Bilingualism," *Journal of Abnormal and Social Psychology* 56:239-244 (1958).

compound bilingual and produce a more selective distrubance in one or the other of the languages of the coordinate. We[5] made contact with a number of bilingual aphasics in the Montreal area and compared their postaphasic linguistic abilities and handicaps with those described in the published medical reports of bilingual aphasics from other parts of the world.

The results of this exploratory study were very encouraging in that they supported the theoretical contrast between compound and coordinate forms of bilingualism, although it became very apparent that much more research on the topic is called for before alternate interpretations can be discarded. It was found that patients whose histories suggested that their languages were essentially in a compound relationship showed a generalized aphasic disorder in the sense that both languages were affected by the neurological disturbance. In contrast, patients whose histories fit the coordinate pattern typically showed a more specific language disorder following injury, one language more affected than the other. The trouble here is that we did not have sufficient information about such factors as the extent of brain damage involved, the type of language retraining given during the recovery period, whether it favored one language only, or, in most published cases, the details of actual language loss suffered at the time of the aphasia.

At about the same time, we were investigating the interesting phenomenon of verbal or semantic "satiation," the effects of continuous repetition of a word on its meaning. We had developed a means of measuring these effects based on the rating scales of the "semantic differential,"[6] and had found that the continuous repetition of a word, such as *house*, would lead to a reliable decrease in the intensity of its connotative meaning. What would happen if a bilingual were given this treatment, and we examined the repetitions's effect on the translation equivalent, say *maison*, for a French-English bilingual? And, more particularly, would there be more cross-language satiation for compounds than for coordinates, as one would expect? The results[7] were in the predicted direction, in fact a little too much so: the compound bilinguals showed cross-language satiation in meaning, as expected, while the coordinates went to

[5]W. E. Lambert and S. Fillenbaum, "A Pilot Study of Aphasia among Bilinguals," *Canadian Journal of Psychology* 13:28-34 (1959).

[6]W. E. Lambert and L. Jakobovits, "Verbal Satiation and Changes in the Intensity of Meaning," *Journal of Experimental Psychology* 60:376-383 (1960).

[7]L. A. Jakobovits and W. E. Lambert, "Semantic Satiation among Bilinguals," *Journal of Experimental Psychology* 62:576-582 (1961).

an unanticipated extreme in that the other language equivalents showed a slight *generation* of meaning. Thus, the groups differed, but certain questions about the coordinates are still unanswered.

While the satiation study increased our confidence in the differences between compounds and coordinates, another investigation conducted about the same time tempered our enthusiasm and made us realize that the matter may be quite complex. In this instance,[8] compound and coordinate bilinguals were asked to read through a mixed series of English and French words and to remember which words functioned as a signal that an electric shock—a jolting one administered to a finger—was to follow. Subjects rapidly learned that the words *verte* or *boy*, for example, were the critical ones, and when they appeared on a screen, would promptly press a key that, if activated soon enough, would cancel the shock. After these associations were well established, we presented each subject with a new mixed list of words, some of which were the translations of the original "shock" words (e.g., "green" and "garçon"). We expected compounds to be more prompt than coordinates in pressing the shock-release key when these translation equivalents appeared, since cross-language associations (e.g., *green* and shock) would be more automatically built up from the original association (i.e., *verte* and shock) for compound bilinguals; however, we found no differences between compounds and coordinates in this instance, which was surprising since most of these subjects were the same as those used in the semantic satiation study where clear differences had been revealed

We were equally surprised with the outcome of a second study conducted with the same subjects. In this study, each bilingual was asked to memorize a mixed list of English and French words, and, after a waiting period, to read through a longer mixed list made up of some of the original words, some "new" ones, and some *translations* of the originals. For example, *glove* and *printemps* were in the list learned originally, while their translations ("*gant*" and "*springtime*") were on the composite list. Thus, subjects were required to switch languages rapidly in memorizing the list, and they had to remember which words appeared in which language. We expected that compounds would make more "translation" errors in the later recognition tests, confusing, for example, *glove* with "*gant*," than the coordinates; however, no reliable differences

[8] R. M. Olton, "*Semantic Generalization between Languages*" (unpublished master's thesis, McGill University, 1960).

turned up! These studies need to be repeated and carefully reexamined, but until that time we offer the following explanation for our failure to elicit group differences. Both of these procedures required that "errors" be made in storing the originally memorized words, that is, "generalizations" across languages had to occur. We thoroughly believed that such generalization errors would be numerous, that bilinguals, especially compounds, would have difficulty remembering both the words *and* the languages they represented. Actually there were surprisingly few errors of this sort made in either of these studies. Apparently both types of bilinguals can "tag" a lexical item as belonging to one language or the other with little or no additional mental effort. This fact has recently been made clear in the current studies of bilingual organization in free recall, to be discussed below. These investigations show that bilinguals can store and remember as many items from mixed-language lists as they can from monolingual lists, and translation-type errors are really uncommon. Thus, bilinguals, even compounds, may have no trouble remembering that *boy*, and not *"garçon,"* was the critical word in the conditioning experiment where vigilance was demanded, even though, judging from the satiation study, cross-linguistic interactions can take place in other situations. The task still before us, of course, is to delineate which situations do encourage, and which do not encourage, such interactions.

Current Studies: The Stroop Procedure

Recently we have tried different approaches to examine the bilingual's capacity to keep his two languages functionally distinct. The difference is that we are now asking general questions about all bilinguals, and the compound-coordinate continuum is examined only as a second step. The question of central interest is: Does the activation of processes in one language system make the other language system inoperative? Penfield and Roberts[9] suggest that there is some type of switching mechanism in the brain which shuts off one linguistic system while the other is in function. Hebb[10] and Milner[11] have also described possible neurological mechanisms that could explain, at one level of generalization, this capacity to

[9]W. Penfield and L. Roberts, *Speech and Brain Mechanisms* (Princeton, 1959).
[10]D. O. Hebb, *A Textbook of Psychology* (Philadelphia, 1958).
[11]P. M. Milner, "The Cell Assembly: Mark II," *Psychological Review* 64:242-252 (1957).

"gate out" potentially antagonistic or competing systems. However, before one can neurophysiologize fruitfully about such mechanisms, it is necessary to demonstrate that a real phenomenon exists and to describe its behavioral and psychological characteristics.

To explain this problem, we searched for a procedure that would present the bilingual with a conflict wherein both of his languages would be simultaneously brought into play. We fortunately hit upon the possibility of adapting a procedure, the Stroop Test,[12] which has had a long and interesting history in experimental psychology. This test consists of several large cards on one of which are one hundred small patches made of colored inks or crayons arranged in ten rows with ten patches to a row. A subject is timed while naming the colors as rapidly as possible. A second card includes one hundred *common words* (such as APPLE, MAN, HOUSE, etc.), each of which is printed in one of several colors, and again the task requirement is to name the crayon colors as fast as possible. On a third card, there are one hundred *color words* (such as RED, BLUE, ORANGE, etc.) printed with red, blue, brown, and yellow crayons. On this card, a subject would encounter a sequence such as: RED printed in orange ink, followed by BLUE in brown ink, ORANGE in red, BROWN in blue, etc., and he would be asked to name the *crayon* colors (orange, brown, red and blue) as rapidly as possible. The problem lies in keeping the color words from impinging on the requirement of naming the crayon colors, a very difficult task because the word reading tendency is highly automatized for literate people, and the procedure very compellingly calls into play a *decoding* process that interferes with the required *encoding* process. The time taken to work through the interference card is decidedly longest.

We adapted this procedure for use with bilinguals, constructing different sets of three cards for various groups of bilinguals (a French, Hungarian, and German set, for instance), so that the second card would contain common *noncolor* words (e.g., in French MAISON, GARÇON, PRINTEMPS, etc.), and the third card would contain *color* words (e.g., in French ROUGE, JAUNE, BLEU, etc.). Subjects were given a battery of ten test cards: the color-patch card was used once for measuring speed of color naming in English and once for measuring speed of color naming in French; the English

[12]J. R. Stroop, "Studies of Interference in Serial Verbal Reactions," *Journal of Experimental Psychology* 18:643-661 (1935). M. S. Preston is the coinvestigator for this project.

noncolor-word and *color*-word cards were used twice, once when the subject named the crayon colors in English and once when he named the colors in French; and the two French cards were used in a similar fashion. The general scheme for English-French bilinguals is outlined in table 1.

TABLE 1

THE STROOP PARADIGM

Response language	Stimulus material				
	English color words	French color words	English noncolor words	French noncolor words	Color patches
English	1	2	5	6	9
French	3	4	7	8	10

Now we can assess the interference caused by simultaneously activating the decoding and encoding processes of the *same* language or the decoding process in one language and the encoding process of the other language. For example, we would expect more interference in cells 1 and 4, where the encoding and decoding processes of the *same* language are simultaneously activated (the subject in cell 1 has to say "red," for example, to name the crayon color in which the color word BLUE is printed) than in cells 2 and 3 where the simultaneously activated decoding and encoding processes involve *different* languages (in cell 2, for example, the subject must say "red" to name the crayon color in which the color word JAUNE is printed). It is assumed that it is easier to gate out a distractor from the other language than it is to gate one out from the same language, since encoding and decoding processes within a language are likely to be mutually facilitative, thereby providing many opportunities for interference with the Stroop procedure. Furthermore, we would expect the distractors in cells 5 through 8 to be more easily set aside. They could even be processed simultaneously with comparatively less interference. Cells 9 and 10 provide an index of encoding *balance*, and subjects are chosen who are essentially balanced in speed of color naming in their two languages. These cells also serve as a comparison point, since no verbal materials occur as distractors.

Our first investigations were pilot studies conducted with small samples of balanced bilinguals.[13] The results indicated that bilinguals are unable to shut out the other language. If they are naming colors in French, the English noncolor and color words impinge as much as French ones do, and the interference is clearly evident in the extra time taken for color naming on cards with verbal materials compared to the time taken for control cards of color patches. There is, however, a stepwise progression of interference, clearly occurring more when *color* words are used as background distractors than when *noncolor* words are used. Furthermore, subjects revealed that the background language was fully active when working through the color-word cards. Suppose a subject encountered the sequence: ROUGE in yellow, VERT in red, and BLEU in brown, and was required to respond in English with "yellow, red, brown," etc. One of the most common errors in these cross-language tests was to translate the stimulus word from French to English and respond with "yellow, *green, brown," for example. This type of error reveals that the encoding system is dominant at the moment, as though the switch was clearly thrown open for English, but that the other language impinged to the extent of winning out in the choice of the appropriate color name. In other terms, the French decoding process became fused with the English encoding process.

We would have expected, nevertheless, that bilinguals would be better able to shut out distractions from the other language than those from the same language, that is, that cells 2 and 3 in table 1 would have faster color naming scores than cells 1 and 4. In the preliminary studies, there was no indication that this was so; however, when special conditions were established, the expected interaction between cells 1, 2, 3, and 4 came to light. For these conditions, two groups of German-English bilinguals were used. One group worked with color-word cards on which English and German translation equivalents had very similar phonemic beginnings, such as ROT *and* RED, or GRÜN and GREEN. The other group was presented cards with translation equivalents having very dissimilar phonemic beginnings, for example, SCHWARTZ and BLACK, or GELB and YELLOW. It was found that bilinguals can gate out the other language distractors better than same language distractors when the color words (and color names) of the two languages are phonemically dissimilar. Thus, bilinguals apparently need a built-in linguistic

[13]M. S. Preston, *"Inter-lingual Interference in a Bilingual Version of the Stroop Color-Word Task"* (unpublished Ph. D. dissertation, McGill University, 1965).

mode of demarcation to reduce somewhat the interplay of his two language systems.

We are currently repeating these studies with larger samples of English-French bilinguals, and the results so far available already require some important modifications of the generalizations just made. For this investigation[14] we selected twenty compound and twenty-one coordinate bilinguals who were very evenly balanced in their French and English skills. Our definitions of compound and coordinate were simplified: compound bilinguals were defined as those brought up in a thoroughly bilingual home environment from infancy on, while coordinates were those who had learned their second language at some time after infancy, usually after ten years of age and usually in a setting other than the family.[15]

The results are summarized in table 2. Note first the marked increase in interference, reflected in *increased* time scores, from the color-patch to the noncolor-word, to the color-word conditions. Second, note that there is a noticeable difference between compounds and coordinates in the color-word condition. The pattern for the compounds is very similar to that noted in the pilot studies where there is no essential difference between same-language and other-language distractions (cells 2 and 3 are essentially the same as 1 and 4). When tested for significance, the interaction between cells is not significant (testing the difference between differences, $(d_1 - d_2) - (d_3 - d_4)$, $t = 0.70$). On the other hand, the interaction among cells is highly significant for the coordinate bilinguals, the difference between differences produces a $t = 2.88$, significant beyond the 0.01 level. Although these results are exactly in accord with the expectation that coordinates would be better able to gate out the other language than would compounds because of the greater functional segregation of the coordinate's two languages, these findings are not strong enough to give us full confidence on this issue, since an analysis of variance indicates that there is not a statistically significant difference between cell interactions for

[14]Maria Ignatow (now Bandrauk), now at McMaster University, was the coworker on this research.

[15]This change simplifies and clarifies the contrast intended. For example, in our earlier work (see Olton, *op. cit.*), we confused the compound category by including those who learned a second language through the intermediary of the first, i.e., by supposedly indirect methods. We also had stressed current language *usage*, letting it have as much or more weight in the decisions of classification as the manner in which the two languages were originally learned. Clearly, much more research is needed on all of these assumptions.

compound and coordinate groups, even though the interaction in one instance is, by itself, highly significant, and the other, by itself, is clearly not significant. The difference, nevertheless, is very encouraging, suggesting that the coordinate relation between languages, developed through acquisition contexts, permits these bilinguals to encode more easily in one language and set aside the potential distraction that would derive from decoding in the other language, even in this condition where the two processes are so forcibly brought simultaneously into play.

TABLE 2
COMPOUND-COORDINATED COMPARISONS ON THE STROOP TEST*

Bilingual type	Number of subjects	Response language	Distracting Stimulus				
			English color words	French color words	English noncolor words	French noncolor words	Color patches
			1	2	5	6	9
Compounds	20	English	54.41	53.67	42.26	43.27	38.09
			3	4	7	8	10
		French	51.58	54.31	40.40	41.88	37.36
Coordinates	21	English	50.95	44.40	38.53	37.17	35.11
		French	48.31	49.16	38.69	38.27	35.08

*Entries are the average times, in seconds, required by subjects to name the colors of a fifty-item Stroop-type card. The number of items was reduced from one hundred to fifty because, in the pilot studies, we noted marked improvement in color naming with practice and we wanted to examine reactions before practice had a leveling effect.

In the third place, the overall analysis indicated that when the results for the compounds and coordinates are combined, the interaction between cells 1, 2, 3, and 4 is highly significant ($p < 0.001$), indicating that bilinguals, particularly the coordinates, are less distracted by the other language decoding process than by same-language decoding. The major trend, however, is still evident: there is an increasing amount of interference from the other language as the distractors change from patches to noncolor words to color words. Thus, it appears that the other language "seeps in," even though it seems to do so less for the coordinate bilinguals. There are, however, many aspects of this question still to be explored.

Current Studies: Bilingual Organization in Free Recall

The investigations[16] I want to discuss now deal with two matters of current psychological interest: the organization of psychological processes, as inferred from subjects' free recall of word lists, and bilingualism. The purpose of the study is to cast light on theoretical concerns in these two research areas by extending the standard ways of studying both the structure of memory and bilingualism.

Research on free recall, in its basic form, requires subjects to read through a list of, for example, thirty or forty words, and to recall its contents in any order. If there are organizational possibilities built into a list, subjects very readily make use of them. For instance, if subsets of words that commonly associate with one another, or that belong to logical categories (e.g., types of trees or names of cities), are randomly distributed through a list, subjects typically congregate these subsets in recall. Even when lists without obvious organizational sets are used, subjects characteristically create a personal system of organization that aids recall. This tendency to congregate items on the basis of some general form of similarity is reminiscent of an associative theme that has run through the whole history of philosophy and psychology. A modern version of this theme has been brought to bear on the strategies people use in tasks requiring memory, and has led to the valuable concept of "chunking."[17] One of the present concerns is the role of chunking in free recall when two forms of organizational possibilities are available to bilingual subjects, one, logical categories, the other, language. The recent research of Kolers[18] suggests that language may be an important organizational schema for bilingual subjects.

We are also interested here in the comparative importance of the associational principle as a means of explaining congregation in free recall. Three research groups are important in this regard:

---

[16]The coworkers on this research were Maria Ignatow and Marcel Krauthammer, an undergraduate Honours student at McGill.

[17]G. A. Miller, "The Magical Number Seven, Plus or Minus Two: Some Limits on Our Capacity for Processing Information," *Psychological Review* 63:81-97 (1956); G. Mandler, "Organization and Memory," in K. W. Spence and Janet T. Spence, eds., *The Psychology of Learning and Motivation: Advances in Research and Theory* (New York, 1966).

[18]P. A. Kolers, "Bilingualism and Bicodalism," *Language and Speech* 8:122-126 (1965).

Bousfield,[19] Jenkins and Russell,[20] and Cofer.[21] Bousfield, the pioneer in this research domain, at first believed that the category clustering observed in free recall was likely to be the result of activation of some type of superordinate structure that encompassed the specific instances brought to attention at different points in the list. Jenkins and Russell, however, demonstrated that the associative links among verbal items were sufficient as an explanation of free recall congregations. This simpler interpretation, based on associative strength, or the liklihood of co-occurrence of particular pairs or sets of words in samples of the language, swayed Bousfield and his co-workers, as well as Cofer, to the associationistic view. Recent experiments have reopened the issue, and there is now a lively debate about the importance of associative strength in free recall clustering.[22]

Also of interest are the interdependencies of the bilingual's two languages. The present experiments examine how bilingual subjects go about organizing materials presented to them in bilingual word lists, where, in certain instances, either language or content category, or both, may be utilized as organizational schemas, while in other instances, the two possible schemas are placed in competition. Although the use of bilingual lists is unnatural for bilingual subjects whose linguistic environments are usually systematically unilingual from setting to setting, still the procedure, like the Stroop Test, of bringing the two into play is extremely valuable as a means of examining how both languages affect psychological processes. Parallel experiments were conducted, one using Russian-English bilinguals, the other, French-English bilinguals, in order to have, for purposes of reliability, evidence from more than one pair of languages.

METHOD

Subjects. — The twenty-four French-English bilinguals, twelve male and twelve female, were young adults, all having received schooling in both languages at the elementary and high school

[19]W. A. Bousfield, "The Occurrence of Clustering in the Recall of Randomly Arranged Associates," *Journal of General Psychology* 49:229-240 (1953).
[20]J. J. Jenkins and W. A. Russell, "Associative Clustering during Recall," *Journal of Abnormal and Social Psychology* 47:818-821 (1952).
[21]C. N. Cofer, "On Some Factors in the Organizational Characteristics of Free Recall," *American Psychologist* 20:261-272 (1965).
[22]H. H. Kendler, "Coding: Associationistic or Organizational?" *Journal of Verbal Learning and Verbal Behavior* 5:99-106 (1966); R. N. Shepard, "Learning and Recall as Organization and Search," *ibid.* 5:201-205 (1966).

levels, and all but two were presently postgraduate students in French. The subjects considered themselves, and were judged by others who knew them well, to be equally skilled in the use of both of their languages.

The twenty-four Russian-English bilinguals, eighteen female and six male, were also young adults, all of Russian origin. Their education from primary school on was in English, although all had attended Russian parochial school one day a week. Seventeen of the twenty-four were Russian language majors at the university level. They all considered themselves to be equally skilled in the audio-lingual use of both languages, although they clearly had much more experience in reading and writing English.

The word lists.—The word lists were constructed on the basis of English, French, and Russian norms of culturally distinctive examples of semantic categories, such as types of fish, men's first names, or types of disease. The (American) English norms of Cohen, Bousfield, and Whitmarsh[23] were considered appropriate for use with Canadian subjects in light of the findings of Lambert and Moore.[24] New norms were developed, however, for French and Russian, using the procedure of Cohen *et al.* as a model. In one instance, sixty seniors in a French-Canadian high school were asked to write the first four examples that came to mind when the superordinate names for forty-three categories were given them, for example, to list four types of fish. The norms place the examples in order from most to least popular. In the other instance, the responses of twenty-five Russian adults (not those used as subjects) were used to compile the Russian norms.

Experimental design.—Each subject was presented ten forty-item lists, one list at a time, with instructions to remember as many items as possible and to be prepared to recall them with no restrictions as to order. Four of the ten lists contained four different categories with ten words to a category (e.g., ten types of fish, ten male first names, etc.); the other six lists did not include category subsets, that is, each list consisted of forty items, one chosen from each of

[23]B. H. Cohen, W. A. Bousfield, and G. A. Whitmarsh, "Cultural Norms for Verbal Items in 43 Categories" (Technical Report no. 22, 1957, University of Connecticut, Contract NONR 631 [00], Office of Naval Research).

[24]W. E. Lambert and Nancy Moore, "Word Association Responses: Comparisons of American and French Monolinguals with Canadian Monolinguals and Bilinguals," *Journal of Personality and Social Psychology* 3:313-320 (1966).

TABLE 3

GENERAL EXPERIMENTAL DESIGN, FRENCH VERSION*

Order	No-category lists			Category lists				No-category lists		
	1	2	3	4	5	6	7	8	9	10
Type	English	French	Mixed	English	French	Mixed concordant	Mixed discordant	English	French	Mixed
Total items	40	40	40	40	40	40	40	40	40	40

*Exactly the same design was used for the Russian version.

forty different semantic categories as represented in the norms. These different list types will be referred to as "category lists" and "no-category lists," the latter serving as comparison and control conditions. To counteract primacy and recency effects, three of the six no-category lists came as the first three lists presented to each subject, and three as the last three in the series of ten. The general schema for the design is given in table 3. Thus, lists 1 and 8 in the design are both no-category lists of forty English items; lists 2 and 9 are similar lists in French. Lists 3 and 10, to be referred to as "mixed," each have twenty English and twenty French items with no built-in categorization possibilities. List 4 is an English list comprising four categories with ten exemplars per category (e.g., ten types of fish) and list 5 is an equivalent French list. Lists 6 and 7 are mixed-language lists, with built-in categories; these are comparable in one respect to the no-category mixed list. The special feature of list 6 is that the twenty items covering two distinct categories with ten examples each are in English, and twenty items covering two additional distinctive categories are in French. In this list there is a *concordance* between languages and semantic categories in the sense that particular categories are reliably marked or set off by one language or the other. List 7, in contrast, has a *discordance* between language and semantic categories; each of its four categories has equal numbers of English and French examples (e.g., five types of fish in French and five in English).

This design, then, permits one to (1) assess the importance of semantic categories in comparison with a no-category base line in terms of total items recalled and degree of clustering in recall (the pairs of no-category lists coming at the start and at the end of the experimental period are averaged); (2) to determine the influence of mixed language lists by comparing them with unilingual lists in both no-category and category conditions; (3) to examine the combined and separate importance of the linguistic and semantic modes of categorizing in a condition where their concordance might be either facilitative or competitively disruptive, and in a condition where their discordance should be disruptive relative to the other category conditions but possibly facilitative relative to the no-category conditions.

For the *no-category* lists, each subject was presented six standard lists but the order of presentation was randomized, that is, one subject would receive the lists in the order shown in table 1, another in the order 9, 8, 10, (5, 6, 7, 4,) 1, 3, 2. These lists were made comparable to all others in terms of the popularity frequencies of category examples taken from the category norms. One constraint in the mixed list was that no more than three words in the same language appeared consecutively.

The presentation order of the category lists follows a 4 factorial plan, all possibilities covered with twenty-four subjects. Furthermore, each subject had a different combination of four categories in his lists, out of sixteen categories chosen for our purposes. Constraints in these lists were that (1) no more than three words in one language appeared consecutively (for the two mixed lists); (2) no two items from the same semantic category appeared consecutively after randomization of the list items; (3) for the discordance list, no translations or synonyms between languages within a category were allowed, for example, BLOUSE and BLOUZKA would not both appear as members of the "articles of clothing" category.

Testing procedure.—In order to create a bilingual atmosphere and to avoid a set in one language, subjects were given instructions in one language with a summary review in the other, half of them receiving English first, half French (or Russian) first. They were told in advance that some lists would be unilingual, others mixed, and that after one run through a list, they would be given two minutes for recall of as many items as possible in any order. For the French study, the items were printed on 3 × 5 cards and flipped at intervals of approximately two seconds. Subjects read the words out loud. For the Russian subjects, who were more experienced at reading English, the words were read to them by a perfectly bilingual experimenter at a two-second rate. Subjects repeated the words after the experimenter. Each subject's recall was recorded on tape for two minutes; a three-minute rest followed each recall period.

Response measures.—Measures were taken of (1) the total items correctly recalled, (2) the extent of category clustering, and (3) the extent of language clustering. The total number of words correctly recalled excluded all types of errors and repetitions. Clusters of items fitting the same semantic category were bracketed and counted. In devising a ratio score, we subtracted one from the total number of items congregated, arguing that the first item is really not part of the run. The ratio was the number of items in a category run over the total of all items recalled. Thus, if the subject recalled *floor, ceiling, door, hall* ($r_1 = 3$), followed by *apple, lemon, pear* ($r_2 = 2$), followed by *knife, gun* ($r_3 = 1$), the ratio would be 6 (i.e., $3 + 2 + 1$) over 9 or 0.67. For the mixed language lists, a similar ratio was devised for clusters of same language responses, and the sum of separate language clusters was divided by the total of items recall. For example, the recall *fox, rabbit, turnip, bear, mouse* (r_1 = 4), followed by *pomme, citron* ($r_2 = 1$), would become 5 (i.e., $4 + 1$) over 7 or 0.71. This ratio is independent of the amount recalled, and it gives more credit than usual clustering methods for longer runs even when the total number of items clustered is the same, that is, the usual methods would give equal credit to four two-item clusters as to two four-item clusters, whereas this method highlights the longer runs, in this example 6 versus 4.

Error Analysis.—Attention was given to two types of errors only: (1) *category intrusions,* items belonging to an appropriate category but not appearing in the actual word list, and (2) *translation equivalents,* semantically correct translations of actual list items. When both these errors occurred in the flow of recall, it was decided that they would not break up (nor, of course, contribute to) the category or language run in which they might be embedded.

RESULTS AND DISCUSSION

The major findings are summarized in tables 4 through 7. Considering first table 4, it is evident that the greater possibilities for organization available in the category lists, compared to the no-category lists, have a general and marked facilitative effect on recall, and this fact is true of both the French and Russian versions of the experiment, with their procedural idiosyncrasies. This outcome was certainly expected in light of a large accumulation of research on categorization and is to be viewed as strong supportive evidence. Nevertheless, there are important variations among conditions in the two major variants of the experiment, that is, the category and no-category comparison.

With regard to the no-category conditions, it is of interest that the mixed list was as well recalled as the unilingual ones for the Russian version and partly so for the French. (One discrepant result is examined separately below.) This finding confirms the results of Kolers' experiment, one that was analogous to the no-category division of the present study. Kolers also found that bilingual subjects recalled mixed lists of English and French monosyllables as well as they recalled unilingual lists. From the perspective of the person who is clumsy in his command of a foreign language, this facility of bilinguals with mixed lists is surprising. It appears, however, that the experienced bilingual makes use of the difference in languages

TABLE 4
GROUP MEAN COMPARISONS, TOTAL ITEMS RECALLED

FRENCH STUDY (Overall F test, 36.86; $p < 0.001$)

	No-category lists[a]			Category lists			
	English	French	Mixed	English	French	Concordant	Discordant
Mean Number Items Recalled (from 40)	10.83	12.65	10.88	19.17	18.21	18.67	15.50

RUSSIAN STUDY (Overall F test, 41.22; $p < 0.001$)

	No-category lists[a]			Category lists			
	English	Russian	Mixed	English	Russian	Concordant	Discordant
Mean number	12.08	12.50	11.40	20.92	17.75[d]	19.04	15.13

[a] Based on two lists.
[b] This comparison just misses significance at the 0.05 level.
[c] Significant at the 0.05 level; Newman-Keuls test of multiple-group comparisons (B. Winer, *Statistical Principles in Experimental Design* [New York, 1962]).
[d] Significant at the 0.01 level.

TABLE 5

GROUP MEAN COMPARISONS, CATEGORY CLUSTERING

FRENCH STUDY (Overall F test, 3.1999; $p < 0.05$)

	Category lists			
	English	French	Concordant	Discordant
Mean category clustering ratio	0.61	0.62	0.62	0.52

RUSSIAN STUDY (Overall F test, 8.65; $p < 0.01$)

	Category lists			
	English	Russian	Concordant	Discordant
Mean category clustering ratio	0.62	0.60	0.59	0.45

°Significant at the 0.01 level; Newman-Keuls test of multiple-group comparisons.

TABLE 6

GROUP MEAN COMPARISONS, LANGUAGE CLUSTERING

FRENCH STUDY (Overall F test, 43.03; $p < 0.001$)

	No category, Mixed	Concordant	Discordant
Mean language clustering ratio	0.49	0.73	0.47

RUSSIAN STUDY (Overall F test, 33.45; $p < 0.001$)

	No category, Mixed	Concordant	Discordant
Mean language clustering ratio	0.42	0.71	0.45

°Significant at the 0.01 level; Newman-Keuls test of multiple-group comparisons.

TABLE 7

GROUP TOTALS, SELECTED ERROR TYPES*

| | FRENCH STUDY | | | | |
| | No-category lists | Category lists | | | |
	Mixed	English	French	Concordant	Discordant
Categorical intrusions	. . . . .	6	12	6	20
Translation equivalents	7	. . . . . .	. . . . . .	3	17
	RUSSIAN STUDY				
	No-category lists	Category lists			
	Mixed	English	Russian	Concordant	Discordant
Categorical intrusions	. . . . .	6	7	13	10
Translation equivalents	7	. . . . . .	. . . . . .	3	34

*Entries are total occurrences for each group of twenty-four subjects.

as just some distinctive feature of words and is not hindered in any way by storing and retrieving words according to the appropriate language, much as a monolingual would distinguish nouns from adjectives in a list without disturbing recall.[25] Furthermore, the bilingual may find that the language variations act as distinctive markers or "tags"[26] that help differentiate list items, thereby aiding recall. The fact that the mixed lists were no *better* recalled may be due to a memory limit reached in this study; with another research design, working below such a limit, one might find that the mixed lists would then be better recalled than unilingual ones.

We set aside for separate comment the finding that the English-French bilinguals showed a stronger capacity to store and retrieve French, in contrast to English, list items. One might view this difference merely as an indicant of the French dominance of these bilingual subjects, but it actually signifies something more. First, Kolers also noted that unilingual lists of French monosyllables were

[25]This interpretation is not incompatible with Kolers'; he argued that "the system properties of the two languages enabled the fluent bilingual to accommodate their respective elements with no loss in efficiency of recall" (p. 126).
[26]D. B. Yntema and F. P. Trask, "Recall as a Search Process," *Journal of Verbal Learning and Verbal Behavior* 2:65-74 (1963).

better recalled than comparable lists in English, even for subjects whose language histories suggest an English dominance. Kolers argued that there might be more lexical and phonemic distinctiveness among French than English words and that this phenomenon might account for the difference. This, or some alternative explanation, becomes more interesting in the light of the present reoccurrence of this difference, this time with real French words, especially since no difference of this sort is apparent in the Russian version of the experiment. However, note also in table 4 that when the same subjects turn to processing the *category* list items there is then a clear equivalence of English and French capacity and a very pronounced English dominance for the Russian-English subjects. The matter of assessing bilingual balance or dominance is of considerable current interest.[27] In this instance, one would conclude from the no-category conditions that the English-French bilinguals are dominant in French and the English-Russian are balanced in skills, while from the category list evidence he would conclude that the English and French skills are balanced and the other group's skill in Russian is inferior. Since lexical and phonemic distinctiveness should be as great in the category conditions as in the no-category case, these data, taken as a pattern, cast some doubt on the adequacy of Kolers' explanation. One can, however, view this pattern from another perspective. The demands made on a subject in the category condition, where he must have the capacity in both of his languages to mentally reshuffle and organize list items according to semantic categories, are quite different from those made on him in the no-category condition: there he must simply store and hold items in rote fashion, encountering difficulties when he tries, within the time limits of stimulus presentation, to organize along purely subjective lines. Assuming that the more demanding case provides the more revealing measure of dominance or balance, the results for the category condition are then seen as fully consistent with the linguistic experiences of both groups of subjects, the French group being balanced in all aspects of language skill, and the Russian being balanced only in the audio-lingual aspects of their two languages. Thus, if consideration is given to the pattern of results, we

[27]Weinreich, *op. cit.*; W. E. Lambert, "Measurement of the Linguistic Dominance of Bilinguals," *Journal of Abnormal and Social Psychology* 50:197-200 (1955); W. E. Lambert, J. Havelka, and R. C. Gardner, "Linguistic Manifestations of Bilingualism," *American Journal of Psychology* 72:77-82 (1959); W. F. Mackey, "The Measurement of Bilingual Behavior," *The Canadian Psychologist* 7:75-92 (1966).

encounter a potentially important distinction between the simple storage demands made on subjects in one instance, and the more complex demands for processing and organizing verbal materials made in the other. This distinction has relevance for the measurement of bilingual balance. Still, further research is needed to explain why French lists are particularly easily recalled. It may turn out that some factor like phonemic distinctiveness has its main effect in instances where less demands of a cognitive nature are made, but is overshadowed by the organizational requirements of complex cases; it is very likely, though, that this puzzle will turn out to be more complex than that.

If we now examine the *concordant* and *discordant* lists, we realize that different types of mixed lists affect the bilingual's recall in particular ways. Turning again to table 4, it is very evident, in both the French and Russian versions of the study, that the discordant lists are the least well recalled of all category lists, even when credit is given for translation errors, but that they are still much more easily recalled than are any of the no-category lists. The intermediary position of these lists indicates that placing language and semantic content in competition, as is done in discordant lists, depresses recall in one sense, but, in another sense, does not depress it seriously. Tables 5, 6, and 7 provide three clues about the subjects' approach to the discordant list: (1) The subjects are handicapped in their capacity to organize items according to their membership in particular semantic categories, that is, the discordant lists are always markedly lower than others in terms of category clustering (see table 5); (2) yet they make as much use of language variations as an organizational schema as they do when recalling the mixed no-category lists (table 6); (3) at the same time, they make many translation and intrusion errors (table 7). These findings suggest that the process of activating a superordinate category (e.g., fruit) is not as easily accomplished when bilingual examples (e.g., APPLE, CITRON, ORANGE, PAMPLEMOUSSE) are used to prime it as when unilingual examples are available for this purpose.

Although handicapped, relatively, subjects can still organize to their advantage, even when forced to use bilingual examples, as is evident when one compares their recall in the discordant and no-category conditions. Thus, although the linguistic mixture in the categories of the discordant list has affected the capacity to categorize, still the presence of categories is a major aid in organizing for recall (compare discordant with mixed no-category lists, table 4.)

What is the nature of this advantage of categories? Because they are built up through bilingual examples, it is difficult to rely on an associationistic explanation of categorization in this instance, that is, one cannot argue that the clustered items are linked through common word-word associations encountered in the language, since it is highly unlikely that the English "orange" is ever followed by the French "pamplemousse" in the written or verbal environments of bilinguals. Nor is it true, in this instance, that the subjects' category clustering scores are artifactually the result of their using only one of their languages to make clusters, since approximately equal numbers of English and French, and English and Russian items were recalled for each category in the discordant lists. Thus, the activation of superordinate structures, rather than word-to-word associations, seems more appropriate as an explanation of clustering in this instance.

These results do not indicate that associations across languages do not take place within the heads of bilinguals. Their capacity to use bilingual examples to advantage indicates that this type of association certainly occurs. Recently it has been found that the separate associational networks of English-French bilinguals are quite distinct,[28] and this fact may mean that the lack of associational overlap between English and French contributed in part to the presumed difficulty in priming a superordinate category with bilingual examples. The possibility also exists that compound bilinguals would experience less of a handicap than coordinate bilinguals in the discordant condition.

Turning again to table 4, there is no advantage in recall for the concordant condition, comparing it with the unilingual category conditions for both versions of the study. (We will presume that the Russian group's superiority with English reflects a language dominance.) The concordant[29] condition is, however, decidedly better than the discordant, or any of the no-category conditions, for both French and Russian versions. Thus in the concordant lists, where all examples of a particular category appeared in one language or the other, language could have been used as a separate and supportive coding schema that could be expected to aid recall. This feature of the concordant condition is of theoretical interest in view of Mand-

---

[28]Lambert and Moore, op. cit.

[29]This condition is analogous in certain respects to the "facilitation" condition of Gonzalez and Cofer, 1959 (see Cofer, op. cit., p. 263), where item pairs made up of an appropriate modifier and a noun (e.g., powerful lion or blue dress) were much better recalled and categorized than were comparable lists of unmodified nouns.

ler's[30] recent suggestion that "parallel" or "separate, though over-lapping organizational schemas" may markedly increase human memory. Certain clues as to why no facilitation actually occurred in this instance are available in tables 5, 6, and 7. Judging from the results in table 5, one might conclude that the ability to categorize has not been affected since the subjects are able to categorize as well in the concordant condition as in the unilingual category con-ditions, and there is no strong evidence that categorical intrusions are more numerous (table 7); however, there is a very large amount of language clustering in the concordant condition (table 6) which holds for both French and Russian versions. These findings suggest that the subjects relied too much on language as an organizational schema which led them to congregate the pairs of categories com-mon to each language, keeping in mind that the examples of two categories were given in one language, and the examples of two other categories were given in the other language. This form of organization would prompt longer recall runs in each language but would adversely detract from the semantic clarity of each category and thereby reduce recall from its potential level. Thus, it appears that bilinguals are vulnerable in the sense that they may be enticed to misuse language as an organizational schema which, to the extent that it detracts from the optimal use of available categories, ad-versely affects recall. These results, then, actually reflect on the limitations of the present design, and the possibility of facilitation in the concordant condition remains open. For example, a fairer test would require a design providing an equal number of categories and languages, that is, either one category for each language, using bilingual subjects, or one category for each of the several languages known by multilingual subjects.

In summary, a good deal of evidence has emerged suggesting that, for bilinguals, language is a quite ancillary means of organiz-ing information in memory when compared with semantic categor-ies, which appear as powerful organizational schemas. The role that language does play is seen mainly in the subtle differences that occur when the two schemas are brought into play. This conclusion is supported, first, by the marked differences in recall between cate-gory and no-category conditions, in contrast with the lack of dif-ferences, or the relatively minor ones, attributable to comparisons of unilingual and bilingual conditions. In fact, in the no-category

[30]Mandler, *op. cit.*, p. 47.

case, where the bilingual cannot do much more than merely store information in a routine fashion, recall is not affected by the bilingual nature of the input, suggesting that in such situations bilinguals regard code variations as simple distinctive features of the elements to be stored and are not hampered in any way by their presence. When more complex demands are made on his language skill, however, as in the category condition where important aids in organization are available, recall can be disrupted when code variations conflict with the process of establishing categories, or it can very likely be enhanced if code variations occur so as to highlight the distinctiveness of the categories. Nevertheless, even when the two coding systems are in a discordant relation and information is presented bilingually, the ability to chunk information, as an aid to recall, is clearly reduced but not seriously so. In this instance, for example, bilinguals are more likely to confuse the code variations, as reflected in the relatively large number of translation errors made, but this fact indicates that they are focusing on categories and are able to do so effectively even with the distraction of language switches. Because they can effectively utilize bilingual information to establish categories, it is suggested that chunking is not based solely on word-to-word associations, but rather, in certain instances at least, on the activation of some type of superordinate structure that works across languages.

It was also shown that a bilingual's capacity to use each of his two languages expresses itself differently according to the task requirements. If, as in the no-category case, he must merely store information first in one of his languages and later in the other, with little opportunity to reorganize, his relative skills in the two languages can be quite different than when, as for the category lists, he can effectively reorganize information. The suggestion was made that bilingual balance or dominance can be more faithfully assessed through the more demanding task.

The final matter I want to discuss has to do with compound-coordinate differences in bilingual organization of list materials.[31] Attention was given only to the concordant and discordant conditions, for which we expected specific outcomes: coordinates should profit more from the language differences that highlight the content

[31]This research is being conducted by Maria Ignatow and myself. We are extremely grateful to Dr. John Macnamara for his discussions of the work and his suggestions for interpretation of the results.

categories in the concordant list then should compounds, whereas coordinates should be more distracted by the bilingual buildup of categories in the discordant list, that is, where French and English examples (such as APPLE, PAMPLEMOUSSE, PEAR, CITRON) are mingled to determine each of the four content categories. Thus, the expectation is that the two groups will differ in particular ways in their performance on the two types of list, the coordinates being better able than compounds to recall items in the concordant list but poorer than compounds in recalling items in the discordant list.

With this purpose in mind, two sizable samples of bilinguals were tested, one of coordinate bilinguals and the other, compounds. Actually these same subjects participated in the Stroop testing, discussed above. The results are presented in table 8.

TABLE 8

COMPOUND-COORDINATE COMPARISONS IN FREE RECALL*

Bilingual type	Number of subjects	Concordant list	Discordant list
Compounds	20	15.55	14.75
Coordinates	23	16.87	13.87

*Entries are the average number of items recalled out of the 40 possible for each list.

An analysis of variance and a group comparison of the differences between recall of the two lists reveal ($F = 3.25$, df 1, 41; $t = 1.80$, df 41, $p < 0.03$, with one-tailed tests) that, as expected, the coordinates show more functional segregation of their two languages than do the compounds. Although these results contribute to a very consistent pattern of differences between bilinguals who develop coordinate or compound relations between their two languages, still there is *much* more to be learned about this and similar contrasts that only more and better research will reveal.

As a final note, I would like to explain, to an audience of linguists, the rationale for conducting a continuous series of investigations around one major theme. This persistence should not be viewed as a dogged attempt to prove a point. Proving a point, especially a complex one, with scientific methods requires a patient, almost endless search. There is no one study or set of studies that ever proves the point, and we certainly make no such claims in this instance. What we psychologists characteristically do in our investigations is to settle on some theoretical notion that is of interest, such as the compound-coordinate idea, usually because of its potential generality, and to regard it as an "hypothetical construct" to be described in every detail imaginable, tested for its validity, and ultimately related to and distinguished from other, better established constructs. This is what we meant by "looking into" or "finding more out" about a particular notion. For most complex constructs there are no reliable criteria for testing validity, and the researcher must attempt to establish what has been referred to as "construct validity."[32] Time-consuming as this process is, still it is the stimulating feature of research where a whole set of one's own hypotheses, derived from personal speculations about the basic nature of the construct, are put to test, and a whole network of empirical relations is gradually built up. One can never *prove* the validity of the construct, nor be certain of its status, because at any point a more incisive research study can cast doubt on the already accumulated evidence, causing at least some major revision of thought about the construct, if not its rejection from serious consideration. At best one can only increase confidence in the existence of the construct and its implications; and, when this confidence is healthy enough, the construct becomes of interest and use to others. Our own confidence in the compound-coordinate matter is still only luke-warm; but, regardless of its fate, the important point is that in our attempts to validate this construct we are "finding out a good deal more about" bilingualism and bilinguals.

[32]For an extremely instructive article describing this whole process, see L. J. Cronbach and P. E. Meehl, "Construct Validity in Psychological Tests," *Psychological Bulletin* 52:281-302 (1955).

Oral Tradition as a Source of Linguistic Information

Shelomo Morag
The Hebrew University
Jerusalem

"Scripta manent, verba volant," says the proverb; but is it really so? Is it true that only those texts that are written down endure, whereas the literature that is committed to memory and transmitted orally from generation to generation does not stand the test of time? The study of world literature does not provide a positive answer to this query. It is a well-known fact that many important parts of world literature have been passed on down orally for generations. So it was with the *Vedas* (and the Sanskrit epics — the *Mahābhārata* and the *Rāmāyaṇa*), the Homeric poems, and the *Avesta*, all of which were transmitted orally before being written. The *Vedas*, as is well known, are still transmitted orally in India today. We might also mention in this connection Early Hebrew and Pre-Islamic poetry and augment our illustrations (without making any attempt to exhaust the field) by citing such present-day orally transmitted literature as Bedouin poetry, recorded and studied by A. Socin[1] and others, or the oral poetry of the Todas of South India, whose significance has been brought to light by M.B. Emeneau.[2]

[1]*Diwan aus Centalarabien*, herausgegeben von A. Stumme (Leipzig, 1900-01). For the transmission of the text of the poems, see Vol. III, pp. 5-7.

[2]See M. B. Emeneau, "The Songs of the Todas," *Proceedings of the American Philosophical Society* 77:543-560 (1937); "Oral Poets of South India — the Todas," *Journal of American Folklore* 71:312-324 (1958), reprinted in Dell Hymes, ed., *Language in Culture and Society* (New York, 1964), pp. 330-340; "Style and Meaning in Oral Literature," *Language* 42:323-345 (1966). It should be noted that it is not the text of the Toda songs which has been transmitted orally, but rather the structural patterns of these songs and a number of their linguistic features. Most Todas produce songs extemporaneously, and in doing so they follow traditional techniques and structural patterns. The language they use for oral poetry is quite different from the vernacular. See further note 8.

It is, however, not the literary aspects of oral tradition which I propose to discuss here, but rather some of its linguistic aspects. Orally transmitted literature is, of course, a source of historical information of a special kind, its special nature being derived from the fact that either all or a part of the information it conveys has not been put down in writing (or, in some instances, was recorded at a rather late stage of the transmission process). We can see, then, that when a historian or a linguist approaches an oral source to extract the information it contains, he is confronted by problems peculiar to such a source. A masterful analysis of oral tradition as a historical, not linguistic, source was presented recently by Jan Vansina in his book *Oral Tradition: A Study in Historical Methodology* (Chicago, 1964).[3] Vansina's inquest into the nature of oral tradition is based primarily upon his own field work among the Kuba of the Kasai (Congo) and in Rwanda and Burundi;[4] his frame of reference, however, is rather broad, and although the book is primarily written for students of history, linguists will also profit from it.

According to Vansina, the central question in the study of oral tradition is whether the special features of orally transmitted information a priori deprive it of validity as a historical source; and if they do not, whether there are any means of testing the validity of the information. His study shows that "oral tradition is not necessarily untrustworthy as a historical source, but, on the contrary, merits a certain amount of credence within certain limits."[5] This is the conclusion of a historian; it may be shown that a linguistic study of oral tradition will also yield similar results.

Before proceeding to discuss the historical validity of orally transmitted linguistic information, we should attempt to present a general classification of oral language traditions. For the sake of clarity, we should observe here that, by the term "oral language tradition" of a community, we denote a language of a literary corpus, which has either been transmitted orally or written down, but is recited in the community in a traditional manner, *only* if this language can be clearly differentiated from the vernacular of the community. The language of the literary corpus and the vernacular may belong to two different families, as is true, for example, in the transmittion of the Vedic literature in a Malayalam-speaking com-

---

[3]Originally published in French: "De la tradition orale: Essai de méthode historique," *Annales du Musée Royal de l'Afrique Centrale, Sciences humaines*, no. 36.
[4]See his preface, p. xii.
[5]*Op. cit.*, p. 1.

munity.[6] On the other hand, the literary language and the vernacular may belong to the same family. This latter category includes the following types: (a) literary languages that represent an older stage in the history of the vernacular of the community, for example, the Arabic reading traditions[7] of the Koran, or the oral poetry of the Todas of South India;[8] (b) literary languages that are historically related to the vernacular in any other way, as is true of the recitations of the *Vedas* in communities whose spoken languages are Indo-Aryan (e.g., Hindi or Marathi), or in the reading traditions of biblical and postbiblical Hebrew in Arabic-speaking communities. This latter class is, needless to say, large and variegated, comprising many different kinds of historical relationships between the vernacular and the literary language.

The case in which the language of an orally transmitted literature is identical with the vernacular, or differs from it in some matters of vocabulary and style only, will not be included in the term "language tradition"; in such a case, the student of historical linguistics may encounter problems of a different kind—those of a historical reconstruction which are proposed in the absence of direct documentation for earlier periods in the history of the language. For these problems one may consult a number of essays, among which I should mention in particular Joseph H. Greenberg's "Historical Linguistics and Unwritten Languages."[9] What interests me in this paper is, however, the evaluation of orally transmitted linguistic information relating to a past stage in the history of a language.

Let us now come back to the question of classifying the oral language traditions. There are, of course, several ways of classifying the traditions, each depending on the point of departure. The classification I shall present here is one based on the examination

---

[6]Malayalam is Dravidian, whereas Vedic is, of course, Indo-Aryan.

[7]For this term see below, p. 131.

[8]Of the language of the oral poetry of the Todas, Emeneau says: "The poetical language is often different, and often markedly so, from the vernacular of the singer ...the morphology, especially of the verb, is different, whether more archaic or merely a contrived difference I cannot yet say. In a few points, by comparison with related languages, it has been possible to identify archaisms of morphology or of vocabulary. But at the same time, there are borrowings from the language of the neighbouring Badagas, who have been in the Nilginis for roughly five centuries", ("Oral Poets of South India: The Todas", *Journal of American Folklore* 71:320, reprinted in D. Hymes, ed., *Language in Culture and Society* [1964], p. 337). For some linguistic features in which Toda oral poetry differs from Toda prose, see Emeneau, *Language* 42:325-330 (1966).

[9]A. L. Kroeber, ed., *Anthropology Today* (1953), pp. 265-286.

of the relation between sound and sign. From this point of view, oral language traditions belong to four major categories.

The first of these is the language tradition that has been transmitted for generations without any recourse to writing, or, to be more exact, that, in some instances, has been recorded in writing at a time later than that of its composition. An example of this language tradition category is Vedic literature, which has been transmitted orally for many generations and is still recited orally in India. In fact, the *śrotriya*, the Brahman who recites the Vedic literature without understanding it, has in India a status comparable to that occupied in Medieval Europe by the monk who copied manuscripts.[10]

Essentially different in character are the "translation languages" extant in a number of Jewish communities. An examination of these languages requires a second category in our classification. In some Arabic-speaking Jewish communities, oral Arabic translations of the Bible have been handed down. For these translations the communities use several forms of Arabic which differ in many respects from the local dialects of the communities. In some of their features the translation forms of Arabic disclose an affinity with classical Arabic, but they are far from being identical with it. These Arabic "translation forms," employed not only for rendering the Bible into Arabic, but also for other purposes, exegetical and literary, are at present transmitted within the communities both orally and in writing; and, in fact, several translations of some of the books of the Bible in these forms of Arabic have been published.[11] The translation languages, however, are always written in Hebrew characters and since Hebrew orthography is, to use the traditional term, "defective," as it represents only some of the vowels, it follows that in the translation forms of Arabic at least a part of the linguistic structure is being transmitted orally. It also appears that the translation languages originated as oral, not written, entities, primarily designated for conveying the meaning of the Scriptures to school children and to the less literate members of the community.

In addition to the aforementioned Arabic-speaking communities, other Jewish communities, such as the Persian, the Kurdish,

---

[10]See J. F. Staal, *Nambudiri Veda Recitation* (The Hague, 1961), p. 17.

[11]For a survey of one of these "translation forms" of Arabic, see H.Blanc, "Notes on the Literary Idiom of the Baghdadi Jews," *For Max Weinreich* (The Hague, 1964), pp. 18-30.

and the Ashkenazi,[12] also possess translation languages. The extent
to which these translation languages differ from the respective ver-
naculars in their phonology and morphology, and not only in matters
of vocabulary and style, has yet to be clarified.

The third and the fourth categories in our classification of oral
language traditions concern what may be called "reading traditions." This term is of importance for our paper, and, therefore,
might be allowed to present here, in a somewhat modified form, an
attempt to define it which I previously gave elsewhere:[13] A reading
tradition (henceforth: RT) may be defined as a corpus of phonological and morphological information, reducible in its main parts to a
set of rules, upon which the correct reading of a text is based. The
reading of a literary text by a native speaker reflects one of the traditional linguistic styles of his community: the extent of his mastery
of this style is disclosed by the manner in which he interprets the
relationship of phonology and morphology to orthography. Since
discrepancy between the literary and spoken forms of a language
is a common phenomenon, the oral transmission of the phonological
and the morphophonemic, as well as, to a lesser extent, the morphological tradition of the literary language, constitutes a significant
part of the teaching of the language within the community. It is by
the transmission of this tradition that the standard oral interpretation of the literary language is maintained. For the linguist, the RT
is a source of the primary linguistic data; for the native speaker, it
is the standard that directs him when he is confronted with both
the literary language of his community and his vernacular.[14]

Some communities have, however, RTs of a different kind,
which relate not to a present but to a past state of a literary language. This literary language is sometimes the ancestor of the
spoken language of the community (or, to be more precise, is closely
related to this ancestor), as is true of the Arabic RTs of the Koran,
or the RTs of Gəʿəz extant in Ethiopia. Other RTs, such as the RTs
of Hebrew and Aramaic preserved by the various Jewish communities, as well as the RTs of Syriac maintained by the Maronite com-

[12]For some bibliographical references for the Ashkenazi translations of the
Bible, see Blanc, op. cit. p. 27, n. 26.

[13]"Oral Traditions and Dialects," Proceedings of the International Congress on
Semitic Studies, Jerusalem, 1965 (in press).

[14]My definition of "reading tradition" comes quite close to what Professor William Labov, in his paper "Phonological Correlates of Social Stratification," American Anthropologist 66:164-176 (1964), calls "reading style," as distinct from "careful speech" and "casual speech."

munity and by a number of other Christian churches, or the RTs of
Coptic, differ from the above in regard to the historical relationship
between the vernacular and the literary language: most of the Jewish
communities spoke for centuries, up to their settlement in Israel,
languages other than Hebrew and Aramaic; the Maronites, who
have a RT of Syriac, and the Copts, who possess RTs of Coptic,
speak Arabic. The RTs in question, of both the former and the latter
categories, are of particular significance in the life of the community, as they are employed in the transmission of those portions of
the literature that have a special religious standing. They may,
therefore, be called liturgical RTs (henceforth: LRTs).

Now, within the bulk of the LRTs, two types are to be distinguished: those in which the graphemic representation indicates
both the phonological and morphological forms, and those in which
the orthography denotes only a part of these forms. Because, in the
first type, more information is conveyed by the graphemic system
than by the traditional reading, our interest lies more in the second
type, that is, in those LRTs where the phonemes not represented
in the orthography are supplied by the reader in accordance with
the tradition of his community.

To the former type belong, for example, the Arabic RTs of the
Koran, the RTs of the Hebrew text of the Bible, the RTs of the Aramaic translations of the Bible (both the Syriac which, as is well
known, is used by Christian communities, and the Jewish Aramaic
translation, the Targum), as well as the RTs of Gə'əz and Coptic.
The second type is best represented by the RTs of postbiblical
Hebrew literature, primarily the Mishna, and of the Aramaic parts
of the Babylonian Talmud. In reading the Mishna, which from the
religious point of view is the most important part of postbiblical Hebrew literature, only the consonantal skeleton of many morphemes
is disclosed by the orthography of the text, their vowel structure
being provided by the reader in accordance with the tradition of his
community. To give a few illustrations: a Hebrew word spelled *dkl*
("palm tree") is read either as *děkål* (the Iraqi community) or
dekel (all other communities); a form spelled *qrḥ* ("bald") is realized as *qereḥ* (the Yemenite community), *qåreaḥ* (the Iraqi community), *qereaḥ* (all other communities); the word spelled *ḥrth*
("regret") is either *ḥårṭå* (Yemenite), or *ḥåråṭå* (all other communities); the spelling *smmnym* ("ingredients") is *sammåměnim* (Yemenite), *sammånim* (Iraqi), *sammåmånim* (Morocco-Tafilalt), or
saměmanim (Lithuania). In Babylonian Aramaic it is up to the

reader to make, for example, the distinction between *něyem* ("he slept"), and *nayem* ("he sleeps"), which are both written *nym*, or between $^c av\underline{d}i$ ("I did"), $^c av\underline{d}ey$ ("they [masc.] did"), and $^c \mathring{a}v\breve{e}\underline{d}ey$ ("they [masc.] do"), all of which are written $^c b\underline{d}y$.

The significance of the RTs of this type is self-evident: they provide information about the phonemics, morphophonemics, and morphology of the language. Moreover, they furnish us with data that in all probability reflect dialectal isoglosses. True, the period to which these isoglosses pertain cannot always be determined with exactness; but all the same we are not altogether at a loss regarding the location in time of these isoglosses in the history of the language. Thus it appears that some of the above varieties of postbiblical Hebrew words are dialectal isoglosses of the period of the Second Temple. My classification of the oral language traditions is summarized in table 1.

We should now come back to the question of the historical evaluation of the information traditions carry. An evaluation of a tradition should be based primarily on the study of its history within the community, and such a study is bound to encompass an examination of a variety of factors, linguistic and extralinguistic. Needless to say, there is much interplay between these two kinds of factors, since the tradition forms a significant part of the cultural heritage of the community. For the individual members of the community, acquaintance with the tradition is a sign of belonging; for the community as a whole, the traditions possess specifying and symbolic values. To some extent, a language tradition is one of the important "community markers." By these "markers" the place of the microsegmental entity, the particular community, within the bulk of the macrosegment, the other communities to which the community in question is related, is determined.

The linguistic study of the history of the community's tradition should mainly be concerned with the question: What is the extent of the distortion suffered by the tradition in the process of being handed down orally for generations? This question is related to the extralinguistic problems of the methods of oral transmission and to the standing of the tradition in the community. As could be expected, those traditions to which mnemonic devices have been applied are more resistant to distortion through failure of memory than others.[15] Another factor plays an important role here: A tradi-

[15]Cf. Vansina, *Oral Tradition: A Study in Historical Methodology*, p. 41.

TABLE 1

CLASSIFICATION OF ORAL LANGUAGE TRADITIONS

Class	Example	Written representation of tradition	Relationship of spoken language of community to language of oral tradition		
			Spoken language and language of oral tradition both belong to same family		Spoken language belongs to a family different from that of language of oral tradition
			Spoken language represents later stage in history of language of oral tradition	Spoken language and language of oral tradition historically related, but spoken language cannot be clearly defined as representing later stage in history of language of oral tradition	
I Linguistic information fully transmitted orally	Oral poetry of Todas (South India)	None	+	—	—

TABLE 1 – *Continued*

	Traditional recitations of *Vedas*	Extant, but recitations are independent of written representations	−	+ (when the spoken language is, e.g., Hindi or Marathi)	+ (when the spoken language is, e.g., Malayalam)
II Translation languages	Semiliterary forms of Arabic used by Jewish communities	Written texts, in "defective" orthography, sometimes used by the community concomitantly with oral transmission; however, not all orally transmitted translations have written representations	+	−	−
III Liturgical reading traditions (LRTs) having full written representation	RTs of biblical Hebrew of all Jewish communities except the Samaritan	Full: Orthography denotes segmental, and some suprasegmental, phonemes	− (before migration to Israel)	+ (RTs of Arabic- or Aramaic-speaking communities)	+ (RTs of communities whose spoken languages are not Semitic)
	RTs of Syriac, e.g., of Maronite community in Lebanon	Full: Orthography denotes segmental, and some suprasegmental, phonemes	−	+	−

TABLE 1 – *Continued*

			(before migration to Israel) + (RTs of Arabic- or Aramaic-speaking communities)	(before migration to Israel) − (RTs of communities whose spoken languages are not Semitic)
IV Liturgical reading traditions (LRTs) having partial written representation	RTs of postbiblical Hebrew and of Babylonian Aramaic extant in Jewish communities	Partial: Orthography denotes only part of segmental phonemes (mostly the consonants)	—	—
	Samaritan RTs of Hebrew and Aramaic	Partial: Orthography denotes only part of segmental phonemes (mostly the consonants)	+	—
	The Yemenite RT of Saadia's Arabic translation of the Bible	Partial: Orthography denotes only part of segmental phonemes (mostly the consonants)	—	+

tion is less susceptible to distortion if it underwent a process of stabilization or normalization by which its form became definitely fixed at an early stage in the history of the transmission. And, if in addition to these two factors, factors of religious or other sociological import are in operation, the tradition becomes even more resistant. That such factors as these militate against the distortion of a tradition may be shown by a host of examples for oral traditions of various kinds, literary,[16] historical, and linguistic.

The transmission of the tradition sometimes has a metaphysical aspect. Thus, the fidelity with which the Brahmans have handed down their Vedic heritage is rooted in the concept of the transcendence of the sacred word and is "identical with the ritual exactitude, *satyam*, 'truthfulness,' with which the Vedic Indians perform the sacrifices."[17] Inaccuracies in oral transmission, as well as in sacrifice, are considered to have disastrous effect on society and the universe.[18] In spite of basic cultural differences, a somewhat similar attitude prevails in Jewish thought regarding the "sacred word." This concern for the sacred word led to the establishment of the requirement for an exact formal transmission of the written text, as well as of those linguistic entities that, owing to the nature of Hebrew and Aramaic orthography, remain unspecified in the text.[19]

In their practice, however, various Jewish communities differ in respect to the importance they attach to the phonetic form of orally transmitted linguistic data. Whereas the Samaritan and the Yemenite are rather strict as to the sound pattern of their RTs, the Ashkenazi (Central and East European) communities appear to be far more lenient. When a community has such a lenient attitude, and this leniency is concomitant with a high degree of interference from the vernacular, a superimposition of one tradition on another may result, as happened to the RTs of the Ashkenazi communities some time between the eleventh and the thirteenth centuries A.D. Before that time, the Ashkenazi communities (or, at least, some of them) had a RT identical with the Sephardi (that is, that of the Jews of Spain); but this tradition has been superseded, in most of

[16]For a comparison of the aspects of accuracy in the oral transmission of literary texts to which a ritual sanction is attached with that of texts that are not associated with such a sanction, see Vansina, *ibid.*

[17]Staal, *op. cit.* p. 12.

[18]*Ibid.*

[19]For the importance of oral tradition in Judaism, see B. Gerhardsson, *Memory and Manuscript: Oral Tradition and Written Transmission in Rabbinic Judaism and Early Christianity* (Uppsala-Lund, 1961).

its components, by a new RT which apparently developed under the influence of the phonological systems of Middle High German dialects.[20]

Valuable information about the ways in which a tradition is handed down within the community may be gleaned from a study of the methods of instruction pursued in the traditional schools, in whose curriculum the language traditions occupy a most important part. As a rule, it can be said that the more mechanical the instruction, the more trustworthy the tradition.[21] The teachers in the traditional school are quite often the carriers of the tradition, their position as tradition carriers being, depending on the community, official, semiofficial, or nonofficial.

We should now come back to the linguistic aspects of the history of the language traditions. For a number of traditions, the most significant of these aspects is that of the contact, of which there are two kinds, tradition-vernacular contact and intertradition contact. The former, contact between the orally transmitted language tradition and the vernacular, is relatively simple, and its consequences are attested primarily in the domain of phonology. The phonemic system of the vernacular interferes in that of the language tradition, and this interference usually results in phone substitution[22] and reinterpretation of distinctive features.[23] Both classes of phenomena are widespread; we shall illustrate them very briefly. Phone substitution occurs, for example, in the Nambudiri recitation of the Vedic texts, and of Sanskrit in general. Thus, since in Malayalam, which is the spoken language of the Nambudiri reciters of the Veda,

[20]Concerning the superimposition of a new RT on the Sephardi RT in the Ashkenazi communities, see H. Yalon, *Quntresim* (Bulletin of Hebrew Language Studies) 1:62-66 (1937-1939); *idem*, *ᶜinyĕney låšon* (1941-42), pp. 16-27; *ibid.* (1942-43), 52-58.

[21]It may be of interest to note in passing that communities that have always lived far apart and have not had any mutual contact in the course of their history are occasionally found to have used similar mechanical devices for the transmission of their language traditions. Thus, the Nambudiri of India use head movements in the recitation of the accents of the *Rgveda* and accompany with hand gestures the realizations of vowels and consonants in the recitation of these texts (Staal, *op. cit.*, pp. 40-41). A similar practice of using hand gestures and finger movements is found in the recitation of biblical accents in the Jewish communities of Yemen (cf. Morag, *The Hebrew Language Tradition of the Yemenite Jews* [Jerusalem, 1963], p. 220, n. 2), in Egypt, Djerba, and Morocco (our information regarding this practice in Morocco is limited to the community of Tafilalt), and in Italy (in which it seems to have originated at a rather late period). For this practice in Jewish communities see now S. Levin, "The Traditional Chironomy of the Hebrew Scriptures," *Journal of Biblical Literature* 87:59-70 (1968).

[22]Cf. U. Weinreich, ed., *Languages in Contact* (New York, 1953), p. 13.

[23]*Ibid.*, p. 18.

phones in final position can be neither plosive nor voiceless, Vedic final *t* is often realized in the recitation as *l*.[24] Reinterpretation of distinctive features is common in the RTs of Hebrew and Aramaic. Thus, as a result of the interference of the spoken languages of the Dutch-Portuguese and the Italian communities, the pharyngeal obstruent / ʿ / has been replaced in the RTs of these communities by a velar or prepalatal /n/, respectively.[25]

More intricate is the contact of the latter kind, intertradition contact, which is usually concomitant with tradition-vernacular contact. What I term "intertradition" contact is a result of the coexistence of a number of different language traditions for specific texts within the same community. An interesting example of such a coexistence is furnished by the Jewish community of Yemen. Geographically isolated in the southern part of Yemen for centuries, the Yemenite Jews constituted a very special phenomenon, both anthropologically and linguistically, as compared to other Jewish communities.[26] In their isolation, the Yemenite Jews preserved six RTs. Of these six traditions, two are Hebrew (the RTs of the Bible and of the postbiblical literature), three are Aramaic (the RTs of biblical Aramaic; of Targum Aramaic, the language of the Aramaic translations of the Bible; and of Babylonian Aramaic, the language of the Aramaic parts of the Babylonian Talmud), and one is Arabic (the RT of Saadia's Arabic translation of the Bible).[27] Such a coexistence of six language traditions in one community is quite rare.[28]

Two kinds of relationships can be discerned where a number of traditions coexist. One kind of relationship results from the coexistence of several traditions of the *same* language (the two traditions

---

[24]Staal, *op. cit.*, p. 38.

[25]For further illustrations, see Morag, *op. cit.*

[26]Anthropologically, the Yemenite community preserved a way of life which, in many respects, reflects that of the Jewish communities of Babylonia from about A.D. 600 to 900.

[27]This translation was made in the first half of the tenth century A.D. Morpho-phonemically and morphologically, the form of Arabic disclosed by the Yemenite RT of this translation differs in a number of points from the Yemenite vernacular.

[28]The members of communities possessing several traditions switch easily from one tradition to another. Thus, for example, when switching from Targum Aramaic to Babylonian Aramaic, the Yemenite reader will immediately replace the Targum Aramaic forms *ᶜiddånå* ("time") or *båråytå* ("external [fem.]") by their Babylonian Aramaic counterparts *ᶜiddanå* and *barraytå*. Both in Targum Aramaic and in Babylonian Aramaic, these words are spelled *'dn'* (or *'ydn'*) and *bryt'* (or *bryyt'*), but whereas in Targum Aramaic the vowels not re resented in the orthography are denoted by specific vowel signs, no such vowel signs exist for Babylonian Aramaic (cf. above, pp. 132-133). The structural peculiarities of these forms in Babylonian Aramaic are, therefore, based solely on oral tradition.

of Hebrew; the three traditions of Aramaic); the other kind originates in the coexistence of traditions of *different* languages (the traditions of Hebrew concomitantly with those of Aramaic and that of Arabic). The latter kind of relationship is, in fact, a special case of multilingualism; the former kind, on the other hand, resembles to some extent the situation known as diglossia. Diglossia, which exists, to use Charles Ferguson's definition, "where two or more varieties of the same language are used by the same speakers under different conditions,"[29] prevails in many speech communities. Oral tradition diglossia differs, however, from ordinary diglossia in that the various traditions are not used under different conditions; they are employed for the recitation of different parts of the literature. The social aspect, which is highly important for ordinary diglossia, where the styles of speech which are used in formal and informal situations are differentiated, is thus missing in tradition diglossia.

Having surveyed the various kinds of contact, we come closer to the problem of evaluating, from a historical point of view, the linguistic evidence conveyed by the oral tradition. It is in this aspect of oral language tradition that the interest of the student of historical linguistics lies. The central question that this student confronts is that of the possibility of reconstructing, in full or in part, the oldest form of the language which the oral tradition reflects (we shall denote this form by F_1).

It should be possible to reconstruct at least a number of the structural features of this form by a process of deduction, that is, by deducing from the present form of the oral language tradition (which we shall denote by F_n) the total amount of interference suffered by the tradition in the various stages of its history.[30] This process of deduction may be carried out successfully only if a significant prerequisite is fulfilled, namely, if the nature and extent of the interference that resulted from the contact of the language tradition with the vernacular(s) of the community. and, in certain instances, with other language traditions employed by the community, can be traced and described. The extent of the interference should

---

[29]C. Ferguson, "Diglossia," reprinted in D. Hymes, ed., *Language in Culture and Society* (1964), pp. 429-439. For the quoted definition, see p. 429.

[30]Needless to say, interference is not the only factor that has stamped the development of oral language tradition. Innovations that resulted from analogy and hypercorrection should be taken into consideration as well. The study of a number of language traditions shows, however, that interference surpasses other factors in shaping the forms of the language tradition. This point is dealt with elsewhere in more detail.

be thus assessed for each of the stages in the history of the traditions which constitute distinct links in their chain of transmission. Needless to say, the performance of this task of tracing the interference may be quite intricate. We shall illustrate this graphically in tables 2 and 3. These tables present the chain of transmission of two traditions of the same community, the Yemenite RT of postbiblical Hebrew and the Yemenite RT of Babylonian Aramaic; they also indicate the various kinds of interference which might have been suffered by the traditions in each stage of their history.

A few words of comment on the tables are in order here.

Table 2. — According to the present state of our knowledge, it appears that by about A.D. 200 postbiblical Hebrew ceased to be spoken in most Jewish communities in Palestine, being superseded mostly by Aramaic. Having ceased to serve as an ordinary means of communication, Hebrew continued its existence in a twofold way, as a literary language and as a liturgical language. In this latter function[31] Hebrew was employed for the reading and teaching of the Bible and postbiblical literature. The reading of postbiblical literature (whose orthography denotes, as mentioned above, only a part of the phonemes) was based, at least in some of its features, on a dialect, or dialects, of postbiblical Hebrew which flourished when the language was still alive.[32] What happened here was a process of transformation, whereby a number of the structural features of a dialect ($= F_1$) that had ceased to live were incorporated in a corpus of phonological, morphophonemic, and morphological information, upon which the correct reading of postbiblical literature was based. This corpus of information (see above, p. 131) constituted the reading tradition ($=F_2$). In fact, there probably existed, in the first centuries following the completion of this process of transformation, several RTs of postbiblical Hebrew. One of these may have been transplanted to Babylonia, where it was employed by the Jewish communities. If this assumption is correct, the Babylonian RT of postbiblical Hebrew had its origins in a Palestinian RT. It should be stressed, however, that our knowledge regarding the transition from F_1 to F_2, and the origins of the Babylonian RT of postbiblical He-

---

[31]The term "liturgical" is used here to include not only the language of the prayer book, but also the language of those parts of the postbiblical literature which were regarded as significant parts of the religious heritage, mainly the Mishna and the Talmud (in its Hebrew elements).

[32]We shall not deal here with the reading of biblical literature prior to the invention of the vocalization signs.

TABLE 2
Chain of Transmission for the Yemenite Tradition of Postbiblical Hebrew

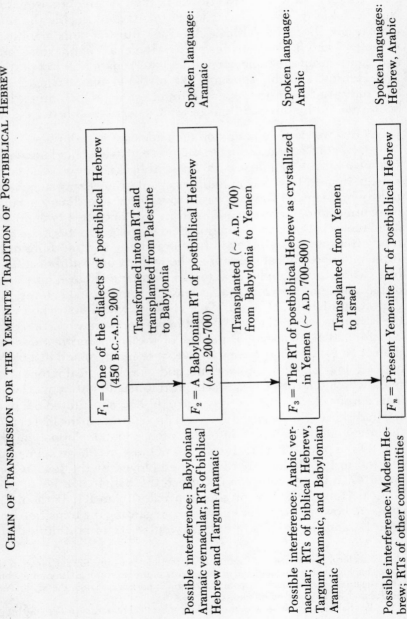

F_1 = One of the dialects of postbiblical Hebrew (450 B.C.-A.D. 200)

Transformed into an RT and transplanted from Palestine to Babylonia

Possible interference: Babylonian Aramaic vernacular; RTs of biblical Hebrew and Targum Aramaic

F_2 = A Babylonian RT of postbiblical Hebrew (A.D. 200-700)

Spoken language: Aramaic

Transplanted (~ A.D. 700) from Babylonia to Yemen

Possible interference: Arabic vernacular; RTs of biblical Hebrew, Targum Aramaic, and Babylonian Aramaic

F_3 = The RT of postbiblical Hebrew as crystallized in Yemen (~ A.D. 700-800)

Spoken language: Arabic

Transplanted from Yemen to Israel

Possible interference: Modern Hebrew; RTs of other communities

F_n = Present Yemenite RT of postbiblical Hebrew

Spoken languages: Hebrew, Arabic

TABLE 3

CHAIN OF TRANSMISSION FOR THE YEMENITE TRADITION OF BABYLONIAN ARAMAIC

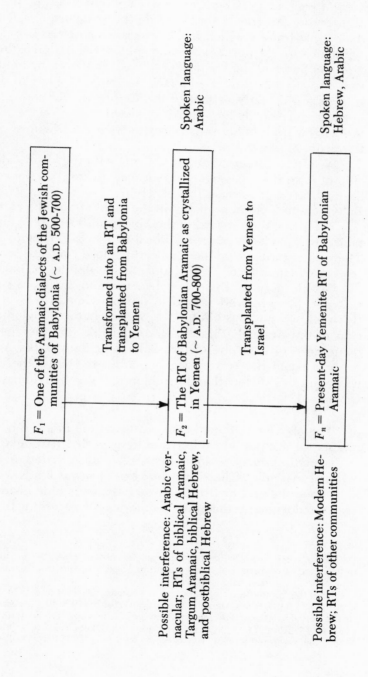

F_1 = One of the Aramaic dialects of the Jewish communities of Babylonia (~ A.D. 500-700)

Transformed into an RT and transplanted from Babylonia to Yemen

F_2 = The RT of Babylonian Aramaic as crystallized in Yemen (~ A.D. 700-800)

Spoken language: Arabic

Transplanted from Yemen to Israel

F_n = Present-day Yemenite RT of Babylonian Aramaic

Spoken language: Hebrew, Arabic

Possible interference: Arabic vernacular; RTs of biblical Aramaic, Targum Aramaic, biblical Hebrew, and postbiblical Hebrew

Possible interference: Modern Hebrew; RTs of other communities

brew in general, is scanty. The Babylonian RT of postbiblical
Hebrew might have been based on the structure of a Palestinian
dialect of Hebrew which had been transplanted to Babylonia earlier than A.D. 200, possibly at some point in the period of the Second
Temple. Some of the features of this RT may even be held, at least
in theory, to reflect those of a Hebrew dialect spoken in Babylonia
in a period as early as that of the Exile (587-538 B.C.); however,
because our knowledge regarding the historical relationship of F_2
to F_1 is far from being satisfactory, this possibility must remain in
the realm of conjecture.

We are on firmer ground in dealing with the historical relationship of F_3 to F_2. It has been shown that several Babylonian RTs of
biblical, as well as postbiblical, Hebrew were transplanted from
Babylonia to Yemen, probably in the eighth or ninth century A.D.[33]

Table 3. — With regard to the Yemenite RT of Babylonian Aramaic, our knowledge of the relationship of F_2 to F_1 is more adequate.
There is historical evidence indicating close contacts between the
Jewish community of Yemen and the Academies of Babylonia in
the Geonic period. It is quite clear that the Yemenite scholars of
that period were well versed in the Babylonian RTs of Hebrew
(both biblical and postbiblical), as well as in the Babylonian recen-
sion of the Aramaic Targum; it is plausible that they became ac-
quainted also with one of the dialects of Babylonian Aramaic in
order to establish a correct way of reading the text of the Talmud. It
was upon this dialect that the Yemenite RT of Babylonian Aramaic
was based.[34]

The above-mentioned task of tracing the interference of community vernacular and other traditions with a particular oral language tradition may, in some instances, be facilitated by the use of
external evidence. There are sources of various kinds which shed
light upon the oral tradition. These sources include historical trea-
tises and documents that provide information regarding the pronun-

[33]The *exact* period when this transplantation took place cannot, at present, be
determined. For historical documentation regarding the transplantation, see S.
Morag, *op. cit.*, Introduction, pp. 24 ff.

[34]For the Yemenite RT of Babylonian Aramaic, see S. Morag, "On the Yemenite
Tradition of Babylonian Aramaic," *Tarbiz* 30:120-129 (1960-61; in Hebrew); "Notes
on the Vowel System of Babylonian Aramaic as Preserved in the Yemenite Tradition,"
Phonetica 7:217-239 (1962); "Oral Traditions and Dialects," *Proceedings of the International Conference on Semitic Studies, Jerusalem, 1965* (in press).

ciation of the community, transcriptions, vocalizations of ancient manuscripts, and so on. Thus, for example, the Yemenite RT of postbiblical Hebrew, which, as noted above, had its origins in a Babylonian RT of postbiblical Hebrew, can be compared with the vocalization of certain manuscripts which disclose the phonology and morphology of the Babylonian RT of postbiblical Hebrew. Our ability to reconstruct past stages in the history of an oral language tradition depends in no small measure on the information gained from such sources. Paucity of external material may prove to be a great hindrance in the reconstruction of any of the past stages. For this reason, and also because of the lack of clarity regarding the relationship of F_2 to F_1 in the history of the Yemenite RT of postbiblical Hebrew (see above), we are in a position to reconstruct, at the most, only a few of the features of F_1.

In arguing that a proposed reconstruction of a past stage in the history of a language tradition is valid, we shall have to substantiate our argument by considering not only the external evidence, but also the internal evidence, which is of prime importance. What we mean by internal evidence is the information obtained from a structural study of the language tradition in question. Both the internal and the external evidence should be applied in testing the validity of the proposed reconstruction; and, in doing so, some general principles of method should be followed.[35] A reconstruction of a past stage in the history of a language tradition is to be considered valid if it shows: (a) that, by deducting from the present form of the oral tradition the total amount of interference the tradition suffered in the course of its transmission from the reconstructed past stage to its present form, a system is obtained that possesses definite features of its own, and these features are sufficient in number and are of such a functional role as to permit the outlining of a distinct structure; and (b) that the affinity of the reconstructed system to that of other dialects of the language which are known to us (or to other related languages) may be systematically formulated in terms of historical linguistics. In other words, the reconstruction may be considered successful if it produces a system that possesses definite features of its own and matches related systems, that is, if it reveals corres-

[35]Cf. also the discussion of these principles in my paper "Oral Traditions and Dialects."

pondences of identical and nonidentical features, and if the latter correspondences can be accounted for.[36]

I have attempted to present here some aspects of the study of linguistic information that has been transmitted through oral tradition. The investigation of linguistic information of this kind can be rewarding. For the student of a particular language, it is bound to yield new data; for the general linguist, more light can be shed on questions such as the permeability of linguistic units, the conflict between primary and secondary systems, and the interplay of extra-linguistic and linguistic factors.[37]

[36]Cf. Professor Werner Winter's discussion of historical relationships in linguistics in his paper "Basic Principles of the Comparative Method." This paper was read at the 1966 Linguistic Institute Conference on Linguistic Method, held on August 1-3, 1966, at the University of California, Los Angeles, and will be published in the proceedings under the title *The Place of Method in Linguistics*.

[37]I am indebted to Dr. Joan Rubin for a number of valuable criticisms and suggestions.

Some Methods of Dynamic Comparison in Linguistics

Joseph H. Greenberg
Stanford University

The comparative method, or more accurately stated, comparative methods, since a multiplicity of them exist, have a fundamental place in the disciplines concerned with man in his social and cultural aspects. These disciplines, in contrast with the physical and biological sciences, never encounter in pure form the phenomena concerning which they seek for understanding and the formulation of regularities. Such entities as culture, society, religion, or language are always encountered in the concrete form of particular, historically conditioned cultures, societies, religions, languages, and so on. One basic approach is, therefore, the comparative one; and a fundamental purpose often served by such an approach is the uncovering of constancies of structure or of developmental tendencies underlying the individual variant forms. Hence we may study culture by means of cultures and language by means of languages.

In linguistics there are two generally recognized methods of comparison, the genetic and the typological. Both of these are associated with language classification, but the classification may be considered essentially a by-product of the application of fundamentally different criteria of resemblance. The classificational aspect is even more a subordinate matter when considered in relation to the overall purposes of the two methods. In the context of the present investigation in which certain additional types of comparison are proposed, because these do not lead to further kinds of language classification, the two latter aspects are the more important, namely the criteria of resemblance and the overall goal of comparison.

In regard to both of these, the contrast between the genetic and typological modes of comparison is of a basic nature. What constitutes a similarity for genetic investigation is determined by some theory of process, that is a theory regarding the classes of possible changes. Thus the acceptance of Latin *sex* as a cognate of Greek *hex* involves, among other things, the assumption of certain sound changes. In this instance one assumption is that Latin continues an earlier $*s$ in essentially unchanged form, while in Greek there has been a change $*s > h$. Where identity is involved, it is merely the limiting case of change (i.e., zero change or stability).[1] Such a method of comparison may be classified as dynamic because it involves, in an essential way, hypotheses about change, while methods in which this feature is absent may be called static.

Of course, often the hypothesis regarding change was arrived at later in order to explain previously noted similarities; but its being so does not nullify the fact that some such hypothesis is integrally a part of the method in that the resemblance is not theoretically accounted for until a satisfactory hypothesis of change has been proposed. It will also generally hold that the genetically accounted for resemblance involves items that are highly similar, so that they could be classified together in some acceptable static scheme. But this is merely a consequence, although in practice a highly important one, of the fact that the outcomes of historical process are, on the basis of static resemblance, similar to their antecedents.

In contrast, typological criteria of resemblance involve no such hypotheses of change. Accordingly as the relevant properties are defined more widely or more narrowly, the degree of resemblance necessary to assign languages to a typological class is greater or less. Once defined, however, providing the definition meets the necessary logical requirements, a language is declared either to have the property or not to have it, without reference to considerations of change, that is, on a purely synchronic basis. Thus, if the criterion is the existence of tone as a distinctive feature of individual segments, then Chinese, Vietnamese, and Yoruba share a common class membership in the class of tone languages.

---

[1]From the purely phonetic point of view, the data over a time span are practically never sufficient for us to posit an identity. It is often possible, however, to assert with some confidence that phonetic feature specifications have not altered through a given period, and this lack of change in phonetic feature specifications is what is intended by "phonetic identity" in the present context.

The differing concepts of resemblance inherent in these two methods are related to their general goals. The genetic comparison of individually related forms, that is, cognates, leads to the positing of reconstructed forms as the source of the later reflexes or the resultants of changes. Inasmuch as, in satisfactory applications of the method, the hypotheses are not *ad hoc* but bring together apparently disparate instances under a single formulation, historical explanations constitute acceptable answers to certain questions and exhibit the common hallmark of satisfactory explanations, namely, generalizing power as shown in the subsuming of particulars under some general rule. Thus the "irregular" plurals of internal change in English (e.g., *tooth–teeth, mouse–mice, man–men*), can be shown to arise from the same succession of changes, fronting of a vowel before *i* of the following syllable in the prehistoric nominative-accusative plural termination, followed by loss of final vowel and subsequent unrounding of the *y* [ü:] of *mȳs* and the [ö:] of *⁎tōþ*, respectively. As is characteristic of satisfactory explanations, it "unexpectedly" also accounts for other phenomena, for example, the variation in the comparative and superlative in *old–elder–eldest* and of certain derived nouns in relation to the underlying adjective, for example, *long–length, strong–strength*.

Typological comparison has had a much more marginal position in linguistics, precisely because, unlike the genetic method, its overall purpose was not easily apparent; however, it now seems clear that the chief value of such comparison is its role as a heuristic for the formulation of universally valid relations among properties of language. Whenever a logically possible class of some typology is null, this same fact is logically equivalent to some statement about languages in general. So-called unrestricted universals, for example, the assertion that all languages have some phonetic segments with the vocalic feature, are merely limiting cases in which the typology is the simplest possible, that is, where there is a single predicate that takes on two values, the presence or absence of some specified property. Thus, corresponding to the above statement regarding the universality of the vocalic feature is a typology in which all languages are assigned to one of two classes defined by the presence or absence of the vocalic feature, and in which the latter class is null. The logical equivalence of null membership of certain classes in more complex typologies to implicational universals has been sufficiently illustrated elsewhere.[2]

[2] See Greenberg (1966a), pp. 9-10.

Thus both genetic and typological comparison lead to generalizations; however, there is at least one important way in which the two types of generalization differ and in respect to which, on the usual view, the explanations arising from typological procedures would be adjudged superior. The generalizations that flow from typologies approach more closely the notion of scientific law in that they are asserted to hold under general, rather than "proper-name," conditions. With regard to genetic explanatory laws, it is commonplace that regular phonetic changes, actually the only kind of linguistic regularities to which the name "law" has ever been commonly attached (e.g., Grimm's Law), hold in each instance for some specified language, or group of languages, and for a specified chronological span. This limitation would cease to exist if it were possible to specify in general terms, in principle applicable to all languages, the conditions under which changes such as those codified in Grimm's statement take place. Such general specification, of course, has not been possible.

In contrast, such an implicational universal as the one discussed later in this paper, namely that whenever a language has voiceless low vowels it always has voiceless high vowels, has the class of all languages as its scope. Its logical form may be paraphrased as follows. If we take any language, if that language has property α it has property β. Because it applies to any language, its limiting conditions are merely the definitional characteristics of language and do not involve specific constants of time and space. Hence such universals conform to the usual requirements of generality for scientific laws, while those based on genetic comparisons do not.

This distinction is no mere quibble about the use of the word "law" with its honorific connotations. Given that the conditions of application of synchronically derived universals are general, when one encounters a new language it is possible, from certain characteristics, to predict others. Such fresh data will also constitute an empirical test of the validity of the hypothesis. On the other hand, it makes no sense to ask such questions as whether there are any languages in the world which violate Grimm's Law, since it only applies to a given language during a specified chronological period.

These results would seem to be a particular exemplification within linguistics of the well-known dichotomy, described, for example, by Windelband in the nineteenth century, between idiographic, historical, particularizing disciplines and nomothetic, generalizing sciences. Within anthropology, the structuralist-functionalist school of A. R. Radcliffe-Brown has similarly divided anthropology into two disciplines, a law-seeking, scientific, social anthropology and a particularistic, historically oriented ethnology, with an undisguised superior evaluation of the former.[3]

This contrast, however, as I will attempt to show, is merely an apparent one. There exists the possibility of a more comprehensive mode of diachronic comparison which shares with synchronic typology the attribute of generality. The individual items of such comparisons are not the cognate forms, but the changes themselves, as formulated in rules and occurring in historically independent cases, and hence subject to classification (corresponding to synchronic typology) and generalization without proper-name restriction. For reasons that will presently appear, it is appropriate to call such comparison processual. That this type of comparison has received only marginal and unexplicit attention rests at least partly on the preemption of the term "comparative" to particular applications of the genetic method, so that diachronic linguistics has appeared already to possess its own comparative method.

Unlike the genetic and the typological methods, the classification involved in the processual approach is not one of languages but of changes. A classificatory scheme exists, although it still stands in need of systematic reformulation, namely the traditional terminology of process, since a process is simply a class of similar changes. Such rubrics as analogical change, dissimilation of liquids, and palatalization each define a class of changes, individual members of which occur in different languages and at different times. As with synchronic typologies, we may have classificatory criteria of lesser or greater breadth. Just as the class of languages with level tones only is a subset of the tonal languages, so palatalization, umlauting, and the like are subprocesses in relation to regular, conditioned sound change.

In this study, processual generalizations are not investigated in isolation from the static universals arising from the application of typological methods. Four methods of processual comparison are proposed here, and each is illustrated by an extended example. Their status as distinct methods, as will appear from later consideration, is more pragmatic than logical, but such a classification

---

[3]It should be pointed out, however, that others, notably Kroeber, accept this division in principle but claim that anthropology is basically history rather than science, without viewing this as a defect.

should prove useful in the initial stages of development. The four methods are called here the dynamicization of typologies, the dynamicization of subtypologies, intergenetic processual comparison, and intragenetic processual comparison, respectively.

Since the first of these, the dynamicization of typologies, has been discussed elsewhere, though not under the same name, it will be treated with relative brevity.[4] Consider any typology in which there are at least two nonempty classes among those defined by the typology. Then, for every pair of nonempty classes, we can ask a processual question regarding the mechanism of change of type in either direction. If, for example, a certain typology contains, among its defined classes of languages, three nonempty ones, A, B, and C, we can ask how a language of type A becomes a language of type B, how a language of type B becomes a language of type A, and so on. The number of such processual questions is evidently $n(n - 1)$, in the present instance, 6. Not all these processes need occur, however. For example, given three types A, B, and C, investigation might show that a language cannot change directly from A to C, but must first change from A to B and then from B to C. It is even theoretically possible, though in practice unlikely, that none of the classes can change into each other. Then, if there are n such classes in existence, there must be at least n protolanguages for mankind, so that no language in one type could have a common progenitor with a language of another type. The assumption of such fixity for any typological criterion is highly improbable and can be refuted in very many instances. For example, the relation of Persian, a non-sex-gender language, to Hindi, a sex-gender language, shows that change in at least one direction is possible in this instance.

A theory that states the set of changes by which a language can move from one typological class to another may be called a theory of relative origin because it applies to the origin of a specific type of language, a type that, in general, arises in a multiplicity of language families and chronological periods. To arrive at such a theory, we will have to compare diverse and historically independent examples which are themselves the results of comparative genetic studies in the ordinary sense. If a single, typical set of changes is found to occur in each instance, we may say that we have a theory of exclusive relative origin. Such theories are obviously the most

---

[4]Greenberg (1966b).

useful, but theories of multiple origin can also be useful, as will be shown later.

We may illustrate the dynamicization of typologies by means of the following example. Consider the synchronic typology in accordance with which languages are classified by the simultaneous application of two criteria, the presence or absence of nasal vowels and the presence or absence of oral vowels. There will then be four logically possible typological classes of languages: (1) oral and nasal vowels both present; (2) oral vowels present but nasal vowels absent; (3) nasal vowels present but oral vowels absent; and (4) oral and nasal vowels both absent.

Of the four classes thus defined, classes 3 and 4 are empty as far as present knowledge goes. Corresponding to this fact, we have the unrestricted universal that all languages have oral vowels, and the implicational universal that the presence of nasal vowels implies the presence of oral vowels but not vice versa. Because there are two nonempty classes, 1 and 2, we have two questions regarding relative origins. The first of these is concerned with change from class 1 to class 2: How do languages with both oral vowels and nasal vowels become languages with only oral vowels? In other words, how are nasal vowels lost? The second question relates to the manner in which languages of class 2 become languages of class 1: How do languages without nasal vowels acquire them?

We shall be chiefly concerned with this second question. Ferguson has already suggested a hypothesis in the form of the following diachronic universal. This hypothesis asserts that a nasal vowel "apart from borrowings and analogical innovations, always results from the loss of a primary nasal consonant."[5] The typical course of events is as follows. A previously oral vowel becomes nasalized nondistinctively through a preceding and/or following nasal consonant. With the loss of the nasal consonant, which is the conditioning factor, a phonological contrast between oral and nasal vowel comes into existence. Where the nasal consonant follows the vowel, the sequence of changes may be schematized as follows: $VN \rightarrow \tilde{V}N \rightarrow \tilde{V}$.

It should be noted that in such diachronic universals of exclusive relative origin, no assertion is made about the period of time in which the change takes place. Indeed, if VN remained in some language indefinitely, it would not refute this thesis. It is not even

<hr>

[5]Ferguson (1963).

refuted by the fact that, in certain languages (e.g., Polish), in certain environments (normally before stops), nasalized vowels have changed back into sequences of oral vowel + homorganic nasal consonant (e.g., $\tilde{e}b = > emb =$). All that is asserted is that, if a language has nasal vowels, at some time in its past, if their origin can be discovered, they arise from the loss of nasal consonants in the environment of nondistinctively nasalized vowels. Such universals might be considered diachronic implications, in which certain facts about a language at time t_2 imply certain other facts about the same language at time t_1, provided t_1 precedes t_2 at some unspecified interval. Since the implied is the hierarchically superior in an implication, the statement in terms of which certain facts at a specified time imply certain facts at a previous time, but not vice versa, is in accord with the historian's intuitive feeling that events of an earlier period explain those of a later period, and not the other way around.

The connection between synchronic and diachronic universals can be illustrated by showing how a specific synchronic universal about the relationship of oral and nasal vowels can be explained in the sense of logical deduction from a set of premises which includes the diachronic hypothesis of relative origin which has just been stated. For simplicity of exposition, I confine the illustration here to the situation in which nasalized vowels developed from the phonetic nasalization of oral vowels with a following nasal consonant, but what will be said is applicable *mutatis mutandis* to instances in which it precedes, or both precedes and follows.

The synchronic universal with which I am concerned is again one already stated by Ferguson and voiced still earlier by Hockett.[6] It is particularly well attested, and I know of no contrary instances. It is the thesis that the number of nasalized vowel phonemes in a language is always less than or equal to the number of oral vowels.

The most frequent situation before loss of the following nasal consonant will be that in which the set of vowels which occurs with following nasal consonants is identical with the set of vowels which occurs in all other environments. If this condition holds, then, to begin with, each oral vowel will be matched by a corresponding nasal vowel. Hence the number of oral vowels is here equal to the number of nasal vowels.

Sometimes the number of vowels which may be followed by a nasal consonant is smaller. If this condition holds, then the number

[6]Ferguson (1963), p. 46; Hockett (1955), p. 90.

of nasal vowels will, in their initial period of autonomous existence, be fewer in number than the oral vowels. On the other hand, no instance is known to me of a language in which the number of vowels which may be followed by nasal consonants is greater than that of vowels which may occur in all other environments. We may, therefore, consider that a synchronic universal asserting that the number of distinct oral vowels preceding nasal consonants is always less than or equal to the oral vowels occurring in any other environment will be another premise in deducing the universal under discussion.

To this premise we must add a further diachronic factor, namely that merger among nasal vowels seems to occur more often than merger among oral vowels. A strong statement may be cast in the form of a further diachronic hypothesis. Merger between any pair of oral vowels implies the preceding merger of the corresponding nasals if they exist. Thus in contemporary French æ̃ has become ɛ for many speakers, merging with the latter, while the corresponding oral vowels œ and ɛ have shown no such tendency. From this diachronic universal it follows that there is a mechanism that will decrease the number of nasal vowels relative to the number of oral ones, but there is none working in the opposite direction. The various generalizations just described, both synchronic and diachronic, seem sufficient as premises to deduce the synchronic universals regarding the relation of nasal to oral vowels and may, therefore, be said to explain them.

It has been noted that, in considering the problems of change of type to and from the two classes of languages under consideration, that is, those with oral but without nasal vowels, and those with both oral and nasal vowels, the two types were not, as it were, treated symmetrically. A change from the first type to the second was considered as a theory of the acquisition of nasal vowels, and from the second to the first, as a loss of the same property. In fact, it appears to be more than an artibrary terminological convention that nasality is treated as a property and nonnasality as its negation, rather than vice versa. There is an obvious phonetic justification here. On this basis a great many instances of change of type may be viewed as coming under the general heading of acquisition and loss of contingent properties, such as nasality in vowels. Usually the proportion of languages with a contingent property is a relative minority of the world's languages.

The second method to be discussed is the intensive comparison of the languages which have such a property. It thus corresponds to the method of "comparison within the type" advocated by functional theorists in the social sciences. In applying this method, we first consider such languages with a view to the formulation of synchronic universals concerning the property in question. We then "dynamicize" the results by procedures to be described later, in order to establish developmental courses of events typical of the subtype.

The example chosen to illustrate this method is a study of languages that have phonetically voiceless vowels. This type is one that occurs within a typology embracing all languages based on the criteria of presence or absence of voiced vowels and presence or absence of unvoiced vowels. In such a typology the class of languages with voiced vowels only constitutes the vast majority, the languages with both unvoiced and voiced vowels is a minority, and the class of languages with voiceless vowels only and the class without either voiced or voiceless vowels are both null. The universals associated with the parent typology are then the following: All languages have vowels. The presence of voiceless vowels implies the presence of voiced vowels.

This study, which makes no claim to exhaustiveness, deals with approximately fifty languages.[7] In most of these the feature of voicelessness in vowels is nondistinctive. There are a number of languages, however, including the Keresan languages of Santa Ana and Santo Domingo, the Shoshonean languages Comanche and Ute, Mayan Chontal and Galla, and Teso and Bagirmi in Africa, in which a phonemic contrast between voice and voiceless vowels exists.[8] On the basis of this sample, we will first seek to establish synchronic generalizations relating to voiceless vowels, and then illustrate the process of dynamicization.

[7]The sources regarding languages with voiceless vowels are enumerated in Section B of the bibliography. Footnote references to titles in this section of the bibliography are marked B. The phenomenon of voiceless vowels is probably more widespread than would appear from the literature. It is reported from every major world area. The apparent predominance of occurrence in American Indian languages is probably a by-product of the phonetic training of linguists involved in this area. It should be noted that, for certain languages listed in the bibliography, the information is too vague to be utilized for some, or even all, of the general statements proposed here, as is tacitly indicated by their omission.

[8]The existence of phonemic contrasts of voice in vowels was denied by Jakobson but asserted by Comanche specialists. On this matter see especially Canonge (1957-B). Since that time further examples have been adduced. Recently Harms (1966-B), in a binary transformationally oriented restatement of Southern Paiute phonology, has treated voicing in vowels as phonemic (I believe incorrectly).

Before proceeding further, however, some discussion of phonetic matters is called for.[9] In general, languages have been considered to have voiceless vowels if this term is used in the phonetic description; but, as will presently appear, this criterion is not entirely adequate. The problem concerns the relation between voiceless vowels and whispered vowels on the one hand, and aspiration and *h*-sounds on the other. Presumably voiceless vowels have an open glottis with the same adjustment as for voiceless consonants, while whispered vowels involve a different glottal adjustment which includes the closing of the arytonoid part of the glottis.[10] An early investigator, Harrington, in his description of Ute draws a clear distinction along these lines: "Voiceless sounds are not whispered. Whispering requires a special adjustment of the larynx."[11] It is evident, however, from some of the descriptions that many linguists consider the terms "voiceless vowels" and "whispered vowels" to be synonymous. Thus Andrzejewski, after describing four Galla vowels that "have no voicing," states that "several alternative terms could be suggested ... voiceless vowels, semi-mute vowels, or whispered vowels."[12] In regard to Bannack, Liljeblad refers to certain vowels as unvoiced, and in a passage immediately following and obviously alluding to the same sound, calls them whispered vowels.[13] Furthermore, Yamagiwa refers to vowels of Japanese which other writers have generally called voiceless as "devocalized (whispered)."[14] In view of this apparent equivalence of usage, a few instances have been included in this study; for example, Karok, for which the only source describes certain vowels as whispered. Moreoever, Holmer's description of Gosjiro, which contains the statement that " ... final short vowels are usually voiceless (or whispered) ... ," is susceptible to interpretation either as a synonymous use of the two terms, or as free variation between voiceless and whispered.[15]

---

[9]I am particularly indebted to Paul Postal for several comments regarding voiceless vowels raised during the discussion of this paper as given orally at the 1966 Linguistic Institute at the University of California, Los Angeles.

[10]Smalley (1962), especially pp. 392-393 and the accompanying tapes. The study reported in Lehiste (1964), pp. 150-159, supports the acoustic distinctness of *h* and whispered vowels in American English.

[11]Harrington (1910-B), p. 22.

[12]Andrzejewski (1957-B), p. 264

[13]Liljeblad (1950-B), p. 130.

[14]Yamagiwa (1942-B), p. 2.

[15]Holmer (1949-B), p. 51. Also the remarks of Heffner (1964), p. 85, indicate the precariousness of the distinction.

In contrast to *h*-sounds, voiceless vowels should theoretically show a lack of glottal friction. And, indeed, several sources indicate phonetic differences along this line. For example, Chontal Mayan is stated to have final segments of vowels in the utterance-final position containing "light aspiration." The same phonetic symbolization is employed here as for vowels in medial position explicitly stated to be unvoiced. It is then stated that "this aspiration is much lighter than that which is interpretated as phonemic *h*."[16] In Kaiwa, aspiration and devoicing are stated to be in free variation in final unaccented syllables. They are thus treated as being distinct phonetically. A further statement concerns Cayuvava in which "voiceless trailoff" of a vowel is called "slight aspiration." Further, "this aspiration differs markedly in quality and distribution from the sound that is interpreted as phonemic *h*. It is more lenis and does not have the friction of the *h*."[17]

It is well known, however, that *h* as a phonetic symbol is frequently used to represent voiceless vowels of the same quality as adjacent voiced vowel segments. In this instance the difference is purely distributional. Such a view is clearly expressed by Lounsbury in reference to Oneida. "Voiceless vowels are assigned to the |h| phoneme in those positions in which their vowel color is environmentally determined but their voicelessness is not. They are assigned to the respective vowel phonemes in those cases ... in which their voicelessness is environmentally determined but their vowel color is not."[18]

It we conclude, as appears necessary, that sounds assigned to the |h| phoneme in some languages in existing descriptions are, in fact, voiceless vocalic segments, then there are four possible cases: (1) Vowel color is predictable but voicelessness is not. Here we have *h*. (2) Vowel color is not predictable but voicelessness is. These are nonphonemic voiceless vowels of the quality of the corresponding voiced segments. (3) Neither vowel color nor voicing is predictable. Such segments are likewise considered voiceless vowels but phonemically distinct from their voiced counterparts, as is true of Comanche. (4) Both voicelessness and vowel color are predictable, as is true in Secoya, a language in which strongly stressed vowels have a voiceless final mora which is of the same quality as the initial voiced portion, and which only appears as a free variant before

[16]Keller (1959-B), p. 45.
[17]Key (1961-B), p. 146.
[18]Lounsbury (1953-B), p. 30n.

a following voiceless consonant. Such a voiceless vowel segment is to be considered an *h* because its quality is predictable, and in traditional phonemic analysis it is eliminated as nonphonemic.

We have chosen as our definitional feature for voiceless vowel, as distinct from *h*, absence of predictability of vowel quality from an immediately adjacent voiced vowel segment.[19] Wherever this condition does not hold, we do not consider the sound in question to be a voiceless vowel, unless there is an explicit indication of phonetic difference from an *h* in the same language. On this basis only one instance in which the existing description specifies a voiceless vowel has been eliminated from the sample, namely, that of Secoya, just mentioned. It seems likely that, because the voiceless vowel segment in this language is always followed by a voiceless consonant, this example is to be assimilated to that of preaspirated consonants which are always unvoiced and medial.

The consistent application of this criterion eliminates one possible universal, namely, that which would assert that the existence of voicelessness in the initial portion of a vocoid implies its presence throughout the segment. What would be forbidden by this statement would include sequences of the type *a̯a*. These do occur but are everywhere analyzed as *ha* in practice and according to the above definition. The universals proposed here are valid, to my knowledge, for the sample considered here and do not rest on the unlawfulness of combinations that occur phonetically, but are to be analyzed as containing occurrences of segments labeled *h* according to the present definition.

We turn now to a consideration of synchronic universals relating to voiceless vowels. Basically we are looking for hierarchical preferences regarding properties associated with voiceless vowels. These may be properties pertaining to the voiceless vowel segments themselves, to sequential characteristics, or to prosodic features over longer stretches. For example, among the present results, preference for low stress over high stress refers to properties of the voiceless segments as such, the preference for adjoining voiceless

[19]On the basis of this definition, voiceless segments constituting "echo" vowels after the glottal stop are considered voiceless vowels because they are not immediately adjacent to the voiced vowel with which they agree in quality. Huasteco, in which there is only terminal unvoicing of the vowel segment, is considered to have voiceless vowels for present purposes, as these sounds are stated to be less fortis than the *h* that occurs in the language (Larsen and Pike, 1949-B, p. 275). For the merely heuristic value of the present definition, see note 66, below.

consonants is sequential, while that for voicelessness of the final vowel in a statement over a question intonation is prosodic. These synchronic results are summarized in a series of numbered universals, each of which is accompanied by discussion of the supporting evidence.

The first set which, in accordance with the foregoing division, refers to features simultaneous with vocalic voicelessness, has as a common motif the preference of voiceless vowels for nonculminative features, that is, weak stress, short length, and low pitch. By culminative features are meant those that figure in rules of the following type, taking stress as an example. Every phonological word has exactly one occurrence of strong stress. No such rules seem to exist for the opposite, nonculminative feature. Thus there is no language in which every word has one and only one weak stress.

1. In languages with stress, every vocalic segment that is voiceless has the weakest degree of stress.

There are explicit statements regarding the co-occurrence of the weakest stress with all voiceless vowels for the following languages: Acoma, Chama, Comanche, Dagut, Kaiwa, Nyangumata, Oneida, Papago, Southern Paiute, Tadjik, Tunica, Uzbek, and Yana. Arizona Tewa, Bagirmi, Galla, Japanese, and Teso are tonal or tonal accentual, and they are not described as possessing stress phenomena. The Yaitepec dialect of Chatino, the only one with voiceless vowels, is a tonal language with automatic stress on the final syllable. The rules are so stated that the vowel of this stressed syllable cannot be voiceless. For Totonac and Korean, neither stress nor tone is mentioned.

Cayuvava, which has been included in the sample on the strength of the statement quoted earlier that the voiceless vowel is distinct from the stronger aspiration of a true *h*, has certain occurrences of the voiceless vowel as the terminal portion of a stressed syllabic. The transcription is neutral regarding the participation in stress of the voiceless portion. There are a number of languages in which the rules as stated do not necessarily exclude stress in voiceless vowels. Nowhere, however, in the literature examined was there an example cited in which a voiceless vowel is unambiguously marked as stressed. The above generalization is considered highly probable on this basis. The absence of stress on voiceless vowels may, of course, rest merely on the physical impossibility of a voiceless vowel having sufficient prominence to produce the acoustic impression of stress.

2. *In languages with distinctive vowel length, the existence of voiceless long vowels implies that of voiceless short vowels but not vice versa.*

For a number of languages with distinctive vowel length, there are explicit or easily deducible statements regarding the nonoccurrence of voiceless long vowels. These include Bannack, Comanche, Galla, Goajiro, Japanese, Karok, Nyangumata, Oneida, Santa Ana, Southern Paiute, Tadjik, and Yana. In other cases there is no statement explicitly denying their existence, but no examples are cited. In Acoma there is a cited example of a voiceless long vowel. For all the languages with vowel quantity, however, the presence of short voiceless vowels is well attested; hence, the above implication holds. Unlike stress, there is no question of physical impossibility, as shown by the Acoma example.

We would correspondingly expect voicelessness to be favored for low-pitched, as against high-pitched, vowels. Because few of the languages with voiceless vowels are pitch languages, the evidence is necessarily limited. In view of the close relation between voicelessness and whisper in vowels, alluded to above, we have a phonetic issue closely allied to the much-discussed question regarding the preservation of distinctive pitch in whispered speech. There is a corresponding difference of opinion in the literature on the present topic. Thus McKaughan mentions voiceless allophones of *i* and *u* in Chatino "whose tone registers (if indeed they exist), have not been discovered."[20] In regard to Arizona Tewa, it is stated that, when a vowel or vowel cluster is completely devoiced, it has no tone.[21] On the other hand, Tucker and Bryan give tone markings for all three levels found in the languages for the voiceless vowels of Galla, Teso, and Bagirmi. What evidence there is wholly favors low pitch over high pitch for voiceless vowels, as exemplified most clearly in Japanese, for which Han says that the "vowels *i* and *u* in low pitched *onsetsu* are regularly unvoiced between voiceless consonants."[22] For Cheyenne, it is stated that single short vowels not

---

[20]McKaughan (1954-B), p. 27.

[21]Yegerlehner (1959-B), p. 5.

[22]Han (1962-B), p. 51. Compare also the statement of Doke (1931-B), p. 33: "A common occurrence in the Bantu languages is the devocalization (almost whispering) of final vowels, particularly *i*, when the tone in careful pronunciation would be a very low one." Trager (1940-B), p. 29, describes the final vowel in Serbo-Croatian disyllables with falling accent pattern and hence low final pitch as "very weak — often voiceless."

characterized by high pitch are voiceless in final position.[23] In other languages, for example, Karok and Chama, the unstressed vowels that are voiceless are stated to have low pitch as a concomitant feature. Such linguistic evidence appears definite enough to support the following statement:

3. *If any language has high-pitched voiceless vowels, it has low-pitched voiceless vowels.*

We now consider the quality of voiceless vowels.

4. *To every voiceless vowel in any language there is a corresponding voiced vowel of the same quality, but not necessarily vice versa.*

This statement implies that the number of voiceless vowels never exceeds the number of voiced vowels in any language, and parallels the relationship of nasal to oral vowels. The present statement is, however, stronger in that one fairly commonly finds nasal vowels that do not match any oral vowel in quality, whereas in our sample every voiceless vowel can be matched by a voiced vowel of the same quality.

5. *The existence of voiceless vowels of less than the maximal degree of vowel height implies the existence of some vowels of the maximal degree.*

The favoring of high vowels with regard to voicelessness is apparent in table 1, which includes all the languages of the present sample in which voiceless vowels do not occur with all the qualities of voiced vowels.

[23]Davis (1962-B), p. 36. The inference here is that low-pitched final short vowels have *become* voiceless. There is no indication that these voiceless vowels have distinguishable pitch.

TABLE 1
HIGH VOWELS AND VOICELESSNESS

Language	Voiceless and voiced	Voiced only
Awadhi	*i, u, e*	*a, o*
Campa	*i*	*o, e, a*
Chatino	*i, u*	*o, e, a*
Dagur	*i, u, e*°	*o, a*
Huichol	*i, ʌ, e*°°	*u, a*
Serbo-Croatian	*i, u*†	*o, e, a*
Tadjik	*i, u, a*	*e(:), o(:), ú(:)*‡
Tunica	*u*	*i, e, ɛ, a, ɔ, o*
Uzbek	*i, u*	*e, ɔ, o, a*

°I follow Martin's symbolization here; *e* is phonetically [ə].

°°Huichol /ʌ/ is described as a high, central, unrounded vowel in McIntosh (1945-B).

†Trager (1940-B) seems to imply, however, that all Serbo-Croatian vowels may be voiceless under certain accentual conditions.

‡Since the investigations of Polivanov, it has become customary to categorize the Tadjik vowels *e, o, ú* as stable in contrast to *i, u,* and *a,* which are categorized as unstable. Traditionally the former were considered long, and the latter, short; and the comparative evidence suggests that this was formerly true phonetically. The stable vowels do not differ in length from the unstable in stressed syllables. In unstressed syllables the unstable vowels are subject to voicelessness in an unvoiced consonantal environment and quantitative reduction or loss in general, while the stable vowels are only slightly shorter than in stressed syllables. We may conjecture that the unstable vowels became voiceless in a period when the phonetic distinction was still one of length in all environments.

Additional evidence for the favoring of high vowels can be found in some instances in which voiceless vowels exist with all the same qualities as voiced. In Japanese and Papago, the high vowels are devoiced in a more extensive set of environments than low vowels. Regarding Japanese, Gensen Mori states that "... *a* is subject to devocalization in a lesser degree than *i* or *u*. Those who regularly devocalize *i* and *u* in certain positions will not always do the same with *a*."[24] For Comanche and Nyangumata there are explicit statements that the lowest vowel *a* is much more rarely devoiced than the others. In Shawnee, of the four vowels *i, e, a* and *o*, all of which are pausally devoiced, only *i* exerts a further regressive force in devoicing a vowel of the preceding syllable under certain conditions.

We now consider some environmental limitations on the appearance of voiceless vowels.

[24]Mori (1929-B), p. 41.

6. Every voiceless vowel is either preceded or followed by silence or a voiceless plain (i.e., nonglottalic) sound.

For example, no voiceless vowel occurs between two voiced consonants. In some languages the stronger statement holds that every voiceless vowel is both preceded and followed by a voiceless plain sound or silence. Silence almost always follows, rather than precedes, because, as will be shown later, a favorite position for voiceless vowels is utterance final, while occurrences in utterance, or indeed in word initial are excessively rare.[25] Among the languages for which this stronger statement holds are: Acoma, Cayuvava, Chama, Chatino, Chontal, Comanche, Huasteco, Japanese, Nyangumata, Pame, Serbo-Croatian, Tadjik, Tunica, Ute, and Yana.[26] In some of these languages, voiceless allophones of otherwise voiced nasals, liquids, and semivowels are found adjacent to voiceless vowels.

The preceding statement also excludes the occurrence of voiceless vowels flanked by two glottalized consonants, glottal stop and glottalized consonant, voiced consonant and glottalized consonant, or voiced consonant and glottal stop. There is additional evidence regarding the disfavoring of voiceless vowels adjacent to glottalic sounds. In Acoma only plain consonants occur before final unvoiced vowels, and nonfinal vowels are devoiced only when neither preceded nor followed by glottalic consonants.[27] In Chatino *i* and *u* are unvoiced in unstressed syllables, provided the following consonant is not a glottal stop. In Papago *i* and *i̵* are voiceless in pause, except after a laryngeal. In Southern Paiute after a glottal stop preceded by a vowel, a final vowel is said to be only partly reduced in voice, becoming a "murmured" vowel.

The tendency of vowels to voicelessness is particularly powerful in the final of words and of longer units such as sentence or utterance. For many of the languages, voiceless vowels can only occur in the final position of some such unit. Thus, in the following languages, voiceless vowels appear only in the final position of utterance, sentence, or some extensive intonational contour: Arabela, Arizona Tewa, Basque, Galla, Hawaiian, Huichol, Ignaciana,

---

[25]The only examples encountered were in Southern Paiute.

[26]It is not clear from Harrington's description whether voiced consonants occur adjacent to voiceless vowels in Ute.

[27]More precisely, a final vowel can be devoiced only if the preceding consonant is a plain aspirated occlusive or /h/. A short, unaccented vowel that does not come after the last accent is optionally devoiced if it is preceded and followed by plain obstruents (Miller, 1965-B, pp. 16-17).

Kaiwa, Karok, Maori, Nyangumata, Oneida, Shawnee, Tunica, and Yana. Languages such as Shawnee, in which voicelessness extends to nonfinal vowel under specified conditions and only when the final vowel is itself voiceless, have been included here.

In most of the languages of the foregoing list, there are further limitations, so that finals are unvoiced only under certain conditions. These limitations are usually in terms of variables already mentioned. For example, in some languages only unstressed final vowels are devoiced, or only high final vowels, and so on. For another considerable group of languages, voiceless vowels occur only in the word-final position, thus embracing a fortiori final position in longer units. These include Bagirmi, Bannack, Campa, Chama, Cofan, Huasteco, Serbo-Croatian, Teso, and Totonac. Most of the remaining languages of the sample have voiceless vowels in both word-medial and word-final positions. Where they do, final occurrences are more frequent, sometimes overwhelmingly so. There are, however, four languages, Mayan Chontal, Chatino, Tadjik, and possibly Japanese,[28] in which voiceless vowels occur in initial and medial position, but not in word-final position. Chatino and Tadjik share the feature of regular final stress, and it has been seen that voicelessness is incompatible with loud stress. Mayan Chontal has most commonly, but not exclusively, final stress. Japanese will be considered later for its methodological interest. For the moment, we consider it a possible exception to the following generalization.

7. *If a language does not regularly have high stress on the word-final syllabics, then, if it has voiceless vowels in word initial, it has them in word medial; if in word medial, then in word final; if in word final, then in the final of some longer unit or units such as an intonational contour, sentence, or utterance.*

The disfavoring of laryngeal sounds, including the glottal stop in the environment of voiceless vowels, was discussed earlier. In sentence-final position, a special relationship of opposition sometimes exists between glottalization and voicelessness. For example, in Chama "the plain glottal stop distinguishes the open juncture terminally when it is preceded by a primary stressed vowel or when the final vowel is not unvoiced under weak stress."[29] In other words, a final, unstressed vowel varies between voicelessness and voicing

[28]Japanese is included on the basis of Bloch's analysis; however, some earlier accounts indicate the presence of voiceless vowels in word final, e.g., Lange (1903), p. xvii.

[29]Firestone (1955-B), p. 53.

followed by the glottal stop. In Arabela, a nondistinctive glottal stop appears in most sentence finals and is incompatible with voiceless-ness of the preceding vowel. In Karok, whereas a short final vowel is optionally devoiced, a long vowel is voiced and glottalized. In Bannack, final unstressed vowels vary freely between voiceless-ness and voicing. In the latter instance, the preceding consonant is glottalized. In Oneida, in pause a final glottal stop is lost, and the preceding, now final, vowel becomes voiceless. In some instances, the two alternatives of voicelessness and glottal closure are con-nected with types of sentence intonation. In Nyangumata, in which most sentences end in voiceless vowels, glottalization occurs in place of voicelessness most commonly in questions and accompa-nied by rising intonation. In Walapai, there is a similar opposition, though without concomitant glottalization. Terminal statement juncture has decrease in stress, pitch, and voicing. Question final juncture is characterized by a sharp rise in pitch and amplitude, and there is no devoicing. A parallel situation exists in Galla. Those short, final vowels that are subject to voicelessness have this characteristic in statement-final position but keep their voicing in the corresponding yes-no question. Those short final vowels that are not subject to devoicing retain it in statements and are replaced by the paired long vowel in the corresponding yes-no question. In Mikasuki, a Muskoghean language without voiceless vowels, "the glottal catch occurs most frequently with questions of the type 'Is it a _____ ?' and 'Is he ____ ing?,' in which a tone change often combines with glottal catch to change a statement to a question."[30] The further observation is made that a terminal vowel with falling tone indicates "rest" or "completion," while level tone with fol-lowing glottal stop indicates "nonfinality." These phenomena are evidently allied with the "rhetorical lengthening" described by Sapir for Southern Paiute. "Final vowels, instead of being elided or unvoiced, are sometime, for reasons of rhetorical emphasis, lengthened and generally followed by a glottal stop."[31]

Just as the preferred position for voiceless vowels is final, so that for glottal stop is initial. The existence of glottal attack for the vocalic sentence-initial or word-initial position is a well-known phenomenon. A particularly striking example in the present sample is Totonac, in which all word-initial vowels are laryngealized, and all sentence-final short vowels are voiceless. Corresponding to the

[30]West (1962), p. 86.
[31]Sapir (1930-B), pp. 20-21.

preference of voiceless vowels for nonculminative prosodic elements is the widely reported occurrence of glottal accent in which
glottalization fulfills the function of a culminative pitch accent.
This complex of oppositions is diagramed in table 2. The manifold
connections involved in table 2 suggest a number of possible universals. In the present connection, only those involving voicelessness are considered. The connections between voicelessness and
final position, and weak stress and shortness in vowels have already
been stated. The following additional universal holds on the basis
of the evidence just cited.

TABLE 2

COMPLEX OF OPPOSITIONS BETWEEN VOICELESS VOWELS
AND GLOTTAL STOPS

Marked	Unmarked
Initial	Final
Glottalization	Voicelessness
Question	Statement
Emphatic statement	Normal statement
Rising pitch	Falling pitch
Strong stress	Weak stress
Vowel length	Vowel shortness

8. *The presence of voiceless vowels in the final of yes-no questions implies their presence in the corresponding statements.*

As a final observation concerning synchronic generalizations
about voiceless vowels, it may be pointed out that in Yana voiceless
vowels occur in "woman's speech" but not in "men's speech."
What is meant here by woman's speech is that of women talking to
women, men to women, or women to men. Men's speech comprises
only those instances in which men speak to men.

Thus far, the method of subtypologies has been applied in a
purely synchronic manner. Comparison of a set of languages containing voiceless vowels has led to the formulation of a number of
synchronic universals concerning them; however, every implication in which both the implying and implied have empirical exemplification can be mapped into a diachronic process by which the
former develops from the latter. For example, from the synchronic
universal that voiceless vowels of lower tongue heights imply those
of the highest tongue height, we can frame the hypothesis that voice-

lessness in vowels begins with those of the highest level and then spreads to the others. This statement is a hypothesis, because there is nothing contradictory involved in the assumption that in some languages only the high vowels become voiceless, while in others all of the vowels become voiceless through a single change. What is excluded, though, is the hypothesis that low vowels are the first to become voiceless and that voicelessness subsequently spreads to high vowels. If this latter statement were so, such languages in the initial stages would have low voiceless vowels without having high ones and thus contradict the original hypothesis.

The revelance of the proviso that both implier and implied must have empirical exemplification can be shown by reference to the universal regarding stressed and unstressed voiceless vowels. The implication that every language with stressed voiceless vowels has unstressed voiceless vowels holds. There are, as has been seen, no authenticated examples of stressed voiceless vowels. Hence we cannot hypothesize that languages first have unstressed voiceless vowels, and that voicelessness then extends to stressed vowels because this, as a limiting case, is a hypothetical stage that is never reached.

Purely synchronic evidence can be relevant in demonstrating that the hypothesized succession does take place. There are, here, two assumptions which, for phonological change at least, receive considerable support outside of the present examples. The first of these is that, whenever a sound change takes place, the older form and the innovating form are, for a period of time, in free variation, with the innovating free variant increasing in frequency until the change is accomplished. Hence, if in one environment variation is free, while in another complimentary distribution shows that the change has been accomplished, change in the first environment must be more recent. The other assumption has to do with style. The situation is no doubt more complex than the mere coexistence of two styles, lento and allegro; however, it is only in reference to this distinction that a large body of data exists which can be exploited for theoretical purposes. There is much evidence in the area of phonology which shows that the allegro form is the innovating form which only later spreads to the lento style. Both the free variation and style assumptions can be neatly documented from the detailed observations regarding voicelessness in Japanese vowels made by Bloch and summarized in table 3.

TABLE 3

FREE VARIATION AND STYLE ASSUMPTIONS

Vowel type	Speech style	
	Lento	Allegro
Low	a	$a > A$
High	$I < i$	$I > i$

Here, a, A, i, and I represent voiced low vowels, voiceless low vowels, voiced high vowels, and voiceless high vowels, respectively. The symbol $>$ means "more frequent than," and $<$ means "less frequent than."

The information in table 3 may be stated as follows: The voiceless high vowels are more frequent than voiced high vowels in allegro, less frequent in lento. The low vowels are voiced only in lento. They occur in allegro; but, unlike the high vowels, the voiceless variants are less frequent than the voiced. We may translate these assertions into dynamic terms as follows: The high vowels have progressed further in becoming voiceless than the low vowels, inasmuch as they have penetrated into lento from allegro, although they are still less frequent in the former style than the latter. The voiceless low vowels have not yet penetrated the lento style, and even in the allegro style, unlike the voiceless high vowels, they are still less frequent than their voiced variant.

Note that these data constitute an empirical confirmation of the thesis that innovations first appear in allegro, then in lento. The hypothesis arrived at independently of the present evidence from a variety of languages was that voicelessness in vowels could not begin with low vowel because such a beginning would produce, in the first stages, a nonexistent language type. Had, for example, low vowels in voiceless form been found in lento but not in allegro, or had low voiceless vowels been more frequent than their voiced correlates in either lento or allegro, while the reverse held for high vowels, our thesis about the relation between lento and allegro styles would have been empirically refuted.

In these instances, in which the nonpreferred or implicating state is not known to exist, we must construct our historical theory in such a manner that we do not assume its existence at any stage.

Thus, as was pointed out earlier, the language state mentioned in the *implicans* of the universal that stressed voiceless vowels imply unstressed voiceless vowels has no empirical realization. As far as appears from the present materials at least, there are no instances of stressed voiceless vowels. An application of this principle can be made in Southern Paiute. In this language internal evidence shows that an original system of high stress in alternate syllables existed before the unvoicing of certain vowels. Stress is now found in the syllable preceding that of the voiceless vowel in those instances where the general rule would predict a stress on the voiceless vowel. It is evidently inadmissible here to posit the following sequence of events: voiced stressed vowel, unvoiced stressed vowel, shift of high stress to preceding syllable leaving the voiceless vowel with low stress. We must rather posit a simultaneous change in stress and voicing, so that the historical sequence is that a voiced, high stressed vowel becomes an unvoiced, low stressed vowel, and the stress moves back to the preceding syllable. In such instances, we may talk of correlated changes, that is, of unvoicing with simultaneous change from high to low stress in vowels.

Since the aim of this study is primarily methodological, I do not propose to treat all of the changes in unstressed vowels which may be investigated by means of comparison within the subtype of languages with voiceless vowels. In addition to those already mentioned, it is of interest to note the existence of evidence in the form of free and style variation that voiceless vowels tend to be replaced by zero (i.e., lost). In Shoshone, voiceless vowels maintained in careful speech (i.e., lento) are suppressed in ordinary conversational style, whether intervocalic or final.[32] In North Carolina Cherokee, without reference to style difference, vowels preceding phrase boundary are often "whispered or dropped."[33] In Goajiro, they are "whispered and eventually suppressed."[34] In Dagur, the vowels subject to unvoicing (*i, u, e*) "often seem to disappear, especially in rapid speech."[35] As noted by Gensen Mori for Japanese, "from devocalization to complete elimination is but a single step."[36] According to Yamagiwa, once more in reference to Japanese, "*i* and *u*

[32]Shimkin (1949-B), p. 175.
[33]Bender and Harris (1945-B), p. 17.
[34]Holmer (1949-B), p. 49.
[35]Martin (1961-B), p. 16.
[36]Mori (1929-B), p. 22.

are often 'devocalized' (whispered) or lost between two voiceless consonants."[37]

In Cheyenne, a voiceless front vowel following *t, s, š, m, n,* or *w* is "very unstable." Forms that in careful speech contain a vowel in this position often lose the vowel in rapid speech. This loss is normally accompanied by a compensatory lengthening of the previous consonant, for example, *néše~něs·.*[38]

It was noted earlier that Japanese was the only language that constituted an exception to the universal according to which languages with voiceless vowels in word-medial position also possess them in word-final position. In view of the evidence just cited regarding the tendency to loss of voiceless vowels, the explanation is now evident. Voiceless *i* and *u* formerly existed in word final but have already been lost precisely because this position is the one that is favored and the one in which they are likely to appear first.

In such forms as *x·tots·* ("one"), and *arimas·* ("is"), cited by Bloch, there is both internal evidence in the form of a distributional gap (the nonappearance of word-final *°tsu* and *°su* in Bloch's material), and external evidence from the kana orthography, of the loss of final *u* after an unvoiced consonant. Bloch gives *hatš·* ("eight") as an allegro form in alternation with *hatši.* That these final vowels were formerly devoiced is made likely by the coincidence of the conditioning factor with that operative in word medial in present free variations, and from the earlier observation of Gensen Mori regarding devoicing, particularly of *u,* "at the termination of a breath-group." Moreover, Mori gives examples like *moši* and *mainitši.* For a still earlier period, R. Lange observes that "final *ssu* usually loses the vowel and becomes *ss,* and the vowel in final *tsu, shi,* and *chi* is barely audible."[39] It may be noted that the consonantal length specified by Bloch in instances where a following voiceless vowel has been lost is exactly parallel to the situation in Cheyenne already referred to.

As can be seen in Japanese, the true regularity lies in the dynamic tendency rather than in the static situation. It is not merely that an exception is "explained" by reference to historical process. The implication is that the valid generalization pertains to the form and the conditions in which a historical change occurs.

---

[37]Yamagiwa (1942-B), p. 2.
[38]Davis (1962-B), p. 36.
[39]Lange (1903-B), p. x.

Reverting to the tendency to loss of voiceless vowels, the suggestion may be advanced that, in many historical instances of loss of vowels, there was, in fact, a period of voicelessness which could not find expression in the orthography. A number of conditions fit quite exactly. The greater tendency of final vowels, unstressed vowels, and short vowels to loss hardly needs documentation. There is also some evidence that high vowels are more easily lost than low vowels, and such loss is a well-known phenomenon in Romance languages. Meyer-Lübke summarizes the situation regarding final vowels in the statement that "l' *a* est la plus résistante des voyelles finales."[40]

The only important respect in which a real difference seems to exist between the conditions for voicelessness in vowels and the conditions for vowel loss is in the preference for a voiceless consonantal environment for the former which does not appear in most formulations regarding vowel loss. The fact is that the rule for vowel loss in modern Japanese requires a previous voiceless consonant as a conditioning factor, and in this instance we can be sure that loss was preceded by voicelessness of the final vowel. This fact suggests that there might be two types of vowel loss: one with a stage of vowel voicelessness and another without. In some instances of final vowel loss, the preceding consonant has become voiceless. For example, in most of Slavic at least the obstruents that preceded the disappearing final *jers* ($\breve{i}$ and $\breve{u}$) appear as unvoiced in word final (e.g., *rogŭ* > *rog* > *rok*, "horn" in Russian). The *jers* would seem to be good candidates for voicelessness before loss, since it is precisely the high and shortest vowels in word final which are affected.[41] Considering the frequency of regressive spread of voicelessness, it is reasonable to assume, instead of the succession of events as described above in accordance with the usual formula, rather *rogŭ* > *rog̊ŭ* > *rog̊ŭ̥* > *rog̊* > *rok*. Since the voiceless g was lenis, it would still be distinguishable for a time from *k*, and would hence be retained in orthographies. In languages such as Serbo-Croatian, voicing could have been restored analogically from forms in which it was never lost (e.g., from *roga*, "genitive singular").

The detailed instrumental phonetic observations of Sokolova on Tadjik, however, show that whereas unstressed short vowels in

[40]Meyer-Lübke (1890-1906), I, 260.

[41]The *jers* are always lost in vowel final. They were also lost in so-called weak position word internally, that is whenever there was a full vowel (non-*jer*) in the next syllable.

an unvoiced environment varied between voicelessness and complete loss, in a voiced environment the same vowels varied between a fully voiced variant and loss, though such loss was substantially less frequent.[42] This fact perhaps indicates that under otherwise favorable conditions for vowel voicelessness this loss occurs in a voiceless consonantal environment, while loss without a stage of vocalic voicelessness takes place in a voiced consonantal environment.

Further investigation is obviously required in this instance, but the theoretical point to be made is that the vast literature of synchronic description, with its numerous instances of free and style variation, is capable of throwing important light on the phonetic nature of sound changes of the past which are only known from documentary sources. The principles involved may be illustrated by another example. Even if we had no historical evidence of an intermediate *h*-stage, in considering the correspondence of *s* in Romance and other Indo-European languages with modern Greek zero (e.g., Italian *sette*, Modern Greek *eftá*, "seven"), we should assume ($s > h >$ zero) for Greek, rather than, directly, $s >$ zero. There are well-attested instances of free variation $s \sim h$ and $h \sim$ zero in contemporary languages but apparently none of $s \sim$ zero.[43]

We may briefly compare the two methods that have been discussed up to now, the dynamicization of typologies and of subtypologies. In both we are interested in the establishment of lawful

---

[42]Sokolova (1949-B). In voiced environments, in addition to less frequent loss of unstable vowels, where these vowels are not lost, their duration is significantly greater. The greater length of vowels in voiced environments, particularly before voiced consonants, is a widely known phenomenon.

A supporting instance for the hypothesis that final vowels are more likely to be lost after unvoiced consonants may be found in the German loss of final unstressed vowel. Modern Standard German is rather irregular in this regard, but Paul noted that there was a preference for the retention of the vowel after *b*, *d*, *g*, and *z* (Paul and Stolte, 1951, p. 74).

Furthermore, Whiteley's material on Ci-miini, a dialect of Swahili, indicates that *i* and *u* have been lost before unvoiced, and not before voiced, consonants (Whiteley, 1965).

[43]Of course free variation is not the only source of internal evidence for sound change. Complementary distribution resulting from accomplished conditioned change, and morphophonemic alternations representing still older processes, are also relevant. Free variation, however, is the only internal source regarding unconditioned merger, and it also provides the most direct information about the phonetic conditions of change because there has been, as yet, no chance for intervening phonetic changes.

successions of types. This statement was not made explicitly with regard to the subtypological method but should be evident. For example, the statement that voiceless low vowels imply voiceless high vowels but not vice versa, and the dynamic evidence that there are instances in which voicelessness spreads from high to low vowels but not vice versa, can be restated in terms of typology. The language type defined by the presence of voiceless high vowels may be succeeded by the type in which all vowels may occur voiceless, but the opposite succession of types is excluded. In the subtypological method, however, the pragmatic emphasis was on the discovery of significant types and their successives based on typological comparison. In the first method, the types were treated as given, and the mechanism of change of type was investigated. A further difierence was the emphasis on the use of the comparative and direct historical approach in the first method. The origin of nasal vowels was to be investigated chiefly by comparing the results of historically independent instances of reconstruction and of historically documented examples of change. In the subtypological method, the emphasis was on the use of internal change phenomena for individual languages without essential regard for their genetic connections. In fact, both methods can be utilized for either case, for internal reconstruction with regard to nasal vowels and for the comparative study of voiceless vowels. For the latter, comparative study of the Keresan and Shoshonean languages, which has already been initiated, is a potential source of enlightenment regarding the problems considered here.[44]

The third method that will be illustrated is that of intragenetic processual comparison. Historical independent reconstructions are compared as a test of the extent to which they are mutually corroborative, and to help in the selection among mutually exclusive hypotheses in individual instances by reference to other typologically similar cases. As with the other methods with which we are concerned, the emphasis here is dynamic, that is, we compare lines of development rather than reconstructions viewed statically. It has been proposed, as a basic contribution of synchronic typology to historical linguistics, that synchronic universals serve as a touchstone for the validity of reconstructed systems.[45] And it is certainly true that a violation of principles, valid for directly documented lan-

<hr>

[44]See Davis (1966-B) and Voegelin, Voegelin, and Hale (1962-B), p. 48, for Uto-Aztecan, and Miller and Davis (1963-B) for Keresan.
[45]Cf. Jakobson (1958).

true that a violation of principles, valid for directly documented languages, precisely for an only indirectly attested language is always a suspicious circumstance which throws doubt on the reconstruction.

This criterion has been applied to Proto-Indo-European; but the question we shall ask here is not the one hitherto and quite justly asked, namely, whether the reconstructed Indo-European phonological inventory conforms to the universal norms of such systems. Instead we will ask whether the sequence of changes in the key instance of laryngals is plausible when considered with reference to other reconstructible or historically documented instances of change. A study that would illustrate this method should ideally be complete in that all instances of changes in systems of laryngals accessible to internal reconstruction, direct historical documentation, and comparative reconstruction should be included. In keeping with the present purpose, however, which is merely illustrative, a single non-Indo-European instance will be considered, that of Coptic, and only in limited detail. There will also be occasional reference to non-Coptic materials.

The Coptic data are of special interest from the methodological point of view for the following reason. They have come down to us in the form of five literary dialects, from the comparison of which it is possible to construct at least the general outlines of a Proto-Coptic. The Coptic dialects do not have laryngal consonants; but, as will be shown here, a comparative study will lead to the reconstruction of several consonants not known in existing dialects. In this instance earlier Egyptian, as written in the hieroglypic script and the structurally equivalent hieratic and later demotic, attests their actual existence where they would be postulated on the basis of Coptic, and the comparative evidence of Semitic and other Afro-Asiatic languages, as well as the transcription of Semitic words of an earlier period, gives evidence regarding their phonetic nature.

The results presented here are part of a more extensive reconstruction effort. All previous work has been in terms of tracing the Egyptian antecedents of items found in Coptic. It has doubtless been done with substantial correctness, and the changes posited here do not differ in essentials from those usually assumed. Such an independent comparison of Coptic dialects in relation to Ancient Egyptian is similar in procedure to that of Romance linguistics in relation to Classical Latin. This approach is even more justified in the present instance because of the defective and arbitrary nature of hieroglyphic and demotic orthography.

We shall be chiefly concerned with two Proto-Coptic vowels symbolized here as *ɔ́ and *ɛ, and we shall proceed by the discussion of a number of instances of correspondences among the dialects. The five standard literary dialects will be indicated by their usual abbreviations, and forms will be cited in accordance with a transcription system described in the accompanying footnote.[46]

1) SBɔ́, AA²Fá. *ɔ́

Every Coptic word has a single high stress on one of the last two syllabics. All other vowels are reduced, and in reduced position only a limited set occurs, for example, never ɔ, o, or e in any dialect in native words. When, as for example in compounds, a form with Vy or Vw diphthong occurs with low or (possibly) intermediate stress, the vowel may be lost and the y or w become syllabic. Compare, in Sḷ stɔ́j ("smell") with stì-núfə (lit. "smell-good," i.e., "perfume").

The above correspondence never occurs in word-final position, and it never occurs before certain consonantal correspondences. Examples containing 1 are:

1a) SB sɔ́n, AA²F sán ("brother"). *sɔ́n.

1b) S sɔ́tməf, B sɔ́thmɛf, AA²F sátmɛf ("to hear him"). *sɔ́tm-(ə)f.[47]

1b contains the third person masculine dependent form -(ə)f. The aspiration in Bohairic th is automatic before any sonant.

2) SBAA² á, F ɛ́. *ɔ́

Correspondence 2, unlike 1, is not restricted to nonfinal position. When nonfinal and followed by a consonant, it is limited to environments in which one of the three following consonant correspondences occurs, these being precisely the environments in which 1 is not found. These three correspondences are:

3) SBAA²F h. *h

4) SA²F h, BA x. *x

5. SBA²F š, A x. *ç

---

[46]The abbreviations used for the dialects are as follows: S, Sahidic; B, Bohairic; A, Achmimic; A², Subachmimic; F, Fayumic. The transcription is self-explanatory except for the following: The vowel symbols *epsilon* and *eta* are rendered as ɛ and e, respectively, and *omicron* and *omega* as ɔ and o. Geminate vowel writings are transcribed by length. For a justification of both of these interpretations, see Greenberg (1962). The supralinear stroke that apparently symbolizes a reduced vowel is transcribed ə . *Beta* is rendered by b, although its phonetic value seems to have been a bilabial unrounded semivowel. For a standard account of vowel changes from Egyptian to Coptic, see Steindorff (1951). What is said here regarding the development of Egyptian laryngeals is subject to the qualification that it is not impossible that larynegeals still survived in Coptic, particularly in Achmimic. On this see Till (1929).

That 1 and 2 represent the same protophoneme is shown not only from this complementary distribution but from morphophonemic alternations. No verb of the same class as *sɔ́tm(ə)f (1b above) occurs with correspondence 1 before *h, *x, and ç, but instead correspondence 2 makes its appearance. The following is an example in which 2 is followed by *h.

2a) S náhməf, BAA² náhmɛf, F néhmɛf ("to save him"). *nɔ́hm(ə)f.

All of the dialects except B have long vowels indicated orthographically by geminate vowel symbols. Long vowels occur only as the syllabic of stressed syllables, and they never appear in word-final position. Among the correspondences involving long vowels is the following:

6) SAA² á:, B á, F é:

An example of this correspondence is:

6a) SAA² ká:f, B kháf, F ké:f ("to put him").

Correspondence 6 is evidently the same as correspondence 2, except for vowel length, in those dialects in which this feature occurs. Moreoever it is found in verb forms with the same formation as that of 1b and 2a. The present example belongs more exactly to the most important class of verb stems with two consonants. It is thus parallel to the following form:

6b) S bɔ́ləf, B bɔ́lɛf, AA²F bálɛf ("to loosen him"). We therefore have reason to see here an occurrence of the protophoneme *ɔ. Moreover, it cannot be accidental that, except for length, 6 is identical with 2, the form that *ɔ takes before *h, *x, and *ç. The natural conclusion is that the same conditioning factor (i.e., a back continuant) must have been present. Note that Proto-Coptic has front continuants *s, *š, and f which do not exercise this effect. That the last conditioning factor should be voiceless is not a necessary assumption because all the reconstructed fricatives are voiceless and the distinctive features need only be fricativity and back articulation. Because, when consonants are lost, it frequently happens that the preceding vowel is lengthened, we may consider the long vowels of the dialects other than B to be the historical continuation of *ɔ plus the lost consonant. We will symbolize this consonant as H_2 and thus reconstruct 6a as *kɔ́H_2f. Further evidence for the second mora of a long vowel in 6 representing a consonant at an earlier stage is that in A, one of the Coptic dialects, a final unstressed vowel written ɛ develops after a sequence of final consonant plus sonant. For example, A has satmɛ as the qualitative (i.e., stative) of the verb "to hear" corresponding to S *sótəm* (**sót(ə)m*). A similarly has final ɛ when a long vowel precedes a sonant, for example, A *yɔ́:rɛ* ("canal") as contrasted with S *yɔ́:r*. A therefore treats the last mora of a long vowel as though it were a consonant.

It was noted earlier that the long vowels do not normally appear in word-final position; therefore, where correspondence 2 occurs in word final, we should also assume the disappearance of H_2. Hence we reconstruct the following word as *lɔH_2:

6*b*) SAA²B *lá*, F *lɛ́* ("slander").

Compare 6*c*) SA² *sáh*, AB *sáx*, F *sɛh*. *sɔx ("scribe").

The absence of vocalic length preceding word-final, as contrasted with length before word-medial, preconsonantal H_2 can be accounted for in two ways. Either $VH_2 > V$: in all environments originally and word-final long vowels were shortened, or word-final H_2, unlike medial H_2, was lost without lengthening the preceding vowel.[47]

The identify of correspondences in vowel quality between internal long vowels and final stressed vowel is not confined to correspondence 2 but is general throughout Coptic. This fact can hardly be an accident. We, therefore, interpret the pairs of internal long vowels and final stressed short vowels as representing the same vowel in each instance. Whether length in every instance results from loss of a consonant remains provisionally undecided. The evidence outlined below regarding the same vowel *ɔ, however, strongly suggests a second lost consonant.

We find another matching pair of correspondences between word interior long vowel and final short vowel as follows:

7) SAA² *ɔ́:*, B *ɔ́*, F *á*:

8) SBAA² *ɔ́#*, F *á#*

Examples of 7 and 8 are:

7*a*) SAA² *bɔ́:nɛ*, B *bɔ́ni*, F *bá:ni* ("be bad").

8*a*) SBAA² *rɔ́*, F *lá* ("mouth").

Besides the phonetic resemblance of this correspondence to 1, we have morphophonemic evidence that 8, and hence 7, must involve **ɔ́*. In the independent pronominal forms of the second and third person, we have a uniform base followed by the pronominal suffixes already quoted in 1*b* and 6*a*. This base appears before an overt consonant in the third masculine singular and elsewhere.

8*b*) S (*ə*)*ntɔ́f*, B (*ə*)*nthɔ́f*, AA²B (*ə*)*ntáf*. **(ə)ntɔ́f* ("he").

---

[47]Medial H_2 usually occurs before a following consonant. Where, however, it is intervocalic, it is normally reflected by a short (i.e., nongeminated) vowel in Coptic.

The stressed vowel here shows correspondence 1 and is, there-fore, reconstructed as $*\acute{ɔ}$. The second person feminine pronoun, however, displays a final stressed vowel with correspondence 8.

8c) SAA² (ə)ntɔ́, B (ə)nthɔ́, F (ʌ)ntá.

We therefore interpret it as containing the same vowel $*ɔ$. Since correspondence 8 differs from 2 which we interpreted in final position as $*H_2$, the consonant involved must be a different one. We symbolize it as H_1, and hence reconstruct 7a, 8a, 8b, and 8c as $*bɔ́H_1nə$, $*rɔ́H_1$, $*(ə)ntɔ́f$, and $*(ə)ntɔ́H_1$, respectively.

We now consider the front vowel corresponding to $*ɔ́$. The fol-lowing correspondence of stressed internal short vowel is frequently found:

9) SB á, AA²F $\acute{ɛ}$.

It is possible to cite at least one minimal contrast with $*ɔ$:

9a) SB bɔ́l, AF bál. $*bɔ́l$ ("outside").

9b) SB bál, AA²F bɛ́l ("eye").

We symbolize this new vowel as $*ɛ$, hence $*bɛ́l$ ("eye").

For $*ɛ$, we find a contrast between other second and third per-son suffixes and the second person feminine suffix parallel to that for $*ɔ$ cited in 8b and 8c.

10) SBAA² $\acute{ɛ}$, F é.

The pair of contrasting forms just alluded to are:

10a) SB náf, AA²F nɛ́f. $*nɛ́f$ ("to him").

10b) SBAA² nɛ́, F né ("to you [f]").

In 10a we naturally reconstruct $*ɛ́$ since it represents correspon-dence 9 as above. In view of the parallelism with (ə)ntɔ́H₁ ("you [f]"), we posit nɛ́H₁ as the protoform for 10b.

We should now expect a correspondence word internally in-volving long vowels and identical in quality with 10, representing $ɛ́H_1$, in this position as follows:

11) SAA² $\acute{ɛ}$:, B ɛ, F é:

It is in fact found, as in the following example:

11a). SAA² mɛ́:rə, B mɛ́ri, F mɛ́:ri. $*mɛ́H_1rə$. We have now found correspondences representing $*ɔ́H_2$, $*ɔ́H_1$, and $*ɛ́H_1$. We have yet to find evidence for $*ɛ́H_2$. Here there are apparently no morphophonemic clues; however, we do find another pair of corre-spondences identical in quality, one involving long vowels in word medial, the other, short stressed final vowels.

12) S á:, B á, AA²F $\acute{ɛ}$:

13) SB á#, AA²F $\acute{ɛ}$#

13a) S *máːtə*, B *máti*, AA² *méːtɛ*, F *méːti*. *méH₂tə ("to reach").

13b) S *wá*, AA²F *wɛ* ("one"). *wɛH₂.

Several observations, however, are to be made regarding 12 and 13. It will be noted that 13 is, in fact, identical with 9, and 12 is also identical with 9, except for vowel length. Thus, *ɛ, unlike *ɔ, does not show special protoallophones before those back fricatives that survive in the existing dialects. Hence it is not surprising that before presumed H_2 it only shows length in word medial and is identical in word final. The other observation to be made is that examples of 13 are difficult to find and the one cited was probably, as shown by Bohairic *wai*, not word final. This form should probably be reconstructed as *wɛH₂jə. The rarity of H_2 in word final suggests that perhaps **H₂#* > **H₁#* at an earlier stage. With this reservation, as indicated by parentheses, the results thus far are summarized in table 4.

TABLE 4

SUMMARY OF CONSTRUCTED PROTO-COPTIC FORMS

Reconstructed protoform	Corresponding forms in existing dialects					Remarks
	S	B	A	A²	F	
**ɔ́*	ɔ́	ɔ́	á	á	á	Except before *h*, *x*, *ç*, and *H*
**ɔ́H₂#*	á	á	é	é	é	Before unvoiced back fricatives as well as before $H_2#$
**ɔ́H₂*	áː	áː	éː	éː	éː	
**ɔ́H₁#*	ɔ́	ɔ́	ɔ́	ɔ́	á	
**ɔ́H₁*	ɔ́ː	ɔ́ː	ɔ́ː	ɔ́ː	áː	
**ɛ́*	á	á	é	é	é	
(**ɛ́H₂#*)	(á)	(á)	(é)	(é)	(é)	
**ɛ́H₂*	áː	áː	éː	éː	éː	
**ɛ́H₁#*	é	é	é	é	é	
**ɛ́H₁*	éː	éː	éː	éː	éː	

We now consider evidence for the existence and identity of H_1 and H_2 when not immediately following a stressed vowel. In post-stressed syllables, which are always final syllables, only one vowel phoneme is reconstructible. It appears as *ɛ̧* or *ə* (the supralinear stroke) when followed by final consonant, and as SAA² *ɛ*, BF *i*, when immediately followed by word boundary. In both instances in the earlier examples it is symbolized as *ə. There is evidently no chance of distinguishing H_1 from H_2 in this position.[48]

In prestressed position, a considerable variety of correspondences is found involving absence of vowel, or differing patterns of occurrences of a or ε. In addition we find unstressed i and u which can be shown to represent syllabic forms of j and w in reduced syllables. Earlier the example of S stɔ́j ("smell") and stì-núfe ("smell-good," i.e., "perfume") was cited. We may add here S hɔ́w‚ ("day") as compared with hù-mísə ("birthday," lit. "day of birth"). There are also instances of liquids and nasals in reduced forms, that is, preceded by the supralinear stroke here transcribed ə. In such instances, some scholars interpret ər as syllabic r, and analogously for other liquids and nasals.[49] An example is S sor ("to scatter") as an independent verbal form, and the reduced form sə̀r- (interpreted by some as phonetically sr̩̀-) with the following nominal object.

Where in prestressed syllables there is evidence for H_1 or H_2, we find a reduced vowel appearing as a and ε in different dialects in a variety of patterns not yet fully accounted for. That, however, a reduced vowel followed by H_2^- may appear as a in all dialects is shown by the verbal forms with final stem H_2. Thus, parallel to such alternations as S sór ("to scatter"), sɔ́r-əf ("to scatter him"), sə̀r- ("to scatter [something]"), we have S jó ("to wash"); já:f ("to wash him"); jà- ("to wash [something]"). The second of these, já:f, shows correspondence 6 as indicated by its form in other dialects, and is, therefore, to be reconstructed as *jɔ́H₂f. Hence jà-, which takes this form in all the dialects, goes back to j(ə̀)H₂-. We shall number this correspondence 14.

14) SBAA²F a (with low or secondary stress).

At this point we resort to the causative formations with prefixed t- to give us information regarding the reflexes of H_1 and H_2 in prestressed syllables. A verb such as *çópə ("to become") has a causative which, on the basis of correspondences previously cited, is tçp ɔ́H₁. Hence, when we find SB ašáj, AA²F ašéj ("to be many"), alongside its causative SBAA² taš ɔ́‚ F tašá, we may, in conformity with our interpretation of ja- with vowel correspondence 14 as j(ə)H₂, reconstruct *(ə)H₂šéj and *t(ə)H₂šɔ́H₁‚ respectively. A different correspondence, 15, is found in other causatives:

---

[48]However, as Polotsky (1939) shows, H_2 is under certain statistically rare conditions reflected as Fayumic c instead of i.

[49]On this point see Till (1951) and the literature cited there.

15) SBF a, AA^2 ϵ

An example is SB $tak\acute{o}$, AA^2 $t\epsilon k\acute{o}$, F $tak\acute{a}$ ("to destroy"), for which the simplex does not exist in Coptic. Since nonlaryngeals have either zero or the supralinear stroke ∂, it seems reasonable to attribute this correspondence to our missing H_1. Hence we posit $^*t(\partial)H_1k\acute{o}H_1$ in this and similar instances.

All verbs that appear in noncausatives with initial vowel without preceding consonant, when they have causatives, show either 14 or 15 in the initial syllable. Thus S $\acute{o}n(\partial)h$ ("to live") has the causative in S $tanh\acute{o}$, in which the initial syllable shows correspondence 14. Hence it seems reasonable to reconstruct the simplex as $H_2\acute{o}n(\partial)x$, and the hypothetical noncausative of $^*t(\partial)H_1k\acute{o}H_1$ ("to destroy") as $^*H_1\acute{o}k$ ("to perish"). Evidently initial H_1 or H_2 is lost before a stressed vowel.

Since we may consider the specific set of verbs which have a t- causative as a reasonable sample of Coptic verbs, the fact that every verb with initial stressed vowel in Coptic displays reflexes of either H_1 or H_2 when it has a t- causative leads to the conclusion that all initial stressed vowels in Coptic formerly had H initially; but, of course, where no alternation exists we can only reconstruct with a cover symbol H because we cannot tell which of the two it is.

Because, in the form $^*(\partial)H_2\check{s}\acute{e}j$ ("to be many"), H_2 appears as correspondence 14, we may expect examples of 15 in similar position to reflect $(\partial)H_1CV\ldots$; as in the following examples:

15a) SB $aw\acute{a}n$, AA^2 $\epsilon w\acute{e}n$, F $aw\acute{e}n$ ("color").

We accordingly reconstruct $^*(\partial)H_1w\acute{e}n$.

A further fairly common initial unstressed vowel correspondence preceding $C\acute{V}\ldots$ is the following:

16) SBAA^{2}F ϵ

as is found, for example, in

16a) SBAA^{2}F $\epsilon s\acute{e}t$ ("ground").

Because we have not accounted for initial sequences in which the laryngeal is in the second position and have seen that before an initial stressed vowel H is simply zero, we may suspect that 16a represents an earlier $^*(\partial)sH\acute{e}t$. Here again, before a stressed vowel there is no way in the absence of alternations to decide between H_1 and H_2. Evidently H_1 and H_2 may modify the quality and length of preceding vowels but exercise no such effect on the succeeding vowel.

We have gone about as far as it is possible to go on Coptic alone. The reconstructed units symbolized here as H_1 and H_2 appear consistently in earlier Egyptian as consonants that can be considered phonetically a glottal stop (ʔ) and voiced pharyngeal (‘), respectively.[50] The only real point of discrepancy is that, in all dialects, forms with prestressed a, which, on the basis of alternations in causatives, was reconstructed as $(ə)H_2$, reflects $(ə)H_1$ in a fair number of instances; for example, SB $anɔk$, AA²F $anák$, which goes back to Egyptian $(ə)^ʔnɔ́k$, rather than to $*(ə)'nɔ́k = (ə)H_2nɔ́k$.

We may summarize the reflexes of H_1 and H_2 in the following list; its parallelism to the most commonly posited developments of the Indo-European laryngeals should be obvious.

1) Nonfinal laryngeals following a stressed vowel are lost and produce length.

2) Final laryngeals are lost without producing length.

3) Laryngeals preceding a vowel do not produce length.

4) Certain laryngeals change the vowel quality of certain preceding vowels.

5) Laryngeals in reduced syllables are accompanied by reduced vowels which survive where vowels with nonlaryngeals under the same accentual condition are lost.

6) For this reduced vowel, it is impossible to tell which vowel has been reduced (e.g., $*ɛ$ or $*ɔ$), but the laryngeal involved is identifiable in certain forms (e.g., the causatives).

7) An initial sequence of nonlaryngeal consonant plus laryngeal plus vowel develops a preceding, low-stressed shwa, whereas sequences of nonlaryngeals have no initial vowel.

8) Long vowels developing from laryngeals followed by w or y display a marked tendency to shorten the resulting long diphthong. (This point has not been illustrated. Compare Indo-European treatment of $e{:}u$ and similar combinations.)

9) Laryngeals tend strongly to metathesis, which usually results in their preceding consonants they formerly followed. (An example is S $šópɛ$ ["become"] $< *šóp(ə)H_1$, as compared with the qualitative $šɔ́{:}p < *šɔ́H_1p$ in which Egyptian indicates that the original sequence was s-p-H_1.

10) Intervocalic laryngeals are lost without producing vowel length, but they often change preceding vowel color. (This point, likewise, was not illustrated here.)

[50]Such at least seems to be the situation not long prior to the Coptic period. However, ʔ represents two apparently different Egyptian sounds, one y-like and the other possibly a glottal stop. Both of these may appear in Coptic as i in stressed syllables but under further conditions that cannot be specified on the basis of present evidence. In addition, some instances of Proto-Coptic H_1 arise from earlier r and t which sometimes apparently become ʔ.

11) All words that begin in the existing dialects with a stressed vowel originally had an initial laryngeal.

With regard to the development of vowel length in sequences consisting of vowel plus laryngeal plus consonant, it may be pointed out that the common formulation of this process as "compensatory," implying perhaps a feeling of collective guilt at having repressed a consonant, conceals the phonetic problem involved. Here the evidence of Hebrew is valuable because it shows, precisely before consonants but not when the consonant is word final, the development of an extra vocalic segment with the same vowel quality as that of the vowel preceding the laryngeals. These are the so-called *Hatephs* or "hurried shwas," for example, *ya'amóδ* ("he stands") < **ya'moδ*. The sequence *ya'ᵃmóδ* < *ya:móδ* as a possible further development is easily understandable; and this development actually occurred with regard to the glottal stop in Hebrew in the prehistoric period, for example, *yo:mér* ("he speaks") < **ya:mér* < *yaʔmér*. Compare also Western transcriptions of Arabic words such as *Kaaba* = Arabic *ka'ba* and the existence of "echo vowels" in some Amerindian languages after ʔ.

As a final principle of dynamic comparison, we consider the intragenetic mode. The following may serve as a preliminary characterization. The comparison is confined to a genetically delimited group of languages. Empirical hypotheses of a diachronic nature are advanced. They are empirical in the sense that it is clearly stated what would constitute a violation. They are diachronic in that they refer to linguistic changes within the family. Typically they take on one of two forms. Either they state that, of two or more mutually exclusive changes, only one may take place (although the change is not inevitable, its alternatives are denied) or that, of several changes, one must take place earlier than the others.[51] Here again, it is not stated as inevitable that the change *will* take place. Only the order of their occurrence is predicted if they do materialize. Although the hypotheses are stated in terms of properties of a particular language family (e.g., they may mention such categories as "weak verbs in English," "palatalized consonants in Celtic"), they may be viewed as exemplifications of universal diachronic hypotheses in which the variables have been filled in with proper name specifications.

---

[51]These two types of statements are equivalent to the diachronic universals discussed in Greenberg (1966b).

Intragenetic comparison is illustrated here with reference to the Slavic system of nominal declension. Attention was initially directed to this topic, because of a problem that arose in connection with the well-known overall tendency in languages for certain categories (the so-called unmarked) to receive zero expression, while opposing marked categories typically have overt expression. Apparently contravening this principle is the well-known existence in some Slavic languages of extensive classes of nouns (basically the hard feminines and neuters) which show the opposite of the expected phenomenon. Although the singular is to be considered unmarked as against the plural, and the direct cases (nominative, accusative) as unmarked in comparison with the oblique cases (genitive, dative, instrumental, locative), these languages have, in certain classes of nouns, an overt desinence for the doubly unmarked nominative singular and a zero for the doubly marked genitive plural. This fact may be illustrated by the following examples from Standard Czech: *žena* (nom. sing.), *žen* (gen. pl., "woman [f]"); *město* (nom. sing.), *měst* (gen. pl., "city [n]"). On the other hand, there is also an extensive set of nouns which does show the expected type of ending, for example, *hrad* (nom. sing.), *hradů* (gen. pl., "castle" [m]). Hence Czech and the other Slavic languages that show analogous phenomena do not constitute exceptions to the principles stated provided one specifies that in no language does a marked category have zero as a sole allomorph; but such a statement is not really satisfactory because it is well known that the zeroes in both instances, where predicted, as in the nominative singular, and contraindicated, as in the genitive plural, arose by the same sound change, the loss of the *jers* (*ŭ* and *ĭ*) still found in Old Church Slavonic. Thus the present nominative singular *hrad* and genitive plural *žen* at an earlier period possessed overt endings as seen in the corresponding Old Church Slavonic forms *gradŭ* and *ženŭ*.

The loss of *ĭ* and *ŭ* in all word-final and certain word-medial positions conforms to certain typical conditions for vowel loss, as was pointed out in the earlier discussion of unvoiced vowels. As a phonological phenomenon it therefore makes sense; but it is, of course, but an illustration of what has been a commonplace since the time of the neogrammarians. Its effects on the morphological system are random, producing by the very same change zeroes in categories where they are both expected and unexpected. If this were the whole story, how would one find the extensive conformity to certain synchronically stated principles, such as the preference of unmarked categories for zero and marked categories for overt expression, which in fact exists?

The answer may be expected to lie in the direction of certain dynamic selective tendencies. Synchronic regularities are merely the consequences of such forces. It is not so much again that "exceptions" are explained historically, but that the true regularity is contained in the dynamic principles themselves.

These principles, where morphology is concerned, may be expected to lie chiefly in the area of analogical change viewed as the spread of one allomorph at the expense of another. The loss of final *jers* in Slavic produced, in effect, a laboratory situation in that it resulted in zero allomorphs both in a category in which they should be favored (nominative singular) and disfavored (genitive plural). We may now consider the situation resulting from the loss of *jers* separately for each of these two categories, beginning with the genitive plural.

Because the ending of the genitive plural was $\breve{u}$ in most declensional classes, the dropping of final $\breve{u}$ produced a situation in which zero was by far the most common allomorph occurring in all three genders and in the most numerous classes in each; however, after this change, there did remain two overt endings. The masculine *u*-stems, a very restricted class, had in Old Church Slavonic the ending -*ovŭ*, historically the same ending as $\breve{u}$, since -*ov*- derives from an original *o*-grade in stemfinal *u/w* nouns. This -*ovŭ*, of course, became -*ov*. The *i*-stems, which were chiefly feminine but included some masculines in Old Church Slavonic, had an ending -*ĭjĭ* from earlier -*ĭjŭ*. With loss of final -*ĭ*, this ending became -*ĭj*, which takes various forms in the Slavic languages. When the -*ĭj* was stressed, it became -*éj* in Russian, and I shall use -*ej* as the citation form for this allomorph. To summarize, with loss of final *jers* the genitive plural had three allomorphs zero ~ *ov* ~ *ej*, of which the first was by far the most frequent.

In the nominative singular, both -*ŭ* and -*ĭ* existed in certain extensive categories of nouns. When -*ĭ* was lost, it left a trace in the palatalization of the previous consonant (unless this was already "soft" because of an earlier -*i*-). The ending -*ŭ* existed in the nominative singular of hard *o*-stems, the dominant category in masculine nouns, and in *u*-stems, a limited group, as has been seen. In masculine soft stems (i.e., those historically with stem final -*i*), by a regular prehistoric change already exemplified above for the genitive plural of *i*-stems (-*ĭjĭ* < *ĭjŭ*), the nominative singular had -*ĭ*. An example is the word for "man" in Old Church Slavonic, which, in the nominative singular, is $m\rho\check{z}\breve{i} < {}^*m\rho g j\breve{i} < m\rho g j\breve{u}$. In addition the i-stems, whether masculine or feminine, had the ending $-\breve{i}$ in the nominative and accusative singular. All of these categories, therefore, had zero after the loss of the *jers*. On the other hand, no neuter had $-\breve{u}$ or $-\breve{i}$ (most had $-o$ for hard stems, $-e$ for soft stems), and the dominant feminine class of a-stems had the overt ending $-a$ in the nominative singular. In the nominative singular, then, after the loss of *jers*, zero was the dominant ending in masculine nouns, was present in a substantial minority of feminines (the i-stems), and occurred not at all in the neuter. The alternants for the nominative singular were, then, $a \sim o \sim e \sim$ zero.[52] Hence, after the loss of the *jers*, zero was the dominant allomorph in the category in which it should not be expected (genitive singular), and only one of several common allomorphs in a category in which it should be expected (nominative singular and the accusative singular of inanimates that are, in Slavic, identical in the nominative and accusative).

With regard to the genitive plural, we hypothesize that of the three alternants zero, $-ov$, and $-ej$, the first will never replace the second or third. If there are any instances of analogical spread, it will be at the expense of the zero allomorph. The historical evidence is, in fact, in favor of this hypothesis. In particular, $-ov$ has tended to spread at the expense of the zero ending. In one language, Upper Lusatian, except for a small remnant with zero, all of the nouns in the language have $-ov$. In Russian dialects, $-ov$ has spread to hard feminines and neuters (e.g., *knígov, mestóv*) so that practically all nouns have overt genitive plural endings. In the Serbo-Croatian literary language, all nouns have nonzero genitive plural endings, the dominant form being $-a$: of still mysterious origin, but with $-i$ $< ej$ also in certain nominal classes. It is fair to say that, in every single Slavic dialect or standard language, zero has lost ground. Nowhere is it now the dominant allomorph, and in some instances it has almost completely disappeared. The only exception to the spread of nonzero endings of which I am aware is that in Polish, from the fifteenth to the eighteenth century, a small number of i-stems replaced their inherited ending by zero (e.g., *myszy* [gen. pl.,

---

[52]I have not included here the various forms of the nominative singular (or the neuter nominative-accusative singular) which involve truncation of the stem common to the remaining cases, for example, the feminine u-stems that have nominative singular $-y$ and, in the remaining cases, $-ov$ plus the usual consonant stem endings. Such truncations behave like nonzeroes. All of these classes have a severely restricted membership.

"mice"] with *-y* < *-ej* was replaced by *mysz*).[53] This trend was subsequently reversed, and modern Polish has *myszy.*

The inverse hypothesis concerning the nominative singular is, of course, that the nonzero allomorphs will not gain ground at the expense of the zero allomorph. If there is any change, it should be in the opposite direction. This hypothesis appears to be verified by the historical evidence from Slavic languages without exception. I do not know of a single instance in which the zero of the masculine basic *o-/jo*-stems and *u*-stems, or that of the *i*-stems, has been replaced by an overt ending. At the same time, the overt endings *-a* for the feminine, *-o/-e* for the neuter have in general been maintained, since they have a function within the gender system, marking the feminine and neuter as against the zero of the masculine. The situation in the nominative singular in Slavic after the loss of *jers* is represented in table 5 for the major declensional classes.

TABLE 5

SLAVIC NOMINATIVE SINGULAR AFTER LOSS OF JERS

Gender	Hard	Soft
Masculine	zero	'zero
1. Feminine (*a*-stems)	*a*	'*a*
2. Feminine (*i*-stems)	.....	'zero
Neuter	*o*	'*e*

Nevertheless, where there has been change in this relatively stable situation, it has been in the direction of the spread of zero to the feminine *a*-stems, rather than vice versa. This change has taken place in West Slavic and has gone farthest in Upper Lusatian and in Slovak. Here the *i*-stems have coalesced with the soft *a*-stems; and, in the merged declension, it is precisely the zero of the nominative-accusative which has been carried over from the *i*-stems, whereas all the other inflections come from the *a*-stems. The same tendencies are noticeable in Polish and in Czech. In the latter, an intermediate declension has arisen (e.g., *dlaň*, "palm of the hand") alongside the *a* and *i* feminine declensions with the zero of the nominative-accusative singular from the *i*-stems and the remaining forms from the *a* declension. These are former *a*-stems that have

[53]Klemensiewicz *et al.* (1955), p. 299.

replaced their overt endings of the nominative and accusative singular with zero, and not former *i*-stems that have acquired the remainder of their inflection from the *a*-stems.

Both hypotheses then, the favoring of the zero alternant in the nominative singular and the overt alternant in the genitive plural, are verified by the historical linguistic data.

We have seen that, in the genitive plural, after the loss of the *jers*, there were three alternants zero ~ *ov* ~ *ej*. Our first hypothesis stated that zero was disfavored as against the two overt allomorphs. We may now inquire whether it is possible to set up any hypothesis regarding the relation between -*ov* and -*ej*.

There are certain expectations based on the observation of these and similar instances. Thus, other things being equal, we may hypothesize that -*ov*, which was originally the genitive plural of a masculine "hard" (nonpalatalized) declension, will more easily spread into a masculine than a feminine or neuter declension, and into a hard declension than a soft declension. Such statements are easily converted into refutable diachronic implications. Spread of *ov* into a feminine or neuter class implies previous spread into a masculine class, and so on.

In the present instance, there is just one declensional class, the masculine *o*-stems, which agrees in gender and nonpalatality with the *u*-stems. We may, therefore, advance the hypothesis that spread to any other class implies previous spread to this class. Because the third genitive plural alternant -*ej* belongs initially to a soft declension which is predominantly feminine with a few marginal masculines, -*ov* will be favored over -*ej* for the masculine *o*-stems.

Such is, in fact, the case, in that wherever else it may spread, it is also found in this class, and that where it is found in several declensions, the direct historical evidence shows its prior presence in the masculine *o*-stems; however, this development is not an independent event in the various Slavic languages. These two declensions have already largely merged in Old Church Slavonic, the original *u*-stems being distinguishable on the whole by greater frequency of inflectional variants stemming historically from the *u*-declension. Hence, the process started before the loss of *jers* with the consequent zero allomorph in the genitive plural of the *o*-stems. The initial conditions for this merger were the resemblance in gender and nonpalatality, but it may be conjectured that the agreement of both declensions in having -*ŭ* in the most frequent (unmarked) cases, the nominative and accusative singular, was a precipitating factor in the merger.[54] I shall return to this point later.

In the course of the merger, individual Slavic languages often retained inflections inherited from both declensions, sometimes with secondary redistributions of function. Nevertheless, the inflections of the far more numerous o-class were normally dominant. It is precisely in the genitive plural, where the Slavic languages, after the loss of final ŭ, inherited a zero from the more numerous o-stems and ov from the u-stems, that the triumph of the u-stem inflection was most widespread and complete. Thus, Vaillant summarizes the result of the merger insofar as it concerns the survival of original u-stem inflections in the following terms: "L'extension de ces désinences est très limitée. Elle est plus notable au nominatif et surtout au génitif pluriels."[55]

We may seek to generalize concerning the factors involved in declensional merger which were seen to operate in the instance of the hard o- and u-stems. Agreement in palatality, gender, and identity of inflection in the nominative and accusative singular may be conjectured to be necessary and sufficient conditions for merger; and, where other factors such as marking do not intervene, the forms of the more frequent declension will triumph. Such a thesis involves, of course, factors that, while not exclusively confined to Slavic (e.g., gender and the distinction of palatal and nonpalatal stems), are sometimes absent in other instances; therefore, it would have to be restated for certain other families of languages.

This particular thesis is verified in a whole series of instances in Slavic; however, statement in the form of necessary and sufficient conditions is not an empirical formulation, as can be shown from the following example. There were in early Slavic three classes of neuter consonant stems, all small in number and having as a common feature the possession of two forms of stem, a shorter in the nominative and accusative singular (in neuters, the nominative and accusative are the same in all numbers), and a longer, containing what is, from the synchronic point of view, an "extension," for the remaining cases of the singular and the entire plural. On the basis of these extensions, we may call them the en-, ent-, and es-stems.

---

[54]Josselson (1953) reports for conversational Russian a frequency of 50.7 percent for the combined nominative and accusative singular and 49.3 percent for all remaining cases.

[55]Vaillant (1950-1958), II, 91.

TABLE 6

Stem ending	Case		Definition
	Nominative-Accusative Singular	Genitive Singular	
-en	*vremę*	*vremen-e*	"time"
-ent	*otročę*	*otročet-e*	"infant"
-es	*slovo*	*sloves-e*	"word"
-o	*sel-o*	*sel-a*	"village"

In table 6 the shorter stem of the nominative-accusative singular is given along with the genitive singular to exemplify the extended stem. In addition the hard thematic *o*-stem neuters, the dominant neuter class, and one without extensions, are included. The forms cited are from Old Church Slavonic. The conditions for merger between the *es*- and *o*-stems are evidently present because, in addition to gender and nonpalatality, there is the factor of agreement in the nominative-accusative singular *-o*. We likewise hypothesize that the more frequent *o*-stems will triumph, so that we may expect that, as the result of merger, words like *slovo* will have genitive singular *slova* in place of *slovese*, and will similarly coincide with *selo* in the remaining forms of their declension. Here again the process has already commenced in Old Church Slavonic, and the dominance of *o*-stems is clear in that, on the whole, only original *es*-stems have variant forms from the two declensions. The process is complete in practically all contemporary languages; however, that Old Church Slavonic probably represents the merger in incipient form not yet carried through everywhere in Slavic territory is shown by modern Slovene, which still retains the distinction between *o*- and *es*-stems. We can always say that the merger will eventually take place in Slovene also, but we have waited roughly 1,000 years and it has not occurred. Hence predictions of this kind without a stated time limit are not empirically refutable. We can always wait longer for it to occur. On the other hand, Slovene has also kept the other neuter consonant declensions separate from the *o*-stems; hence, the familiar implicational thesis holds here as elsewhere in Slavic and can be stated in the following terms: Merger of the *en*- and *ent*-stems with the *o*-stems implies previous merger of the *es*-stems with the *o*-stems. The decisive importance of identity in the nominative-accusative singular is further shown by the occurrence of merger of these other classes with the *o*-stem, or its palatalized counterpart, the *e*-stems, when further phonetic change produces identity in the unmarked nominative-accusative singular (e.g., *en*-stems in Ukrainian).

We may note that in the three neuter consonant classes we are once again close to a "laboratory" situation in which *cetera* are indeed *paria*. The three consonant classes agree in gender and non-palatality but differ in the factor of identity in the unmarked cases with the thematic neuter declension.

Because the combined frequency of the oblique singular together with the entire plural is roughly equal to that of the nominative-accusative singular, we might have expected that, in merging with the *o*-stems, the *es*-stems could have analogized in the opposite direction, generalizing the extended stem to produce a declension *sloveso* (nom.-acc. sing.), *slovesa* (gen. sing.), and so on. In fact, such a development has taken place rather widely with just one noun of the *es*-class, namely *kolo* ("wheel"). Russian, Ukrainian, Lower Lusatian, and Slovak all agree in generalizing the extended stem in just this word, and Upper Lusatian has *koleso* and *kolo* as doublets. Kuznetsov conjectures that the survival of the *-es* form in this word in Russian is the result of the frequency of its use in the plural.[56] If his conjecture is correct, then the nominative and accusative plural may be expected to be the most frequent cases, and these, of course, have the *-es* extension.

Thanks to the data provided by Steinfeldt, who gives the frequencies for individual inflectional categories of all the more frequent nouns in modern Russian, it is now possible to test this thesis, at least insofar as it pertains to Russian.[57] In table 7 are listed all words that have survived in modern Russian of the words cited by Diels in his Old Church Slavonic grammar as belonging to the *-es* declension.[58] We see, indeed, that *kolo* is most frequent in the plural.[59] Generalizing the example of *kolo*, we may say that a set of relative frequencies can be mapped into a chain of diachronic implicational hypotheses. Of course, due regard would have to be

[56]Kuznetsov (1953), p. 83.
[57]Steinfeldt (1965).
[58]Diels (1932), p. 169.
[59]Slovak has doublets *telo–teleso* and *slovo–sloveso*. For both pairs, the forms in *-eso* are neologisms, of lesser frequency and with specialized technical meanings, as noted in Stanislav (1957-58) II, 231. The same is true in Czech. Thus *telo* is "body" in the ordinary sense, *teleso* is a solid in geometry; *slovo* is "word," but *sloveso* is a modern coinage meaning "verb." It should likewise be noted that the modern representatives of Old Church Slavonic, *nebo* ("sky") and *cudo* ("miracle") often have *-es* extensions in the plural only, which is recognized as an example of Old Church Slavonic influence.

TABLE 7
RUSSIAN SURVIVALS OF -es DECLENSION

Modern Russian word belonging to -es declension	Frequencies according to Steinfeldt		Definition
	Singular	Plural	
nebo	97	3	"sky"
telo	95	5	"body"
lico	84	16	"face"
delo	75	25	"thing"
čudo	54	46	"miracle"
slovo	53	47	"word"
derevo	44	56	"tree"
keleso	16	84	"wheel"

given to the statistical significance of the frequency differences. Thus, if any word on this list generalizes the es-stem, it should be kolo. The generalization of the es-stem in slovo implies its generalization in derevo and kolo, and so on.

It will not be possible in the present connection to illustrate the further series of intragenetic hypotheses verified by the historical evidence even in this one relatively restricted domain of morphological change. Other areas of change, not touched on at all, include, for example, the elimination of inflectional categories as such by merger or by replacement through syntactic constructions. An instance of the application to another linguistic family of one of the principles discussed here in reference to Slavic is the following: In Old High German, through phonetic change, the dominant allomorph of both the neuter singular nominative-accusative and the neuter plural nominative-accusative was zero. The single overt allomorph for the plural involved the suffix -ir and internal vowel change (e.g., OHG lamb/lembir), and it was restricted to a handful of nouns. Its subsequent spread would be predicted as a further instance of the principle involved in the expansion of -ov and -ej in the Slavic genitive plural. Ultimately all German neuter plurals acquired overt marking.

Although I believe that the specific examples presented here are novel, I do not imply that the application of such modes of comparison has been completely lacking in the previous literature.[60] What I believe to be an innovation is the attempt to indicate in a

[60]For example Allen (1957-58), Kurylowicz (1964), and Manczak (1957-58).

systematic way the manner in which such studies transcend the comparative method in the usual sense and the proposal to study some particular phenomenon, for example, vowel nasalization or voiceless vowels, by bringing in all the evidence available on a worldwide scale and in historically independent instances. None of the present extended examples could, for obvious reasons, be presented as an exhaustive study. It may be hoped, however, that the details presented are sufficient for illustrative purposes.

In summary, the four approaches described here are basically similar in that they involve, in varying combinations and from varying points of view, the deployment of the methods of internal reconstruction, comparative reconstruction, and direct historical documentation in order to arrive at universal diachronic principles. These take the form of theories of relative origin (e.g., of nasalized vowels, tonal systems, gender), or of implicational relations among changes (e.g., that low vowels do not become voiceless earlier than high vowels). Synchronic typologies function merely as heuristic, though often indispensable, devices in defining the problems and in assembling the relevant data.[61] Thus it makes sense, I would maintain, to compare all the languages exhibiting some particular phenomenon (e.g., voiceless vowels, laryngeals, nominal case systems, etc.). So, likewise, the method of synchronic universals, which is inextricably involved with typological comparisons, has limitations, as has already been pointed out in the body of this paper by the citation of several instances where it was seen that the true regularity lies in the dynamic tendencies, that is, the diachronic universals.

We may illustrate this dominance and the purely auxiliary role to be assigned to synchronic static regularities, at least in regard to contingent linguistic phenomena, by reverting once more to one of the problems raised in connection with voiceless vowels. It was pointed out that we could not state as a synchronic universal that voicelessness in an earlier portion of a vowel implied voicelessness in the remainder because, at least on the hypothesis that h-sounds were, in some instances, voiceless vowels, the sequence forbidden by this law exists but is generally interpreted as h + vowel (e.g., $\mathtt{a} = ha$). If, however, we state the hypothesis as a diachronic implication, it will be true as far as the evidence with which I am familiar goes that when vowels *become* voiceless this process may

[61] For a discussion of some of the limitations of typologies, see Greenberg, 1966a, p. 82.

initially effect only the latter part of the vowel but never merely the initial. On one phonetic assumption, at least, that some sounds labeled *h* are merely voiceless vowels, the difference between the two is that *h* arises from previous consonants, and *V*, from previous vowels.[62] This difference would sometimes, at least, appear in a generative grammar in the form of the rules in the phonological component. This general topic is reserved for later treatment.[63]

Finally, three types of limitations in the present treatment of diachronic hypotheses should be pointed out. The first pertains to the possibility of explaining (i.e., deducing) these from more general phonetic or semantic principles. Such explanations are often feasible, or at least reasonable suggestions may be made. For example, high voiceless vowels are probably more easily distinguishable than low voiceless vowels. Moreover, previous consonants often have initially redundant palatalization or labialization which carries most of the burden of differentiation and may ultimately carry all of it after the loss of the vowels. This limitation of interpretation was purposely adopted as not within the scope of the present paper.

[62]Voiceless vowels seem to be exceptional in that definitions based solely on articulatory and/or acoustic phenomena without regard to distribution or historical origin are normally adequate at least for the heuristic purposes of defining typologically a set of languages within which generalizing comparisons can be carried out. The definition of voiceless vowel given earlier seems adequate for a singling out of the set of languages within which comparison may operate insofar as it delineates the property "to have a voiceless vowel." It is unrevealing, however, in the following respect: Where a voiceless vowel in accordance with the definition occurs, say in final, but in its regressive spread only affects the terminal portion of the vowel of the previous syllable, this latter segment has predictable quality and is, hence, *h* rather than a voiceless vowel by the earlier definition. This definition is clearly unsatisfactory, although it does serve the initial purpose of classifying the language itself as having a voiceless vowel.

[63]The following remarks are of a provisional nature. In phonology, at least insofar as generative rules restate sound changes of the past, regularities in the form of limitations in the types of possible changes can be stated as conditions on such rules as they appear in descriptions. It is, however, not clear in practice to what extent higher level representations are required to represent earlier lower level realizations. Thus Harms, in his treatment of Southern Paiute (1966-B), at one stage of representation puts stress on every syllabic including voiceless vowels and then erases some of them, including those on the voiceless vowels. Perhaps this generative phonology is not satisfactory; but if it is not preferred to alternative statements of the same weak generative power, the evaluation criteria employed will come from the phonetic plausibility of both the representations and the changes, and these are subject to independent verification by the evidence of ordinary phonetics and the well-established methods of internal reconstruction and comparative linguistics proper.

A second limitation is that diachronic changes were studied only in relation to immediate conditioning factors and to the hierarchy among obviously connected changes, not in relation to the rest of the system. Thus we did not ask what other characteristics might exist in languages which might serve to explain why nasalized vowels develop in some languages but not in others. Virtually all languages have the initial conditions, namely nasal consonants adjacent to vowels, which might lead to the genesis of nasalized vowels. It is the largely unfulfilled promise of structuralism that such conditions exist. They deserve continued investigation, but it seemed preferable as a matter of scientific tactics to investigate first those areas in which success seems more likely and is indeed a probable prerequisite for the wider problem. Until we know what hierarchies of change exist in fact, we cannot investigate the synchronic structural conditions of their appearance.

The third limitation is very likely an extension of the one just mentioned. It has been aptly named by Herzog, Labov, and Weinreich the riddle of actualization.[64] Why does a specific type of expectable change materialize in one language and not in another, and why does it come into being at one period of a particular language and not another? Thus we hypothesized that the Slavic *es*-declension would merge with the *o*-declension neuters sooner than certain other declensions; but why have they all remained distinct in Slovene to the present day, while other Slavic languages merged them at earlier dates? When stated in this form, our problem admits of a wider search for relevant variables than the internal structural factors mentioned earlier. We might turn to possible sociolinguistic and cultural conditions, though here also the search has heretofore been largely profitless, and it may be that, in the words of Poincaré, we must, in the end, say *ignorabimus*.

---

[64]M. Herzog, W. Labov, and U. Weinreich (1967).

Bibliography

Abbreviations

AL   *Anthropological Linguistics*
BSOAS   *Bulletin of the School of Oriental and African Studies*
IJAL   *International Journal of American Linguistics*
WZKM   *Wiener Zeitschrift für die Kunde des Morgenlandes*
ZPAS   *Zeitschrift für Phonetik und allgemeine Sprachwissen-schaft*

A. REFERENCES EXCLUSIVE OF DATA ON VOICELESS VOWELS

Allen, W. S.
  1957-58 "Some Problems of Palatalization in Greek", *Lingua* 7:113-133.
Diels, Paul
  1932   *Alkirchenslavische Grammatik* 1. Teil: *Grammatik.* Heidelberg.
Ferguson, Charles A.
  1963   "Assumptions about Nasals: A Sample Study in Phonological Universals." In *Universals of Language*, ed. J. H. Greenberg (Cambridge, Mass.), p. 42-47.
Greenberg, Joseph H.
  1962   "The Interpretation of the Coptic Vowel System", *Journal of African Languages* 1:22-29.
  1966a   *Language Universals, with Special Reference to Feature hierarchies.* The Hague and Paris.
  1966b   "Synchronic and Diachronic Universals in Phonology", *Language* 42:508-517.
Heffner, R. M. S.
  1964   *General Phonetics.* Madison.
Herzog, M., W. Labov, and U. Weinreich
  1967   "Empirical Foundations for a Theory of Language Change", *Proceedings of the Symposium in Historical Linguistics, Austin, 1966.* In press.

Hockett, Charles F.
  1955   *Manual of Phonology*. Baltimore.
Jakobson, R.
  1958   "Typological Studies and Their Contribution to His-
          torical Comparative Linguistics", *Proceedings of the
          Eighth International Congress of Linguistics*. Oslo.
          Pp. 17-25.
Josselson, Harry Hirsch
  1953   *The Russian Word Count and Frequency Analysis of
          Grammatical Categories in Standard Literary Russian*.
          Detroit.
Klemensiewicz, A., T. Lehr-Spławinski, and S. Urbanczyk
  1955   *Gramatyka historyczna języka polskiego*.
Kuryłowicz, Jerzy
  1964   *The Inflectional Categories of Indo-European*. Heidel-
          berg.
Kuznetsov, P. S.
  1953   *Istoriceskaja grammatika russkogo jazyka: Morfologija*.
          Moscow.
Lehiste, Ilse
  1964   *Acoustical Characteristics of Selected English Conso-
          nants*. Baltimore.
Manczak, W.
  1957-58 "Tendances générales des changements analogiques",
          Lingua 7:298-323, 387-420.
Meyer-Lübke, W.
  1890-
  1906   *Grammaire des langues romaines*. Paris. 4 vols.
Paul, H., and H. Stolte
  1951   *Kurze deutsche Grammatik* (2 ed.). Tübingen.
Polotsky, H. J.
  1931   "Zur koptischen Lautlehre. I.," Zeitschrift für *Ägyptis-
          che Sprache und Altertumskunde* 67:74-77.
Samarin, William J.
  1966   *The Gbeya Language*, Berkeley and Los Angeles.
Smalley, William A.
  1962   *Manual of Articulatory Phonetics*. 2 pts.
Stanislav, Jan
  1957-58 *Dejiny slovenskeho jazyka*. Bratislava. 3 vols.
Steindorff, Georg
  1951   *Lehrbuch der koptischen Grammatik*. Chicago.
Steinfeldt, E.
  1965   *Russian Word Count*. Moscow.

Till, Walter
  1929   "Altes aleph und ^{c}ajin im Koptischen", *WZKM* 36:
         186-196.
  1951   "Der Mittelzungenvokal im Koptischen", *Le Muséon*
         64:63-69.
Vaillant, Andreé
1950-58 *Grammaire comparée des langues slaves.* Lyon. 2 vols.
West, John David
  1962   "The Phonology of Mikasuki", *Studies in Linguistics*
         16:77-91
Whiteley, W. H.
  1965   "Notes on the Ci-miini Dialect of Swahili," *African
         Language Studies* 6:67-72.

B. References on Voiceless Vowels

Andrzejewski, B. W.
  1957   "Some Preliminary Observations on the Borana Dialect
         of Galla," *Bulletin of the School of Oriental and African
         Studies* 30:354-374.
Aschmann, Herman P.
  1945   "Totanaco Phonemes", *IJAL* 12:34-43.
Bender, Ernest, and Zellig S. Harris
  1945   "The Phonemes of North Carolina Cherokee", *IJAL*
         12:14-21.
Biggs, Bruce
  1961   "The Structure of New Zealand Maori," *AL* 3:3, 1-54.
Bloch, Bernard
  1950   "Studies in Colloquial Japanese IV. Phonemics," *Lan-
         guage* 26:86-125.
Borman, M. B.
  1962   "Cofan Phonemes," *Studies in Ecuadorian Indian Lan-
         guages* (Norman, Okla.) I, 45-59.
Bridgeman, Loraine
  1961   "Kaiwa Phonology," *IJAL* 27:329-334.
Bright, William
  1957   *The Karok Language.* Berkeley and Los Angeles.
Canonge, Elliot D.
  1957   "Voiceless Vowels in Comanche," *IJAL* 23:63-67.
Casagrande, Joseph
  1954   "Comanche Linguistic Acculturation I," *IJAL* 20:140-
         151.

Davis, Irvine
  1962   "Phonological Function in Cheyenne," *IJAL* 28:36-42.
  1964   "The Language of Santa Ana Pueblo," *Bureau of American Ethnology Bulletin* (Washington) 191:53-190.
  1966   "Numic Consonantal Correspondences," *IJAL* 32:124-140.
deAngulo, Jaime
  1932   "The Chichimeco Language," *IJAL* 7:152-194.
Dirks, Sylvester
  1953   "Campa Phonemes," *IJAL* 19:30-44.
Doke, Clement M.
  1931   *A Comparative Study in Shona Phonetics.* Johannesburg.
Firestone, Homer
  1955   "Chama Phonology," *IJAL* 21:52-55
Gibson, Lorna F.
  1956   "Pame Phonemics and Morphophonemics," *IJAL* 22:242-265.
Gleason, Henry Allan
  1962   *Workbook in Descriptive Linguistics* (New York). Esp. p. 62 (Chatino).
Haas, Mary
  1946   A Grammatical Sketch of Tunica," In *Linguistic Structures of Native America*, ed. H. Hoijer (New York).
Halpern, A. M.
  1946   "Yuma I. Phonemes," *IJAL* 12:25-33.
Han, Mieko S.
  1962   "Internal Juncture in Japanese," *Studies in Linguistics* 16:49-61.
Harms, Robert T.
  1966   "Stress, Voice and Length in Southern Paiute," *IJAL* 32:228-235.
Harrington, J. P.
  1910   "The Phonetic System of the Ute Language," *University of Colorado Studies* 8:199-222.
Hodge, Carlton T.
  1946   "Serbo-Croatian Phonemes," *Language* 22:112-120.
Holmer, Nils M.
  1949   "Goajiro (Arawak) I. Phonology," *IJAL* 15:45-56.
Jimbo, K.
  1925   "The Word-Tone of the Standard Japanese Language," *BSOAS* 3:659-667.

Johnson, Orville E., and Catherine Peeke
 1962   "Phonemic Units in the Secoya Word," *Studies in Ecuadorian Indian Languages* (Norman, Okla.) I, 78-95.
Keller, Kathryn
 1959   "The Phonemes of Chontal," *IJAL* 25:44-53.
Key, Harold
 1964   "Phonotactics of Cayuvava," *IJAL* 30:143-150.
Lange, Rudolf
 1903   *A Text-book of Colloquial Japanese.* Eng. ed. by Christopher Ness (Tokyo).
Larsen, Raymond S., and Eunice Pike
 1949   "Huasteco Intonation and Phonemes," *Language* 25: 268-277.
Liljeblad, Sven
 1950   "Bannack I. Phonemes," *IJAL* 12:126-131.
Lochak, Dorita
 1960   "Basque Phonemics," *AL* 2:3, 12-31.
Lounsbury, F.
 1953   *Oneida Verb Morphology.* New Haven.
McIntosh, John B.
 1945   "Huichol Phonemes," *IJAL* 11:31-35.
McKaughan, Howard
 1954   "Chatino Formulas and Phonemes," *IJAL* 20:23-27.
Martin, Samuel E.
 1951   "Korean Phonemics," *Language* 27:519-533.
 1961   *Dagur Mongolian Grammar, Texts and Lexicon.* Bloomington.
Miller, Wick R., and Irvine Davis
 1963   "Proto-Keresan Phonology," *IJAL* 29:310-330.
Miller, Wick R.
 1965   *Acoma Grammar and Texts.* Berkeley and Los Angeles.
Mori, Masatoshi Gensen
 1929   *The Pronunciation of Japanese.* Tokyo.
O'Grady, Geoffrey
 1964   *Nyangumata Grammar.* Sydney.
Ott, Willis, and Rebecca Ott
 1959   *Fonemas de la lengua Ignaciana.* La Paz.
Polivanov, E. D.
 1928   "Karšinskij govor," *Doklady Akademii Nauk SSSR* (Uzbek), no. 5.
Preuss, K. Th.

1932   "Grammatik der Cora-Sprache," *IJAL* 7:1-84.
Pride, Kitty
1961   "Numerals in Chatino," *AL* 3:2, 1-106.
1963   "Chatino Tonal Structure," *AL* 5:2, 19-28.
Ramanujan, A. K., and C. Masica
1966   "Toward a Phonological Typology of the Indian Linguistic Area" (Awadhi). Unpublished MS.
Ransom, Jay Ellis
1945   "Duwanish Phonology and Morphology," *IJAL* 11:204-210.
Rich, Furne
1963   "Arabela phonemes and High-level Phonology," *Studies in Peruvian Indian Languages* (México) I, 193-206.
Redden, James E.
1966   "Walapai I. Phonology," *IJAL* 32:1-16.
Riggs, Venda
1949   "Alternate Phonemic Analyses of Comanche," *IJAL* 15:229-233.
Sapir, Edward
1930   "The Southern Paiute Language," *Proceedings of the American Academy of Arts and Sciences* 65:1, 1-296.
Saxton, Dean
1963   "Papago Phonemes," *IJAL* 29:29-35.
Seiler, Hansjakob
1957   "Die phonetischen Grundlagen der Vokalphoneme des Cahuilla," *ZPAS* 10:204-223.
1965   "Accent and Morphophonemics in Cahuilla and in Uto-Aztecan," *IJAL* 31:50-59.
Shimkin, D. B.
1949   "Shoshone I. Linguistic Sketch and Text," *IJAL* 15:175-188.
Sjoberg, Andrée F.
1963   *Uzbek Structural Grammar*. Bloomington.
Smith, William B. S.
1949   "Some Cheyenne Forms," *Studies in Linguistics* 7:77-85.
Sokolova, V. S.
1949   *Fonetika tadžiksogo jazyka*. Moscow and Leningrad.
Trager, George L.
1940   "Serbo-Croatian Accents and Quantities," *Language* 16:29-32.

Tucker, A. N., and M. A. Bryan
  1966   *Linguistic Analyses: The Non-Bantu Languages of North-Eastern Africa* (Galla, Teso, Bagirmi).
Voegelin, C. F.
  1935   "Shawnee Phonemes," *Language* 11:23-37.
Voegelin, C. F., and F. M. Voegelin
  1964   "Indo-Pacific Fascicle Two," *AL* 6:7, 20-56 (Hawaiian).
Voegelin C. F., F. M. Voegelin, and Kenneth L. Hale
  1962   *Typological and Comparative Grammar of Uto-Aztecan I. (Phonology).* Baltimore.
Wurm, Stephen
  1949   "The (Kara-) Kirghiz Language," *BSOAS* 13:97-120.
  1947   "The Uzbek Dialect of Qïzïl Qujaš," *BSOAS* 12:86-105.
Yamagiwa, Joseph K.
  1942   *Modern Conversational Japanese.* New York and London.
Yegerlehner, John
  1959   "Arizona Tewa I. Phonemes," *IJAL* 25:1-7.

Vocative and Imperative *

Werner Winter
University of Kiel

        The field of specialization assigned to the Collitz Professor is the field of comparative Indo-European studies. In the context of a Linguistic Institute, it is but one of many fields, and, for all its great tradition, perhaps not even one of the most important fields — certainly not if one were to measure importance in terms of student interest. I think there is absolutely no point in deploring this state of affairs and in casting back longing glances to the nineteenth century when linguistics and Indo-European philology were, for all practical purposes, taken to be synonymous expressions: this identification was nothing but a mistake, and it is not to be deplored, but to be applauded that other fields have come very much into their own.

        Still, it is a very fortunate fact that a Collitz Professorship should continue to be an integral part of every regular Linguistic Institute; for in this way the continuity that is to be found in our science, in spite of all surface changes, is made manifest year after year. Now, the fact that the Indo-Europeanist speaks for the oldest branch of our science need not imply that he should hold on most tenaciously to old methods and old interests; if indeed he thinks of himself as a

---

*In preparing this paper for publication, I decided to preserve the form in which it had been presented to the fullest possible extent. For better or worse, this decision led to the exclusion of the paraphernalia of an article as distinguished from a lecture: no additional documentation, excursus, or bibliographical references have been given, and no attempt has been made to delete some of the peculiarities of a text planned for oral delivery.

205

participant in a continuum of scholarly endeavor, he will constantly feel and face the challenge posed by new developments, and will ask himself what new assessments of old facts might contribute to the work in his own domain, and, conversely, what the findings of an old, and by no means inexperienced, discipline might contribute to the work on new frontiers.

The task of a Collitz Professor in the context of a Linguistic Institute is thus, among other things, that of a builder of bridges. In his contributions to the Institute, of which the lecture to this captive postbanquet audience tends to be the most conspicuous one, he should try to show how methods and techniques developed in other fields can be made to work in his own, and that his own observations can serve useful purposes in other branches of linguistics. To achieve this end, he will have to persuade his audience that the things he is doing are not only things somewhat off the beaten path, but also things interesting, relevant, and necessary.

What I propose to do here today is to study a small segment of Indo-European grammar, a segment that has received considerable attention in the past, to describe problems connected with the analysis of this segment, and to suggest new solutions to at least some of these problems. For reasons that will become obvious later, I will treat the segment as referred to in the title of this lecture in two installments, turning to a discussion of the imperative only after having drawn a number of general conclusions concerning the vocative; moreover, the comments on the imperative will be limited in scope and depth for reasons that again should become clear.

When a vocative in Indo-European languages is found set off against other forms of the nominal paradigm, the vocative is characterized by (a) special accent features, and (b) special features of the word end. Attested languages vary as to the occurrence of (a) and (b); yet, the data are sufficient to ascribe a combination of (a) and (b) to the parent language.

The special accent features are as follows: A vocative form is either unaccented, or it shows a retraction of accent to the frontmost position permitted under the accent-distribution rules of the respective language. Absence of accent is found (the data are primarily obtained from Vedic Indic) when a vocative occurs in second position in a sentence, that is, when it is used as an enclitic. Retracted accent is a characteristic of a vocative in sentence-initial position (with the decisive data again coming from Vedic).

As concerns the word end, the traditional description of the forms found has always stated that the vocative, where it differed from the nominative, represented the mere stem of a noun without an ending attached as in other case forms. The data are briefly as follows: For stems in obstruents, no special vocative forms can be reconstructed as concerns the segmental features. Stems in continuants have special vocatives of the singular: s-stems, a vocative in -es (Skt. *durmanas*, "annoyed", Gk. *dúsmenes*, "hostile"); r-stems, a vocative in -er or -or (Skt. *pitar*, Gk. *páter*, "father"; Skt. *dātar*, Gk. *dôtor*, "donor"); n-stems, a vocative in -on (Skt. *rājan*, "king"; Gk. *kúon*, "dog") and probably in -en, though the crucial Greek evidence is lacking; y-stems, a vocative in -ey and probably in -oy (Gk. *pótei*- in the name of the god Poseidon, and Skt. *mate*, "mind," and *sakhe*, "friend"), plus a vocative in -i, as in Greek *óphi* ("snake"); finally, w-stems have a vocative in -ew (Gk. *Zeû*, Lat. *Iuppiter*) or -ow (Goth. *sunau*, "son"), plus one in -u, as in Gothic *sunu*. To turn to vocalic stems (vocalic at least in traditional terms), we have a vocative in -a with ā-stems (Skt. *amba*, "mother"; Gk. *númpha*, "nymph," *déspota*, "lord"; OCS *ženo*, "wife"; Umbr. *Tursa*); the vocative singular of o-stems ends in -e in Greek, Latin, Umbrian, Lithuanian, and Old Church Slavonic, and Sanskrit -a is readily enough derived from earlier -e.

As the few examples cited indicate, the vocative form is limited to paradigms with masculine or feminine gender; only marginally, in Old Indic, do we find transfer of a masculine vocative form to the neuter (cf. *mitra*, "friendship").

Let us begin our discussion of vocative forms by first considering those associated with continuant stems. We may raise the question: Is there any way to explain the striking variation in ablaut grade found between, say, Sanskrit nominative *sūnúṣ* ("son"), accusative *sūnúm*, and the vocative unaccented *sūno*, accented *sū́no*, or between Sanskrit nominative *matíṣ* ("mind"), accusative *matím*, and its vocative unaccented *mate*, accented *máte*? Wherever we find another form used in the syntactic slot of the vocative, it is a nominative form; and in other declension classes, the form of the vocative appears to be particularly closely associated with that of the nominative (witness Gk. *Zeû* as against nominative *Zeús* and accusative *Zên(a)* or *Día*). Why then should we encounter a sharp break between vocative and nominative singular in the forms of the y- and w-stems just cited?

To answer this question, we must first try to determine more precisely the nature of the association of the vocative with the nominative singular in other forms. Let us consider the relationship of, say, Greek *páter* with its nominative singular *patḗr* ("father"). Descriptively speaking, the vocative contains an unextended form with full grade in the suffix, which can be projected back into Proto-Indo-European as *pAter* on the basis of the exact agreement between Greek *páter* and Sanskrit *pitar, pítar.* The nominative singular can be reconstructed as Proto-Indo-European *pAtér* with lengthened-grade vocalism on the basis of such forms as Greek *patḗr,* Armenian *hayr,* Gothic *fadar,* and Tocharian B *pācer.* The immediate outcome of our inspection is what we conclude that the distinction between short and long (historically speaking: lengthened) vowels marks the distinction between vocative and nominative singular. Such a formulation would adequately describe the pattern found in *r*- and *n*-stems, in a form such as Greek *Zeû,* and last, but not least, in *ā*-stems; but it would in no way be usable as a description of the relation between *mate* and *matíṣ.* Unless we want to be content with the existence of several rules for the formation of the vocative (or the nominative, as the case may be), or even with a mere enumeration of heterogeneous forms, we must try to find a different formulation for the description of the relationship between vocative and nominative forms. To arrive at such a formulation, we will have to cross over from the field of comparative reconstruction to the more complex field of internal reconstruction based on the results of comparative reconstruction.

Oswald Szemerényi has recently presented a strong argument for the equal treatment of -*s* nominatives and lengthened-grade nominatives in Proto-Indo-European consonant-stem nouns. He proposes to derive a form such as Proto-Indo-European *pAtér* from an earlier form *pAter-s*, with an intervening assimilation of tautosyllabic -*rs* to -*rr* and elimination of the double consonant with concurrent compensatory lengthening of the preceding short vowel. This proposal impresses the reader with its neatness; however, before it can be accepted, certain difficulties will have to be taken into account. The assimilation-and-reduction-plus-lengthening hypothesis will, of course, also have to be applied to Proto-Indo-European *n*-stems, which would lead us to derive, say, Proto-Indo-European *k'wōn* ("dog") from an earlier form *k'won-s*; however, the sequence -*ons* has to be reconstructed as unchanged for Proto-Indo-European on the comparative evidence of such forms as Cretan *lúkons,* Gothic *wulfans,* dialectal Lithuanian *vilkuns* ("wolves"), all plural accusatives.

Obviously, in a context in which phonological rules are assumed to operate without exception unless an interference can be demonstrated, a development of former -*ons* in syllable-final position to both -*on* and -*ons* cannot be postulated unless different conditions can let us account for the difference in the results of change. Differences in the environment of the sounds in question are hard to imagine; therefore, the conditioning factor may have to be sought not in differences in adjacent phonological or morphological features, but rather in a chronological difference. We, therefore, surmise that the change as postulated by Szemerényi occurred at a time when a cluster of final -*ns* in an accusative plural form had not yet developed.

The assumption that forms of the nominal plural were developed through a combination of singular case forms with a suffixed plural marker -*s* is an old one. What I would like to add here is the proposal to interpret the distinction between a singular case form in the role of a base and the plural marker -*s* in the role of an extension as a reflection of two stages in a historical development: it is not only assumed that the plural forms require the existence of the singular forms to be synchronically derivable from them, but that singular forms of the shape incorporated in plural forms existed at a time when plural forms had not yet been developed. To this earlier period we would then assign the sound changes leading to the development of lengthened-grade forms in nominatives ending in *-ēn, -ōn, -ēr, -ōr*.

As it turns out, the assumption of an early date for the development of lengthened grade from an assimilation of syllable-final -*s* also provides us with a means to decide among various possible reconstructed forms in another position of the nominal paradigm; we shall return to that question very soon. For the moment, we must consider a troublesome matter, at least in passing: If indeed, as we seem to have reason to believe, the addition of final -*s* in the nominative singular of *r*- and *n*-stem nouns led to the development of *s*-less lengthened-grade nominatives, what happened in other stems ending in continuant? The answer is simple for *s*-stems. Forms like Sanskrit *durmanās* ("annoyed"), and Greek *dusmenḗs* ("hostile") contain lengthened-grade -*es*; forms like Sanskrit *uṣás*, Homeric Greek *ēṓs* ("aurora") contain lengthened-grade -*ōs* in close parallelism to *-ēr, -ōr*, and so on.

What, however, is to be assumed to have been the result of the addition of a final -*s* to the full-grade form of a *y*- or *w*-stem? Do forms like Sanskrit *sákhā* ("friend"), Greek *Lētṓ*, or Sanskrit *dyaús* ("heaven"), and *gaús* ("bovine"), attest a regular development of, say, -*oy* plus -*s* to first *-oyy*, then *-ōy*, with or without the secondary addition of a final -s as, *mutatis mutandis*, in *dyaúṣ*?

The answer to this question can probably be in the negative. Full-grade diphthong with -y or -w followed by final -s recurs in forms outside the nominative singular, notably in genitive-singular forms such as Sanskrit *matéṣ* and *sūnóṣ*, without any trace of a lengthened-grade development. It seems, therefore, that we may take a form like Vedic *véṣ* ("bird") to contain the regular nominative-singular development from -y diphthong plus -s, and not a form like *sákhā*. Rather than consider the lengthened-grade nominatives in y- and w-stems, whether with or without final -s, as something extremely archaic, we will want to interpret them as the result of a transfer of the vocalism regularly developed in other continuant stems because of the high degree of paradigmatic agreement in forms outside the nominative singular. Thus, the paradigm of "friend" in Old Indic as reconstructed here would have agreed in all forms but the nominative singular with that of the word for "donor": accusative singular, *sákhāyam–dātāram*; vocative singular, *sakhe–dātar*; nominative plural, *sákhāyas–dātáras*; accusative plural *sákhīn–dātṝn*, and so on, but nominative singular, in its older form, **sákheṣ* but *dātā́*. In a form like Sanskrit *dyaúṣ*, what was transferred was simply the feature of vowel length found in a nominative such as *pitā́* ("father"). Once the priority of the unlengthened form has been recognized, the question, of course, arises whether a form like Greek *Zeús* must be interpreted as the result of a Greek shortening of a long diphthong, or rather as the survival of the expected form, with the lengthened form **dyēws* reduced to **dyēs* (cf. Lat. *diēs*) reflected only by the accusative form *Zên(a)*. A detailed discussion of these questions would lead us too far afield.

To sum up our conclusions reached up to this point: The nominative singular of continuant stems can be set up as involving full-grade vocalism, with a secondary split into -e and -o vocalism, depending on general properties of the form, plus a suffix -s. This form represents the result not of a comparison of surviving forms only, but includes conclusions drawn from internal reconstruction.

It is against this series of nominative forms ending in **-ers*, *-ens*, *-ess*, *-eys*, and *-ews* that the vocative forms we find attested in a variety of Indo-European languages must be plotted. To **-ers* in Greek *patḗr*, there corresponds -er of the vocative in *páter*; to **-ons* in Greek *Apóllōn*, -on of the vocative in *Ápollon*; to **-ess* in Greek *dusmenḗs*, -es in the vocative *dusmenés*; to **-eys* in Sanskrit *véṣ* ("bird"), -ey in Greek *Poseidáōn*; to -ews in Greek *Zeús*, -ew in the vocative *Zeû*. We thus obtain a pattern of the utmost consistency: Nominative equals vocative plus -*s*, or, stated in reverse, vocative equals nominative minus -*s*. Which of these two formulations is to be preferred? Generally we like to think of morphological processes as leading from lesser to greater complexity of forms; therefore, it would seem most reasonable to assume that the nominative should be derived from the vocative. In slightly different terms, this is very much like what has always been the contention of Indo-Europeanists (down to, among others, W. P. Lehmann eight years ago): it has always been held that the vocative represented an unextended form, a base, and important conclusions have been drawn from this identification—that the vocative, like at least some forms of the imperative, hailed from extremely remote days in the history of Proto-Indo-European, days when the syntactic relationships within a sentence were not yet expressed by inflectional signals, and it was thought to be quite logical that such a situation should have been left unchanged in the case of a vocative, since this form by itself constituted what we would now call a clause and did not enter into any syntactic relationship with other forms, be they verbal or nominal. Part of the interest in the past in questions of the vocative has probably been caused by this very belief in its archaic nature; however, is such an assessment of the general problem justified?

We shall not dwell on the theoretical difficulties of the traditional interpretation. The notion that unmarked forms once constituted the whole inventory of a language, a notion implied in the statement that the vocative dates from a time when there were no case forms, can be maintained only if it can be shown that syntactic relationships signaled later on by case forms either were nonexistent or were indicated by different devices such as order, particles, intonational features. That cases should have sprung up from nowhere is not likely. However, there seems to be precious little to document an alleged precase stage of development in the history of Proto-Indo-European. A Hirtian labeling of elements extracted from longer forms as particles is not very helpful. That there were unmarked case forms can scarcely be doubted (witness such items as Gk. *gónu*, "knee", *méli*, "honey"); but that the entire system of nouns-within-clauses should have remained without marking seems incredible. There seems, however, to be little point in concentrating on these matters of speculation when more tangible issues remain unsettled.

If the vocative forms as we have them were relics of an extremely remote period, we would expect them to be formed in agreement

212 Substance and Structure of Language

with ablaut rules to the extent that we can be sure of these; but they were not. As I have stated earlier in this paper, the evidence found in various Indo-European languages indicates that the vocative singular (and in Vedic, also the vocatively used form of the dual and plural) was primarily an unaccented form; accent in sentence-initial position was a secondary phenomenon, as shown by the occurrence of the same accent-retraction phenomena as found in the reaccentuated verb forms of Greek. We must then posit accentlessness as a basic characteristic of Indo-European vocative forms, both in individual languages and in the reconstructed protolanguage.

When we inspect, though, the forms of the vocative enumerated a short while ago, we find that all of them show full-grade vocalism. This feature decidedly does not agree with the property of accentlessness. If the vocative forms are ascribed to a time when vocalization was a function of accent distribution, these forms, if they are highly archaic, point to source forms with primary accent and not with weak accent or no accent at all — whatever condition one wants to posit for a zero-grade vocalism.

There seems to be no easy way out of this dilemma. If one were to choose some of the *-u* and *-i* vocatives, instead of those ending in *-ew* and *-ey*, as the starting point of one's argument, one could circumvent part of the difficulty; but one would still have to explain the deviant forms in diphthong, which is particularly awkward when they occur alongside zero-grade forms of the nominative and accusative, as in many Old Indic paradigms, and worse than that, one would have to explain away the quite unambiguous evidence of the *r*- and *n*-stems that consistently show full-grade vocalism in the vocative. Thus it would seem that the full-grade forms should be made the basis of the argument, provided of course that an explanation for the zero-grade vocatives can be provided in due time.

To state the problem once more: We have before us very strong evidence for an old set of vocative forms without accent, but with full-grade vocalism. To explain these forms, it seems necessary to introduce an interpretation of the facts that deviates substantially from those proposed earlier. It is assumed here that the vocative forms reconstructed on the basis of the evidence found in various Indo-European languages came into existence at a time when a change in accent was no longer automatically accompanied by a change in vowel grade, that is, at a time when ablaut had ceased to be a regularily operating phenomenon. Furthermore, it is assumed that vocatives were formed from nominatives by the elimination of the accent characteristic of the nominative and the deletion of the case marker at the end of the form. Rather than having a situation expressed by the formula *Stem equals vocative singular*, we have one to be subsumed under *Nominative singular minus accent minus case marker equals vocative.*

The double deletion postulated here can be conceived of as a one-step or a two-step development. In this paper, I prefer the first alternative; but it may be stated briefly what the second one would involve. A vocative is derived from a full clause, and a full clause as such would be reconstructed with a principal accent, at least as long as it remained an independent clause. At the state of independence, the subject marker would have been deleted, and the deletion of the accent would have taken place only at the next stage of development when the now vocative clause was subordinated to another clause. One may even ask whether, under the conditions sketched here, a derivation from a nominative would still be required; I would answer this question in the affirmative as the explanation of the vocative of *ā*-stems, to be discussed later, as a parallel to that of continuant stems would otherwise have to be replaced by another more complicated one.

Whether we posit a two-step or a one-step development, the formula given accounts fully for the vocatives included in the earlier enumeration; however, there are still difficulties to be considered before we can accept the formula as adequate. The relationship between Sanskrit nominative *sūnús* ("son") and its vocative *sūno*, and between Sanskrit nominative *matís* ("mind") and its vocative *mate*, is not covered by the above formula. Does this mean that we have to abandon the formula? We approach this problem in a somewhat circuitous manner.

Reference was made earlier to the assumption found with Brugmann and others that at least a number of the plural forms of Indo-European nouns were to be derived from case forms of the singular extended by a suffix *-s*. Formal matches to support this contention are found in the accusative (singular *$\ast wlk^{w}om$*, "wolf" [Gk. *lúkon*] : plural *$\ast wlk^{w}ons$* [Cretan *lúkons*]) and in forms of the instrumental (singular *$\ast$-bhi* : plural *$\ast$-bhis*). For other case forms, greater or smaller difficulties remain.

Let us suppose that the plural forms, with some exceptions, are indeed based on the corresponding case forms of the singular. We then note immediately a considerable difficulty in one of our crucial forms, once we move away from the nonablauting *o*-class: While we can derive the ending of the accusative plural from the ending of the accusative singular in a pair such as Sanskrit *pitáram*, "father" : *pitŕn* (the replacement of *m* by *n* can be explained by the simple assumption that an assimilation took place), we have no way to account for the difference in ablaut grade between the two forms.

Our notions about the distribution of grades in ablauting paradigms have always been very much influenced by the facts observed in Greek and Indo-Iranian plus Armenian; however, these are languages that form a geographic continuum, and it is well to ask whether the evidence they provide should be rated higher than conflicting evidence from other languages.

It is a well-known fact that Latin has in its paradigm of "father" a distribution of full (or lengthened) versus zero grade quite different from that occurring in Greek or Sanskrit: only the nominative (and possibly the vocative, if a form like *Iuppiter* can be used as evidence) has full grade; all other forms show zero grade, while in Greek zero grade is limited to genitive singular, one variant of the dative singular, one variant of the accusative plural, one variant of the genitive plural, and all forms of the dative plural. The comparative evidence has traditionally been interpreted as permitting a reconstruction of lengthened grade for the nominative singular, full grade for vocative, accusative, and locative singular, nominative-accusative dual, and nominative plural. This enumeration of so-called strong cases disregards the evidence of Latin and the parallel evidence of Tocharian, where only the nominative singular and possibly the vocative singular (which cannot, however, be extracted as an inherited form from our Tocharian materials) show full grade.

Let us consider the possibility that the Latin-Tocharian pattern of grade distribution may be of even greater antiquity than that of the southeastern languages. In a paradigm like that of Sanskrit *súnúṣ*, the accusative singular *sūnúm*, the vocative *sūno*, the accusative plural *sūnún*, as well as the other weak cases, would then be old forms, and the nominative singular, as well as the nominative plural *sūnávas*, would be innovations. In a paradigm like that of *pitā*, the accusative singular *pitáram* and the nominative plural *pitáras*, (disregarding here, for the sake of simplicity, the locative singular and the nominative-accusative dual) would be innovations. Compared with the amount of leveling found in related paradigms, say, in Old Church Slavonic, the extent of analogical spread of forms to be assumed for Greek and Sanskrit under this hypothesis would not be excessive; but such a statement is clearly not enough. Is there other evidence that would make the claim for the antiquity of the Latin-Tocharian pattern more likely?

Let us consider the Sanskrit forms again. In the paradigm of "father," we have to assume, under the hypothesis proposed, an extension of the stem form of the nominative-vocative to the accusative singular and the nominative plural. In the paradigm, say, of *matíṣ* ("mind"), where we posit an old nominative in -*eys* on the basis of *véṣ* ("bird"), we have to assume the spread of the stem form of the nominative-vocative singular to the nominative plural, and a subsequent spread of the stem form of the accusative singular and plural to the nominative singular. Analogical spread then operates, so it would seem, at random and at cross purposes.

We have, however, some data that permit us to assess the situation more adequately. The *r*- and *n*-stem nouns of Old Indic are typically animate, the *y*- and *w*-stems, while containing some animate nouns, are made up to a large extent of verbal abstracts and thus of inanimate nouns. A study of large bodies of text in various languages, on which I reported a number of years ago at an annual meeting of the Linguistic Society of America, showed clearly two quite different frequency patterns in regard to the distribution of subject and object case of animate and inanimate nouns. For animate ones, the subject was of about equal frequency with the object, or even was more frequent; for inanimates, accusative forms were roughly four times as frequent as nominatives. At that time, I was concerned with the implications of such observations for an assessment of hypotheses about specific analogical changes. It turned out that a statement seemed borne out by the facts that, given two or more forms in juxtaposition, say, within a paradigm, the more frequent one was more likely to prevail if a leveling occurred; frequency here could refer either to text frequency or to paradigmatic frequency, with text frequency apparently of paramount importance. The observations seemed to me significant as they appeared to offer a useful tool for one's attempts to classify a hypothesis about analogical change as probable or improbable, since they seemed to indicate that there were testable regularities to be found in analogical change, regularities more tangible than those suggested by Jerzy Kuryłowicz.

If we apply these findings to our Indic paradigms, we come to the conclusion that a spread of the nominative form is to be expected in the animate class of *r*- and *n*-stems (e.g., *pitáram*), but that an extension of the accusative stem is likely in the inanimate *y*- and *w*-stems (e.g., *matíṣ*).

Another observation to be made with texts from various languages was that the frequency of singular forms tended to be very much higher than that of plural (let alone dual) forms. Whenever an analogical spread occurs, it is, therefore, likely that the singular form should be generalized at the expense of the plural or dual. This observation turned out to be independent of animateness or inanimateness of the nouns considered; therefore, it is not surprising that we should find that the full-grade stem of the nominative singular recurs in the plural nominative of both *pitá* and *matíṣ*. Note, by the way, that Latin, which does not have extension of the full grade vocalism of the nominative singular to such forms as *patrem* or *patrēs*, shows at least a trace of the spread from singular to plural in forms like nominative *ouēs* ("eggs") beside accusative plural *ouïs*. Likewise, Tocharian seems to have a reflex of the *-eyes* form of the nominative plural in such items as *lyśi* ("thieves").

If our conclusions so far have been justified, we now have a partly established paradigm for continuant stems at an early stage in the development of Proto-Indo-European. We can posit, say,

> a nominative singular in *-tér-s*
> a vocative singular in *-ter*
> an accusative singular in *-tr-m*
> an accusative plural in *-tr-n-s*

What can we say about the form to be reconstructed for the nominative plural? We note immediately that the attested forms of the type **pAtéres mntéyes* with full-grade vocalism in two adjacent syllables cannot be old — even though they, of course, are to be reconstructed for late common Indo-European. They quite obviously date from a time when ablaut as a phonologically conditioned phenomenon was no longer operative. Are there competing forms that might represent an older type?

It has been customary to consider plural nominatives like Vedic *aryás* ("the pious ones") and *mádhvas* ("the sweet ones") as the result of an extension of the accusative vocalism to the nominative; in the light of our earlier observations concerning the direction of analogical change, this explanation is at least unlikely for *aryás*. Let us assume that *aryás* and parallel forms are indeed not of a recent origin; what would that imply for the reconstruction of our paradigm? It means that we would have to posit an old nominative plural form in **-trés*, a form supported also by such items as Greek *kúnes* ("dogs") and *ándres* ("men"). Is this the ultimate point in our reconstruction, or can we derive this *-trés* from an even earlier form?

It is very tempting indeed to go one step beyond the form obtained by comparative procedures, and to posit an earlier complex *-tr-és-s*, in which *-és-* (corresponding to *-s* of the singular) would be the case marker of the nominative, and final *-s*, the marker of the plural, as in the form of the accusative or instrumental. But should we then not expect to find lengthened grade *-ēs* in the ending, as in Greek *dusmenḗs*? Again the chronology as reconstructed for the contrast between *-ōn* of the nominative singular and *-ons* of the accusative plural has to be taken into consideration: If the plural marker *-s* was added to the accusative form at a time when the rule leading to the production of a lengthened grade was no longer operative, then the addition of an *-s* in the nominative plural could not produce a form in *-ēs* either, but now the *-es* was the expected result. If our argument is correct, we obtain an old paradigm

nominative singular	*-tér-s*	nominative plural	*-tr-és-s*
vocative singular	*-ter*		
accusative singular	*-tr-m*	accusative plural	*-tr-n-s*

in which the vocative is associated only with the nominative.

It may, perhaps, be in order to make a few comments concerning some implications of the reconstruction of all accusative forms with a zero-grade vocalism. The pattern we have followed will undoubtedly lead to the reconstruction of many accusative forms without a full-grade vowel; is that a reasonable result?

First of all, many zero-grade-only accusatives are included among the forms obtained by comparative reconstruction (e.g., *mntím* underlying Skt. *matím*, Lat. *mentem*). If our basic assumption about an interrelatedness of accent and ablaut grade is correct, we cannot escape the conclusion that we must reconstruct an even earlier form as a form without accent, viz., *mntym*. Is that again a meaningful result?

Now when we look at our inventory of reconstructed Proto-Indo-European forms with a view to agreement or disagreement between ablaut grade and reconstructed accent, one of the most glaring discrepancies is found in the domain of finite verb forms: finite verb forms, with very few exceptions, contain a full-grade vowel (even discounting thematic vowels, which are best left aside), but comparative evidence of an incontrovertible nature points to accentlessness of these forms in the simplest type of clause. We thus get, in a combination of object and verb, a combination of an accusative form with an accent reconstructed comparatively, but with zero vocalism indicative of an earlier accentlessness, and a finite verb form reconstructed by comparative methods as accentless, but pointing, by its full-grade vocalism, to an earlier state at which it was accented. Internal reconstruction thus leads to the positing of an important change in the intonational pattern of the Proto-Indo-European verb phrase: at an earlier stage it was the verb that bore the principal accent of the phrase, and the transfer to the noun belongs to a later time. The vocalism of such forms as *mntym fits the earlier situation beautifully; the fact that the rearrangement in accent distribution did not lead to a change in ablaut grade in the accusative forms seems to indicate that the reorganization of the intonation pattern occurred when ablaut had become obsolete as a phonological phenomenon.

Let us return to the vocative. Our findings thus far have been: The vocative shows the ablaut grade of the nominative singular, but not its accentual properties. The vocalism of the vocative cannot be explained if we consider it an archaic form that originated at a time when ablaut was still fully associated with accent; other noun forms, on the other hand, show the expected ablaut results once internal reconstruction has been carried out. We, therefore, conclude that the vocative as preserved in historically attested Indo-European languages and reconstructible on the basis of this evidence for Proto-Indo-European is a relatively young form and not a relic from a remote period of pre-Proto-Indo-European. It was formed from the nominative singular by the removal of the strong accent and the deletion of the case marker -s; the suffix deletion was also applied to nominatives that owed their vocalisation to analogical transfer from the accusative: Gothis sunu ("son") is thus based on the more recent nominative form sunus, Gothic sunau, on the reconstructed older form *sunaus.

The statement as presented here seems to account fully for the vocative forms of continuant stems; what remains to be discussed are the vocatives of ā- and o-stems. It would obviously be preferable to be able to use a single formula to describe the formation of vocatives; therefore, it is not very attractive to suggest that the voctives in short -a (e.g., Gk. númpha) are to be derived from their nominative forms by shortening of the final vowel. It is equally unattractive to consider the final -a of Greek and Umbrian and the final -o of Slavic the reflex of a shwa alternating with the full-grade vowel -ā in the nominative: doing so places the forms of the ā-stems in complete isolation, and forces us to exclude Sanskrit amba ("mother") from our list altogether. It seems, therefore, preferable to propose that final -*a* (short) was derived from the final long -*ā* of the nominative singular by the deletion of the final element, in this instance not -*s*, but length. Whether this feature of length should still be interpreted as the *a*-coloring laryngeal, or whether one simply wants to speak of a phoneme of length, does not matter much; if the formation of the vocatives in their attested shapes is a relatively late development, even an explanation assuming the development of final long -*a* without any remaining trace of the laryngeal prior to the creation of the vocative on the basis of the nominative would seem reasonable.

We are then left with the problem of the vocative of *o*-stems. Little remains to encourage us to entertain any longer the idea that final -*e* shows the stem form plain and simple; on the other hand, we cannot readily derive -*e* from the -*os* of the nominative. Again, some more general remarks are called for.

It seems that at least a substantial number of *o*-stem nouns owe their declensional pattern to the transfer of postconsonantal material from pronominal paradigms to the paradigm of root nouns ending in consonant; particularly in old obstruent stems, this transfer eliminated excessive morphophonemic variation. The transfer took place after ablaut had ceased to be related to accent; very many *o*-stems violate basic ablaut patterns. One characteristic feature of the pronominal paradigms over against nominal ones is that third-person pronouns lack a vocative form; deviations from this general rule as found in Indic are of no consequence. The pronominal paradigm thus could not furnish morphemic or submorphemic material to mark the vocative of the new *o*-stems; the endingless form of a root noun was particularly apt to be affected by environmental conditions. A vowel was therefore introduced whose presence prevented such changes; this vowel was -*e*, which had no direct relationship to the principal-accent vowel of times past.

There is at least one parallel instance where an -*e* has been introduced in an endingless form which would otherwise have been subject to multiple alllomorphic variation: the third person singular of the perfect is reconstructed on the strength of comparative evidence with a final -*e*; internal reconstruction, however, then shows us that this -*e* has taken the place of an earlier nothing—not a zero suffix, but no suffix at all. The insertion of -*e* in the perfect is later than phonologically conditioned ablaut, as evidenced by the co-occurrence of several full-grade vowels in forms such as Greek *léloipe* ("he has left"). In the same way, -*e* of the vocative may occur next to a full grade of the root (cf. Lat. *eque*, "horse").

What distinguishes the vocative of *o*-stems from other vocatives is then that it is not directly derivable from its nominative. Once we proceed, however, from the assumption that the class of *o*-stems developed from a class of modified root nouns, the pattern common to all other vocatives can be seen to prevail in the *o*-declension too: The expected vocative of a root noun *wlk^w-s* ("wolf") would be *wlk^w* without a final *-s*. The nominative was reshaped, after the model of demonstrative pronouns, as *$wlk^w os$*, with all other cases matched in the pronominal paradigm undergoing an analogous change. There was no model for a vocative in the pronominal pattern; the vocative *wlk^w* thus remained unchanged, but it received a final vowel which, at least initially, had no morphemic significance, but which prevented the form of the vocative from undergoing severe changes caused by the immediate environment.

If the arguments presented here are correct at least in their crucial points, we have before us a clear example of morphological derivation by deletion. We cannot explain the shorter form without prior recourse to the longer one; the direction of the derivational process is therefore clear, regardless of how much this may contradict our (by the way, well-founded) notions of what constitutes normal characteristics of derivational processes.

Let us consider this point in somewhat greater detail. It makes eminently good sense to consider a vocative clause (for it has been pointed out before that the vocative in Indo-European forms a clause by itself) as derived by ellipsis from a normal declarative clause, as there is evidence that the markers identifying the position of the noun with respect to the entire clause have been present. We can draw up a (somewhat simplified) tree and can specify that in such a clause without predicate the subject markers of the noun may be

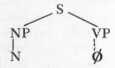

deleted. If (this is a point that has not been mentioned yet) the NP position is not filled by a noun, but by a noun phrase, the deletion takes place either only once, affecting the head of the construction (e.g. Hom. *phílos ô Menélae,* "my dear Menelaos"), or twice, affecting both head and modifier (e.g., Gk. *phíle kasígnēte,* "dear brother"), a pattern widely considered as secondary. If the noun-phrase position is filled by two coordinated nouns, the deletion again occurs only once (cf. *Rig Veda* 1.2.5 *Vāyav Índraś ca cetathah,*

"Vāyu and Indra, take heed!" and 1.3.276 f. *Zeû páter . . . Ēéliós te*, "Father Zeus . . . and Helios").

I find the argument for deletion attractive because I do not have to rely, when I use it, on general considerations concerning the nature of the relationship to be posited between statement and appeal, but can find evidence for the omission of overt formal features in the actual linguistic data at my disposal. Obviously I do have to resort to interpretation of what I find by inspection, but my interpretation, so it would seem to me, is rather directly subjectable to control by overt facts and not just by such criteria as internal consistency of my arguments. I, therefore, think that from my point of view the case for ellipsis in vocative clauses in Indo-European languages is strong; however, even a complete verification of my assumptions by materials not yet considered would merely confirm this analysis for this specific group of languages and the protolanguage of this group. It would not prove that vocative clauses were universally derivable from declarative ones. This proof would have to come separately for any one language; and, because the proof would have to be provided on the basis of overt data, in many a case it could not be furnished. Sometimes the solution offered here for Indo-European remains an unprovable possibility, as for Old Turkish where subject and address form are identical; sometimes, differently marked subject and address forms stand side by side, as in Walapai, offering no formal support for the assumption of a derivational process in either direction. Rather than force the Indo-European solution upon these data, I would prefer to forgo the intellectual satisfaction of seeing a universal pattern of relationship in various languages of overtly vastly differing structures, and would rather be content with fragmentary statements, as long as they reflected faithfully the immediately accessible and therefore provable facts.

I have so far limited myself to a discussion of the vocative in Indo-European. The Indo-European imperative, in its simplest form, with a singular without ending with full grade of the stem in the case of an ablauting verb, and a plural with a suffix -*té* added to a stem in the zero grade, is an instance where the claim of deletion cannot be proved by overt formal evidence. To be sure, these forms can be neatly derived from second-person forms of the indicative unmarked for tense by the deletion of the second-person marker -*s* of the singular and a parallel deletion of an -*s* of uncertain function in the plural, but the imperative forms themselves show no trace whatsoever of the former presence of an -*s*. We cannot, therefore, refute the claim that has been made for the imperative (just as it has been made for the vocative) that the singular form represented a stem pure and simple, unextended by any marker whatsoever. If, however, this analysis is adopted, a derivation of the imperative clause from an underlying indicative one lacks all overt, formal confirmation; therefore, the argument for ellipsis in the imperative is much weaker than that for ellipsis in the vocative.

This condition is rather regrettable. After all, vocative and imperative clauses seem to be neatly complementary as far as included and excluded material goes: the vocative clause contains NP, but not VP; the imperative one has VP, but not a subject NP. Thus it would be good if one could prove, even under the more stringent requirements of overt indications as set up here, that the imperative clause, at least in Indo-European languages, was a kind of mirror image of the vocative clause, with both derived from complete indicative clauses. It seems, however, that this proof just cannot be furnished.

It may be suggested that the covert presence of a second-person subject is indicated by such anaphoric patterns as English *Come here, won't you!* Reasoning from anaphora, however, is not as simple a matter as it may seem. Take an example from German: *Das Mädchen* is clearly a noun with neuter gender selection; compare, for example, the phrase *ein kleines Mädchen*. Anaphorically, *Mädchen* is, however, commonly referred to by *sie,* as though we were dealing with a feminine noun. This deviation from the normal pattern can, of course, be easily enough explained; the question, though, is: Does a covert feature (here female sex) override an overt one (neuter gender selection outside an anaphoric context) in our classification of the form *Mädchen*—or, to return to *Come here, won't you!,* does an overt feature related anaphorically to a form without such overt feature have enough weight to make us attach this feature to the unmarked form, even if it were only to delete it immediately again? Where does our right to project end? Is it acceptable to project when the counterpart of an overt form is a nothing (as in *come here!*)? Or is it even acceptable to override overt evidence to the contrary whenever a projection seems to yield good overall results (as with *das Mädchen* and *sie*)?

It seems that at times we must be content with an unfinished job. I am inclined to think that the limitations to our success in performing exhaustive analyses and in developing all-encompassing theories that really work when put to a test are not just limitations in the abilities of a linguist, but also limitations that reflect real imperfections in natural languages. Because I believe that, I am not unhappy that my presentation did not lead to an infinitely neat statement about vocative and imperative in Indo-European and elsewhere. I would simply say that I have gone about as far as I would dare go here and now; and I would gladly leave it at that.